D0216415

MILITIAS
IN
AMERICA

A Reference Handbook

Other Titles in ABC-CLIO's
CONTEMPORARY
WORLD ISSUES
Series

Books in the Contemporary World Issues series address vital issues in today's society such as terrorism, sexual harassment, homelessness, AIDS, gambling, animal rights, and air pollution. Written by professional writers, scholars, and nonacademic experts, these books are authoritative, clearly written, up-to-date, and objective. They provide a good starting point for research by high school and college students, scholars, and general readers, as well as by legislators, businesspeople, activists, and others.

Each book, carefully organized and easy to use, contains an overview of the subject; a detailed chronology; biographical sketches; facts and data and/or documents and other primary-source material; a directory of organizations and agencies; annotated lists of print and nonprint resources; a glossary; and an index.

Readers of books in the Contemporary World Issues series will find the information they need in order to better understand the social, political, environmental, and economic issues facing the world today.

MILITIAS
IN
AMERICA

A Reference Handbook

Neil A. Hamilton

**CONTEMPORARY
WORLD ISSUES**

ABC-CLIO

Santa Barbara, California
Denver, Colorado
Oxford, England

Copyright © 1996 by Neil A. Hamilton

All rights reserved. No part of this publication may be reproduced, stored in a retrieval system, or transmitted, in any form or by any means, electronic, mechanical, photocopying, recording, or otherwise, except for the inclusion of brief quotations in a review, without prior permission in writing from the publishers.

Library of Congress Cataloging-in-Publication Data

Hamilton, Neil A., 1949–
    Militias in America : a reference handbook / Neil A. Hamilton.
      p.   cm.—(Contemporary world issues)
    Includes bibliographical references and index.
    1. Militia movements—United States.   2. Right-wing
extremists—United States.   3. Government, Resistance to—United
States.
    I. Title.   II. Series.
    HN90.R3H355   1996   96-26538
    303.48′4—dc20   CIP

ISBN 0-87436-859-6

02 01 00 99 98 97 96 95   10 9 8 7 6 5 4 3 2 1

ABC-CLIO, Inc.
130 Cremona Drive, P.O. Box 1911
Santa Barbara, California 93116-1911

This book is printed on acid-free paper ∞.
Manufactured in the United States of America

For my brother
Joel

Contents

A dangerous ambition more often lurks behind the specious mask of zeal for the rights of the people, than under the forbidding appearance of zeal for the firmness and efficiency of government. History will teach us, that the former has been found a much more certain road to the introduction of despotism, than the latter, and that of those men who have over-turned the liberties of republics the greatest number have begun their career, by paying an obsequious court to the people, commencing Demagogues and ending Tyrants.

Alexander Hamilton,
The Federalist

Preface

S ince the April 1995 bombing of the Alfred P. Murrah Federal Building in Oklahoma City, Oklahoma, public interest in the militia movement has increased markedly. Although there is no evidence linking any militia to the explosion, the event reflected an extremist environment that has permeated many aspects of American politics, including the militias, in the 1990s. This book discusses the formation of militias in contemporary society, their roots in the American past, their views, and the controversies surrounding them; it evaluates where they fit within the American constitutional and legal system; and it provides readers with information that should allow them to contribute to the debate respecting the necessity of forming citizen militias and allowing them to operate.

Chapter 1 presents an overview intended to place the militias within the context of historical developments dating from the American Revolution. In this respect, the militias appear not as an aberration, but as another manifestation of the violence and paranoia that has long marked American politics. But they reflect, also, an ideology dating from Revolutionary society that the protection of liberty relies on an armed and vigilant citizenry. Chapter 2 provides a chronology covering militias in early America and since World War II. Chapter 3 presents biographical sketches of people prominent among modern militias—either founders or persons who have greatly influenced the movement. Chapter 4 contains primary material intended to give the reader a sense of the thoughts and actions within militias and among those who have monitored and criticized them. Chapter 5 lists organizations involved in the militia scene, both those opposed to the militias and the militias themselves. The last two chapters provide numerous print and nonprint resources that will give the reader a solid starting point from which to further investigate the militia movement. The book concludes with a glossary of terms commonly used by those who study or participate in militias and a detailed subject index.

Acknowledgments

The problem of research for this book has been twofold: first, the uneven availability of information about militias—scarce prior to the Oklahoma City bombing in April 1995, then substantial afterwards; and second, the heavy use of the Internet by militias and those who analyze them—requiring an ability to work through a maze of connections. Both problems could not have been overcome without the help of knowledgeable and dedicated reference librarians who knew how to acquire materials either difficult to find or, because of their recent publication, not on the library shelves, and who were willing to introduce this author to the intricacies of home pages and computer links. For assistance in these areas I am especially grateful to David Bunnell and Bret Heim at the Spring Hill College library in Mobile, Alabama. Thanks also to Brinin Behrend, a student at Spring Hill College, for helping to electronically scan primary materials.

I am grateful to my mother for her support and to the following people for their cooperation: John Trochmann, David Trochmann, and Randy Trochmann—all of the Militia of Montana; Noah Chandler of the Center for Democratic Renewal; Gail Gans of the Anti-Defamation League; and Mark Vanderboegh, an Alabama militia leader.

Finally, I am indebted to Henry Rasof, senior acquisitions editor at ABC-CLIO, for his receptivity to the idea for this book and for his many helpful suggestions, and to Mary Kay Kozyra, development editor, for guiding the manuscript to final production.

Introduction 1

On 19 April 1995, a bomb explosion ripped through the Alfred P. Murrah Federal Building in Oklahoma City, killing 167 people. Soon after the incident, investigators arrested Timothy McVeigh, a former soldier, as a suspect amid numerous reports he had associated with militias in Michigan and Arizona. Although no evidence has emerged to prove a direct connection between the Oklahoma City bombing and any militia groups, the stories about McVeigh's background reveal a world little known to most Americans: armed citizens organized as militias to protest against what they considered to be an oppressive national government.

Prior to Oklahoma City, when Americans thought about militias at all, they usually recalled images from 1776, the patriotic revolution, when Minutemen and citizen farmers fought the mighty and oppressive British army. So strong is this image in the national mythology that modern militias base their views and patriotism on it and insist that their very existence conforms with the republican principles laid out two centuries ago.

But does it? What do these modern militias stand for? What roots do they have in the more immediate cold-war period that emerged after World War II? What conditions in the 1990s have generated their growth? Are they acting within constitutional provisions? Should they exist? The Oklahoma City bombing has raised these and other questions and intensified the scrutiny of militias.

Militias Defined

Over the years, militias have had a nebulous and sometimes shadowy existence. This has made it difficult to distinguish them from other armed groups, particularly informal ones such as mobs or vigilantes that arise spontaneously, or organizations that use violence as a tactic without establishing paramilitary training. In this book, militias are defined as formal, structured, *private* organizations of armed citizens that declare themselves militias and engage in paramilitary training sessions or preparedness meetings. They are distinct from the regular army or professional soldiers. In American history, militias have been temporary groups that generally arise in reaction to a particular environment or crisis, and their ideological orientation has been diverse.

The discussion herein does not follow the formal, legal definition, as established by federal statute, that states the militia is the entire able-bodied male citizenry between the ages of 18 and 45 (a provision militias consider the lawful foundation for their existence). Nor does it consider the National Guard to be a militia, since it is under the direction of state and national governmental bodies.

The definition of militias for this book, however, begs the question of their legality. Militias claim they have the right to exist because federal law, namely, Title 10, Section 311, of the United States Consolidated Statutes (see chapter 4, document 1), establishes the general citizenry as a militia. But the statute does no more than that—it certainly does not provide any legal sanction for private militias. In addition, many states have laws specifically forbidding paramilitary organizations. Over the years, federal and state governments have not been comfortable with the thought of militias operating outside the realm of governmental supervision—not in the Revolutionary period or since. State governments, in particular, provide for militias to be under their control. In fact, from the very founding of the colonies, rules that placed militias under the supervision of the entire community were clearly laid out.

Militias in Early American Society

Militias existed in America from the beginning of the British colonial settlements. The colonists living in seventeenth-century Plymouth and Massachusetts Bay required all men at age 16 to become part of the militia organized to fight, if necessary, Indians and any invasions by foreign powers, such as France or Spain. This requirement conformed with English custom, although the emphasis in Britain had, in the previous few decades, shifted from citizen militias to armies filled with mercenaries directed by a centralized command. Initially, Massachusetts Bay placed its militia under the governor's council, and later, under a special council of war. Localism characterized the system, however, as individual commanders in the colony's towns were able to order troops into battle. The settlers devised an alarm system among the towns, and riders stood ready to spread the news of any emergency. Concerned with preparedness, these New England communities provided training fields for their militias, while on the other hand they recognized conscientious objection and, under that stipulation, excused some men from serving. The amateur status of the militias may have hampered their effectiveness. In general, they failed to develop good communications, lacked a trained command, and experienced difficulties in securing supplies.

Even though all the colonies had militias, diversity existed. For example, the scattered settlement pattern in Virginia, as opposed to New England's compactness, made it difficult to mobilize the militia. Instead of voluntary militias, Virginians relied on forts and hired soldiers to patrol the frontier. In South Carolina, a peculiar situation emerged: Black slaves existed in large numbers, so the government regulated arms to make sure only whites possessed them. With ever greater frequency, South Carolinians used the militia to defend against slave uprisings. To African-Americans, then, the militias stood not for freedom, but for oppression.

The colonial militias did not function independently from the local settlements; they were extensions of them. In an era when few government agencies existed, militias epitomized the belief, particularly in New England, that true community—the settlers coming together in selfless dedication—underlay harmony, happiness, and survival. Yet change in this arrangement occurred, and in the 1700s (and in some instances even earlier), militias did less and less fighting; instead, the colonists turned to armies manned not by yeoman farmers, but by displaced poor people. This was clearly evident in the early 1760s during the French and Indian War. Additionally, colonists relied increasingly on permanent forts and garrisons manned by forces consisting of men from the lower class under command of middle-class and wealthy officers—a system akin to that in England.

When the American Revolution erupted, militias played a prominent role, at least in its early stages. In 1774, the Massachusetts Provincial Congress ordered the reorganization of militias and the formation of minuteman units—militia fighters trained to take quick action, generally within a half hour. This provision continued the colonial tradition. That same year, the Continental Congress called on the colonies to reorganize their militias so as to make them responsive to the struggle against Britain. In effect, this meant that the militias would reflect the Patriot cause, purged of Loyalists and obstructionists. Then on 19 April 1775, some minutemen in Massachusetts fought the British, first at Lexington and, as the enemy troops advanced, later in the day at Concord—two infamous battles that began the Revolutionary War.

Concord had been a town in decline, experiencing economic stagnation, a flight of people to other settlements, and a loss of community spirit. In the weeks preceding the battle, militia training day had produced a disappointing turnout, and not until near the showdown with the British army had enough men assembled to form a minuteman company. From then on, as the crisis with Britain mounted, the minutemen carried their muskets everywhere—even to church. The Revolution rekindled community spirit, the sense that all could and should care for Concord's development. The militia reflected this environment and became an extension of the entire town, not just one segment of it, and operated within the guidelines laid out by the townspeople and the state government.

At the Concord battle, minutemen and regular militia marched in orderly double-file formation toward the British troops, who had lost an element of surprise by arriving later in the day than planned because a brigade major had failed to get his orders on time. When the British retreated, the New England militia ranks collapsed, and the militia men, boosted by hundreds of reinforcements who had come to the site, began firing from behind trees and fences, an unconventional style disparaged by professional armies as cowardly. "The militia, Minutemen, and alarm companies," according to the historian Louis

Birnbaum, "became hopelessly intermingled as men slipped behind trees or walls and waited for the [British] column to pass. Then they fired their guns and quickly ran into the woods to reload, and sprinted ahead of the column for another chance."[1] After the battle, the Massachusetts Committee of Safety designated the colony's entire militia as minutemen. As the colonies converted their political systems into state governments, they formalized arrangements for maintaining control over the militias. At all times, they considered it essential for the militias to be subordinate to civil authority, both the governor and the legislature, with the latter having the most say in military matters.

As in the pre-Revolutionary period, however, the colonial militias developed along different lines, and they did not always follow the intentions of higher authorities. In Vermont, New York, and Pennsylvania, backcountry settlers had, prior to Lexington and Concord, often aimed their discontent at the revolutionary elite as much as at the British and, in taking up arms, may have desired some form of property redistribution. This reflected years of disputes with the wealthy over land titles. In Philadelphia, the militia radicalized and promoted an internal revolution to advance popular power. Indeed, one historian claims that this militia's lack of discipline and sometimes erratic behavior indicated egalitarian politics at work.

This raises the question of motivation. Why did the colonists in general, and the militias in particular, fight against Britain? The reasons are many, and their complexity prohibits fully discussing them here. Two factors, however, deserve recognition as relevant to militias in the 1990s: conspiracy and economics. The colonists believed in a conspiratorial plot underway to rob America of liberty, one supposedly directed by a small group of the king's ministers and several powerful men in parliament. Hence, legislation such as the Stamp Act, Townshend Acts, Quebec Act, and the infamous Intolerable Acts were not unplanned or misguided endeavors but calculated, incremental efforts to establish tyranny. Even some moderates such as Pennsylvanian John Dickinson believed in this conspiracy theory, and revolutionary writing, including the Declaration of Independence, often reflected it. A conspiracy did not exist, but additional British proposals, such as one in 1777 to outlaw the militia in America, only boosted suspicions. In any event, among the colonists the conspiratorial theories carried a truthful resonance.

In addition, economic conditions influenced the colonists. Opportunity, for many, appeared to be declining. British legislation and the colonial elite had worked their influence to make land less available in the backcountry, and, in cities, wealth concentrated at the top while poverty expanded below. In the late 1760s and early 1770s, when the colonists had boycotted trade with Britain, the economic pinch had worsened. This condition prompted colonists to act outside regular political channels and to direct their frustration and anger at the mother country. According to historian Richard Brown, colonial rebellions such as the Revolution, occurred because in this atmosphere "the ordinary peaceful political means of conflict resolution had proved inadequate."[2]

As the Revolution continued, fewer men volunteered to fight, and the militias receded in importance. In trying to get recruits to fill quotas, many towns, including Concord, relied on lower-class men to join the Continental Army. By and large, the war became a poor man's battle. Nevertheless, the militias served a crucial role during the Revolution and in the years immediately after. Patriot authority as expressed through the militias helped to prevent Loyalists, or Tories, from gaining control of many state and local governments. Additionally, the militias maintained domestic order, helped recruit soldiers for the Continental Army while assisting it in several campaigns, and protected the frontier against attacks by Native Americans. The Revolutionary experience reinforced a faith in local militias, and in fact these units helped carry out governmental functions at a time when national and state polities were too weak to do so.

The founding fathers recognized the role militia groups played in society when, in the Second Amendment to the Constitution, they protected the right to bear arms as part of maintaining a well-regulated militia. Historians today debate whether the founders intended this right to be an individual one, exclusive of militia membership. But they agree in seeing the militia concept as founded on republican ideology prevalent in the late 1700s, particularly the view that militias must exist to protect liberty and property against a tyrannical government. To many Americans, the concept of a citizen soldier as expressed decades earlier by various European philosophers rang true. Thomas Jefferson proclaimed, "What country can preserve its liberties if their rulers are not warned from time to time that their people preserve the spirit of resistance? Let them take arms."[3]

Indeed, colonial and Revolutionary America instilled in society the practice of military units under local control and a distrust of centralized authority. As a result, under the Articles of Confederation (the new nation's first governing document), the states, believed to be more expressive of popular will than the national government, had nearly complete control over the militias.

By the late 1780s, however, many Americans, shaken by Shays' Rebellion, an armed uprising in western Massachusetts that was supported by militias in the local area, distrusted this decentralized approach. As a result, the Constitution established a different form of control: Now Congress (and, under certain circumstances, the president) would regulate militias, a situation that resulted in joint authority over them by the national and state governments. The War Powers clause of the Constitution—Article I, Section 8—stated in part:

> [Congress shall have the power] to provide for calling forth the Militia to execute the Laws of the Union, suppress Insurrections, and repel Invasions;
>
> To provide for organizing, arming, and disciplining the Militia, and for governing such Part of them that may be employed in Service to the United States, reserving to the States respectively, the Appointment of the Officers, and the Authority of training the Militia according to the discipline prescribed by Congress.

Hence, militias were not to be private; where the federal government did not intercede the states would, establishing appointments and providing the authority to train under prescribed rules. That such controls were to exist in the new nation reflected the colonial and revolutionary experience at the local level. The Virginia Bill of Rights, for example, adopted in 1776, clearly stipulated "that in all cases, the military should be under strict subordination to, and governed by, the civil power." In this way, liberty and order could be balanced and protected. Control even meant detailed rules as to the type and kind of weaponry permitted in the militias.

In the early 1800s, the national government developed permanent military institutions, primarily a professional standing army. Despite an act in 1792 that made all able-bodied male citizens a universal militia, this shift to a professional army hastened the decline of militias, already suffering from poor training and equipment, and a shortage of men willing to engage in training. Thus ended the nation's heavy reliance on militia units to perform vital functions, including defending the frontier, although militias continued to serve notable roles in battles against Indians and in large-scale wars, including the War of 1812 and the Civil War. Both major political parties, the Federalists and the Jeffersonians, accepted and promoted the shift to a professional military. They did so, however, with varying degrees of financial commitment while conveying memorable tales of days when citizen soldiers defended the nation. Each party used this tactic of harkening to the past as a way to show itself most attached to republican ideals.

In recent years, many observers have insisted that "violence is as American as apple pie." Early American history attests to this, as evident in the Revolution and the other upheavals discussed earlier. In short, although Americans cherish order, they frequently resort to violence. This characteristic runs like an undaunted current through the nation's development, and is often tied to extremist ideologies.

A Seedbed for Extremism: The 1940s Through the 1960s

We need only look to the years right after World War II to find more immediate roots to today's militia movement, a time of distrust and competition for international supremacy between the United States and the Soviet Union, when the cold war emerged and took form. For Americans, the intense fear of communism that characterized this period, the economic and social development that accompanied military and consumer production, and the sharp disagreement over the Vietnam War, provided a seedbed for extremism—shaping it, encouraging it, propelling it.

The cold war involved propaganda, espionage, and military buildups, first stimulated in the United States by President Harry Truman, who in the 1940s portrayed the Soviets and their Communist system as an evil that must be destroyed. Despite American efforts, the Communists expanded their influence, most notably in China, where in 1949 a Marxist regime gained power. Many Americans could not understand how the United States, so powerful economically and militarily, with a nuclear arsenal unmatched by anyone, and so superior morally, could "lose"

China, as well as Eastern Europe, and on top of that suffer over the next decade, the humiliation of Communist rebellions in Africa and Latin America. The explanation, some concluded, rested with internal enemies.

At the same time that cold-war intrigue raised suspicions, so, too, did the period's economic development. While plenitude after World War II bred substantial conformity among whites, as evident, for example, in the rapid growth of suburbia, it intensified the discontent among African-Americans burdened with an inferior social, political, and economic status. The civil rights movement gained momentum, at first largely through legal action, such as the monumental case *Brown v. Board of Education of Topeka, Kansas*, whereby the Supreme Court, in 1954, declared public school segregation unconstitutional, but later through protests led by the Reverend Martin Luther King, Jr., and others who believed in nonviolent resistance to promote civil rights. Sit-ins, boycotts, and freedom rides soon shook the nation.

All in all, to many in white America, societal order seemed under assault by Communists and blacks, and some wondered if a connection existed between the two groups. Amid this concern, witch hunts began in search of enemies and their conspiratorial evil influences. Congress held hearings on domestic communism, most notably those led by Senator Joseph McCarthy, and labeled all leftists as "Reds." Also so labeled were many who, although not leftists, challenged the status quo: labor officials at odds with big business, teachers who questioned conformist values, witnesses who refused to cooperate with congressional inquisitions, and civil rights leaders, such as King. The director of the Federal Bureau of Investigation (FBI), J. Edgar Hoover, strongly believed that an insidious connection existed involving King, other civil rights activists, and the Communist movement.

Cultural shock waves, international and domestic, thus combined to produce societal tension. In his seminal book *The Paranoid Style in American Politics and Other Essays*, historian Richard Hofstadter referred to these developments as not unlike ones in other tension-filled periods in America's past when paranoid extremists had attacked Jews, Catholics, Mormons, Indians, Freemasons, and financiers. According to historian David Brion Davis, "The American people have...been subjected to continual alarms and warnings of imminent catastrophe."[4] In this cold-war period, the paranoid style in politics emphasized not special economic interests but, at least among conservatives, status, that is, cultural and moral concerns about crime, drug use, pornography, and nonconformist behavior. Senator Thomas H. Kuchel of California complained in the 1950s about "fright mail" coming from his constituents. These letters, approximately 10 percent of all those he received, made hysterical assertions about the American military being commanded by a Russian colonel in the United Nations, and about black troops from Africa stationed in Georgia, preparing to lead an international attack to overthrow the government.

The paranoid style in the cold war involved exaggeration, suspicion, and conspiracy (much as it would in the 1990s). Paranoiacs saw the world in simplistic overtones: black and white, us versus them. In the paranoid style, conspiracy became more than a mere factor in history: It was the primary cause, the engine driving events. Conspiracy brought revolution, war, social upheaval, economic hardship. Mistakes did not occur; what appeared to be mistakes were actually conspirators at work, selling out their fellow citizens. In this situation, only dedicated crusaders could put up the good fight. Compromise could not be condoned: The crusader battles to the finish, and anything short of complete victory means failure.

The extreme right viewed the American Revolution as a fight for individual freedom, and, holding to this ideal, rejected socialism, and, in some instances, big corporations, and longed for a return to an era when small farms and trades prevailed. Extreme rightists did not want to uplift the dispossessed as much as reverse the declining status of particular groups; indeed, they saw themselves caught in deterioration resulting from economic constraints, or challenges to their values, or both. When this status anxiety cut sharply, it cut across class lines and included the wealthy as well as the middle and lower strata.

Such status movements developed scapegoats and indulged in irrational behavior. Although those who authored conspiracy theories seemed to present intellectual arguments within wordy treatises, at some point their writing required the reader to simply have faith and trust the conclusions presented. Surface rationality devolved into unsubstantiated claims.

The cold war would last through the 1980s, until the Soviet Union collapsed, but it is in its early stages, in the 1940s into the 1960s where we find right-wing radicalism taking shape, setting themes and fears that, mixed with newer elements, exist in today's militia movement. Three prominent right-wing extremist groups that appeared during this early cold-war period crafted and perpetuated a far-right ideology: the John Birch Society, the Liberty Lobby, and the Minutemen. But extremism did not belong only to the right, and so two prominent left-wing groups also appeared: the Black Panthers and Weatherman.

The John Birch Society

Contributing to right-wing extremism, the John Birch Society emerged in 1958 after businessman Robert Welch conducted a meeting in Indianapolis, where 11 people—largely fellow businessmen—gathered and agreed to found a new organization aimed at destroying big government and communism, which they believed to be ruining America. The group opposed the federal income tax, saying it stifled individual initiative; it considered social security and other welfare programs—the entire heritage from the New Deal—to be moving the nation toward totalitarianism. As the Birchers saw it, a Communist conspiracy had gripped America, Communists had taken over the State Department, and Communists ran the civil rights movement with the intention of producing turmoil and weakening society. Welch insisted that "the French people under Louis XIV had as little cause to let themselves be led by conspiratorial destructivists into insane horrors and murderous clamor for 'liberty' as the Negroes in America have today in demand for 'freedom'"[5] In his writings and speeches, Welch told of a cabal underway since the late 1700s, led by a mysterious, atheistic Illuminati seeking to establish a One World government. According to Welch, the Illuminati, which had worked its wiles in the French Revolution, continued doing so through communism. In the United States, the conspiracy included establishing the income tax and the Federal Reserve banking system, amending the Constitution to provide for the direct election of senators (a move that diluted the power of the states), and forming the internationalist United Nations.

During the 1960s, Welch opposed the Vietnam War, calling it a plot by Communists in Hanoi, Moscow, and Washington to discredit America. Birch Society literature continued to argue that African-Americans should look not to the government for help, but to their own community. The Birchers still blamed civil strife and racial unrest on a combination of Communist agitators and a weakened American moral fiber.

In *The Invisible Government*, Dan Smoot, a prominent Bircher, argued that the Council on Foreign Relations and other "associated tax-exempt organizations" were engaged in a conspiracy to control Congress and the public for insidious reasons. "The fact is," Smoot argued, "that every step the United States takes toward political and economic entanglements with the rest of the world is a step toward realization of the end objective of communism: creating a One World socialist political and economic system in which we will be one of the subjugated provinces."[6] He called New Deal liberalism nothing less than undemocratic centralism, draining power from the people and the states.

In 1965, Revilio P. Oliver, a professor of classics at the University of Illinois and, like Smoot, a leading Bircher, claimed that the nation's capital was populated mainly by "hordes of thieves, perverts, and traitors."[7] Oliver condemned what he called a conspiracy of Communists, Illuminati, and Jews. His anti-Semitism became so strong that in 1966 the Birch Society forced him to relinquish his membership.

Birchers did not engage in terrorist activities or paramilitary exercises. Their tactics involved writing letters, issuing propaganda, lobbying to repeal the income tax and impeach liberal Supreme Court Justice Earl Warren, and maneuvering to take over the Republican Party, an effort they considered promising, if not successful, with the nomination of conservative Barry Goldwater for president in 1964 (although Goldwater was not a Bircher). The Birchers joined the frenzied hunt for Communists, making accusations and ruining reputations as their crusade equated good Americanism with ideological conformity.

Although the Birchers never attracted a large membership—Welch did not see the group as a mass party but as a "striking force"—they had a substantial sympathetic audience. Those they recruited tended to be well educated, young, and wealthy. Ideologically, the typical Bircher fit the description Richard Hofstadter presented of a paranoiac personality: "He believes himself to be living in a world in which he is spied upon, plotted against, betrayed, and very likely destined for total ruin. He feels that his liberties have been arbitrarily and outrageously violated."[8]

The Liberty Lobby

Extremism reared its head too in the Liberty Lobby, founded in 1957 by Willis Carto, who announced its formation in his publication *Right*. This organization attracted two men who became influential in shaping its agenda, Revilio P. Oliver and fellow college professor Austin J. App. A book also influenced the Liberty Lobbyists and became a standard among right-wing extremists. Entitled *Imperium,* and written in 1949 by Francis Parker Yockey, a law graduate from Notre Dame, it envisioned a beneficent future in which science would serve technology and in which Jews would be controlled by an authoritarian government. Yockey called Jews the destroyers of civilization and implied that Hitler was a hero.

Strongly racist and nativistic, that is, protective of white American culture from any so-called pollution by foreigners and their ideas, the Liberty Lobby supported the segregationist system in the South and, like the Birchers, tried to take over the Republican Party. Toward this end, it often cooperated with the Birch Society, although the latter considered its comrades too anti-Semitic. With radio programs, videotapes, books, publications—especially *Spotlight*, a weekly newspaper—and inside political connections, the Liberty Lobby grew in the 1970s and continued its influence during the growth of militias in the 1990s.

The Minutemen

Cold-war extremism, fed by fears about communism and a One World system, evolved into a militia movement when Robert DePugh, head of a veterinary drug firm in Missouri, founded the Minutemen in 1961. As a member of the John Birch Society, DePugh drew much of his ideology from it. He, too, saw communism on the verge of conquering America and circulated a report in which he claimed that Chinese Communists had massed below the Mexican border, poised to attack. America's salvation, he believed, rested on people who thought as he did, armed and ready to fight for liberty, like their predecessors in 1776. DePugh asserted, "If this nation is saved, it must be by [its] backbone...by those who are willing to sacrifice, by those who are willing to work, by the little people."[9] Although the Minutemen emphasized propaganda and spying on "enemies," DePugh advised in his publication *On Target*, "If you are ever going to buy a gun, buy it now," and insisted that whatever happens to America, "we're going to crawl out of this hole as a well-knit combat outfit."[10] In 1964, DePugh broke with the Birchers after a dispute erupted over his alleged attempt to dominate the group. He then established a training camp in California where some 50 Minutemen learned combat tactics. The fight, he declared, had begun between individualism and collectivism, and the Minutemen, he instructed, must operate in small units to spread propaganda and remain militarily vigilant. Although DePugh's organization never numbered more than a few hundred, he believed it had "the most sophisticated and best equipped underground army movement this world has ever seen."[11]

The Minutemen spread into several states, and numerous paramilitary groups operated in affiliation with them—the Sons of Liberty, Christian Soldiers, and Soldiers of the Cross. Some Minutemen planned to assassinate Arkansas Senator J. William Fulbright, a prominent liberal in foreign affairs, and to release cyanide into the ventilation system at United Nations headquarters in New York City.

In the mid-1960s, the Minutemen suffered a setback when the federal government arrested DePugh for violating the National Firearms Act. He resigned in 1967 as head of his organization, but still oversaw its operation and promoted a stridently violent strategy. Later that year, an explosion at a police station in Redmond, Washington, detonated by Minutemen, and an attempt to rob three banks resulted in DePugh's indictment for conspiracy. He fled the authorities, but his capture and conviction, coming on the heels of his earlier trouble, doomed the Minutemen, until their revival two decades later.

Two Left-Wing Extremist Groups: The Black Panthers and Weatherman

Of course, not all paranoid extremists came from the right-wing; the left-wing had its share, too. But the two differed in world view and goals. Those of the extreme left did not idolize George Washington, Paul Revere, or other heroes of the American Revolution; the group idolized Karl Marx, Ho Chi Minh, and Mao Tse-tung—or other heroes of anti-capitalist revolts—and strove to advance some kind of socialist system that would improve the status of the dispossessed in society.

For extreme leftists, the Vietnam War proved the oppression of capitalism in the United States, and it stimulated a violent attempt to overthrow the system. This effort appeared most prominently within two groups, the Black Panthers and Weatherman, whose emergence in the mid- to late-1960s occurred as the war intensified.

In response to what they considered to be racist oppression, evident in the economic exploitation of African-Americans and the large numbers of them dying in Vietnam, the Black Panthers organized several militia units. This group, founded in 1967 by Huey Newton and Bobby Seale, arose primarily in northern and western ghettos and took a militant position to advance Black Power. The Panthers never clearly defined the concept, but it generally meant self-determination for African-Americans, the promotion of black community and black pride, the replacement of capitalism with socialism, and the use of militias to end police brutality and destroy the existing power structure. The Panthers wore battle fatigues, drilled and marched in military formation, and openly carried rifles and guns. In the ghettos, they formed patrols to monitor the police (whom they labeled a white occupation army) and to prevent mistreatment of those stopped or arrested. Several Panthers engaged in shoot-outs with the authorities. The Panthers, though, insisted they used guns only for defensive purposes.

Also disenchanted with the Vietnam War and the failure of the U.S. government to eradicate economic, political, and social injustice, Weatherman emerged in 1969, committed to fomenting revolution and replacing capitalism with socialism. In one protest—the Days of Rage that October in Chicago—the group took to the streets with bottles, chains, and clubs in an assault on the police. Weatherman considered street fighting a way of showing revolutionary bravery, and one leader, Bernardine Dohrn, organized a women's militia for the Chicago event. The following year, several Weathermen went underground and resorted to bombing public buildings. By and large, though, these Weathermen did not rely on arming and training a militia; instead, they resorted to terrorism.

Right-Wing Extremism Resurgent: The 1970s and 1980s

Even though American military troops gradually withdrew from Vietnam in the early 1970s, extremism continued. While with a few exceptions the radical left receded, in part because the war no longer existed as a rallying point, the radical right expanded, still tied to cold-war fears that communism would take over the world, but obtaining fresh energy from the myriad of cultural changes brought on during the 1960s, such as civil rights for blacks, expanded rights for women, a larger welfare state, and a stronger national government that had been used to advance these changes. Right-wing extremism manifested itself in numerous notable developments, including the formation of the National Caucus of Labor Committees, the modern Ku Klux Klan, the White Aryan Resistance, the Order, Aryan Nations, and the Posse Comitatus; the expansion of Identity Christianity; and the emergence of the New Right.

The National Caucus of Labor Committees

The National Caucus of Labor Committees (NCLC) emerged from the experiences of its founder, Lyndon LaRouche, a 1960s leftist who went to the other extreme in the 1970s and organized a far right militia movement. His right-wing tactics remained largely the same as his left-wing ones and included TV advertising campaigns and violence. By 1973, the NCLC had 600 members in 25 cities and published a newspaper, *New Solidarity*. LaRouche directed members of NCLC to disrupt Communist Party meetings and beat up its leaders (in what he called Operation Mop Up); he held ego-stripping sessions to rid members of their individuality and thus maintain their ideological purity; and he invented stories of assassination plots against himself to keep the group united through hysteria. In 1973, LaRouche organized street-fighting units, or what he called a paramilitary structure, to unite urban gangs and politicize them. This Revolutionary Youth Movement collapsed after police arrested several gang members on weapons charges.

The NCLC displayed a paranoid political style, infused with anti-Semitism. LaRouche declared that an evil dictatorship existed in America dominated by international Zionist bankers. This had to be replaced by an authoritarian regime with a centralized, disciplined economy, along with engineers and scientists trained and totally committed to advance American world domination. In his scenario, all political opposition would be purged by the police, and Jews would be expelled from the country.

In the late 1970s and 1980s, LaRouche entered mainstream politics. He tried to win the Democratic presidential primaries, but never got higher than two percent of the vote; at the same time, he supported Ronald Reagan's campaign to win the Republican presidential nomination. Although Reagan never publicly embraced LaRouche, the NCLC leader briefly wielded considerable influence within the president's administration. While participating in mainstream politics, LaRouche established a secret paramilitary boot camp near Argyle, New York. Those who attended learned how to use rifles and explosives, and from this came several local militia units. In 1988, LaRouche's drive toward power ended with his conviction for loan fraud. The NCLC continued, but in diminished form. In 1996 LaRouche, out of prison, again entered the race for the Democratic presidential nomination.

The Ku Klux Klan

The modern KKK, born amid the cultural and social strife of the 1960s, exhibited a resurgent militancy in the 1970s and 1980s. It was anchored to fears among some whites that the civil rights movement had ruined the nation, and that Communists and socialists stood ready to destroy liberty. Of course, the KKK had a long history that preceded the cold war, and over the years it had undergone several transformations. From 1867 to 1871, during the Reconstruction Era after the Civil War, the original, or first Klan, appeared, and it intimidated African-Americans in the South, and any white Southerners who supported black civil rights. This KKK did not organize militias as such, but enforced its program through terrorist activities—burnings, beatings, and lynchings.

A second KKK emerged in 1915, created by 15 men who gathered atop Stone Mountain near Atlanta, where they burned a huge pine-board cross. This second Klan exerted its influence well beyond the South and became a powerful organization in the Midwest, experiencing its most dynamic growth in urban areas and attracting several million members with its promise to protect white civilization from people it considered to be inferior, namely blacks, Jews, and immigrants. But the second KKK collapsed in the 1920s, after the public became disenchanted with its violent tactics, and a morals scandal involving a Klan leader destroyed the organization's reputation as protector of traditional American values.

The Invisible Empire was perhaps the most militant of several state and regional organizations that identified themselves as part of the Klan. In the 1970s, its leader, Bill Wilkinson, surrounded himself with booted, uniformed bodyguards armed with pistols, rifles, and shotguns. In October 1979, a Klan group under Virgil Griffin earned notoriety when its members fired into an anti-Klan rally held by the Communist Worker's Party in Greensboro, North Carolina, killing five people. The Klan colluded with Nazis in the attack.

In the early 1980s, a Klan organization in Texas under leader Louis Beam provided paramilitary training for its supporters to attack fishing boats in Galveston Bay, ones owned by Vietnamese immigrants. In 1981, the KKK joined other right-wing extremists for military training maneuvers in California's Sierra Nevada mountains, while another Klan group operated a paramilitary camp near Birmingham, Alabama. One newspaper reporter there told of how the mountains echoed with the sounds of war and of how participants talked about fighting a race battle against blacks. In the late 1980s, the Klan, heavily splintered and lacking a single dominant group, increasingly allied itself with neo-Nazis.

David Duke and the Extremist Appeal

Anti-Semitism, racism, Communist conspiracies, fear—these created the atmosphere for an intensified militia movement. At the same time, the appeal traveled beyond extremists to entice a wider range of the nation's disaffected and dissatisfied. David Duke showed this when, in 1989, he ran as a Republican for a seat in the Louisiana legislature and won. The former grand wizard of the Louisiana Knights of the Ku Klux Klan embraced not only racism, but also anti-Semitism, claiming that a Jewish conspiracy existed to oppress America. Although the national Republican Party censored Duke, the state organization refused to follow suit, even after he used his legislative office to sell literature such as *Hitler Was My Friend*; even after he appeared at a rally in Chicago for the Populist Party, an anti-Semitic group, where bodyguards wearing Nazi uniforms protected him, and a crowd cheered as he told them his election represented a victory for the "white majority movement."[12] Duke obtained his greatest support from those in the middle and working classes who felt squeezed from the top by the wealthy and from the bottom by welfare recipients, and from those who experienced or feared declining incomes and job opportunities, and those who believed that blacks did not meet the standard of hard work and individual initiative that had made America great. Although Duke lost his subsequent bids for the U.S. Senate and the Republican presidential nomination, the paranoid politics he represented, immersed in rage, grew in the 1980s alongside other forms of racism and anti-Semitism, prominently displayed in the White Aryan Resistance and the Order.

The White Aryan Resistance and the Order

Tom Metzger, whose activist roots extended back to the Ku Klux Klan, organized young people in the 1980s into the White Aryan

Resistance (WAR), a neo-Nazi Skinhead group. Metzger's Skinheads and other rightist Skinhead groups attacked Jews, blacks, and homosexuals. Numbering a few thousand, WAR considered itself a revolutionary vanguard seeking to overthrow the existing governmental system. Both Metzger and his son John, an equally important Skinhead leader, advocated class warfare against wealthy whites and the formation of terrorist cells—small, secretive groups intended to plan and perform violent acts against public facilities. Further, the Metzgers circulated books telling how to assassinate people and make bombs.

In 1983, Robert Matthews founded the Order, formally the Silent Brotherhood, in Metaline Falls, Idaho. Anti-Semitic and opposed to nearly all federal authority, including taxes, the Order, with approximately 40 members, plotted to overthrow the American government, or what it called the Zionist Occupation Government (ZOG). Toward this end, several Order members went on a rampage, printing counterfeit money, robbing $3.8 million from a Brinks armored truck in 1984, and killing Alan Berg, a liberal Jewish talk show host in Denver. Later that year, the FBI tracked Matthews down and killed him in a shoot-out at Whidbey Island in Washington. Over the next two years, the authorities arrested Matthews' accomplices and the Order dissolved.

In its ideas about Zionist occupation, the Order had reflected the bigotry found in an early twentieth-century work, *The Protocols of the Meetings of the Learned Elders of Zion,* that had attained new popularity, and strong circumstantial evidence exists to indicate the Order consciously modeled itself after the organization described in a more recent anti-Semitic book, *The Turner Diaries.*

Published in Russia sometime between 1903 and 1907, *The Protocols of the Meetings of the Learned Elders of Zion* purports to be minutes from a secret gathering of Jewish leaders in the late nineteenth century. The 24 protocols outline a so-called Jewish conspiracy to dominate Gentiles and establish a world dictatorship. "Even now [control of the press] is already being attained by us, inasmuch as all news items are received by a few agencies," The Protocols proclaim.13 The "minutes" further reveal that Jewish conspirators directed the French Revolution, communism, and numerous upheavals to force the masses to accept authoritarian Zionist rule. In addition, Jews intended to control all money needed by businesses and to make materialism a cult, so that when economic troubles ensued, the lower classes would

015 WALTRIP H.S. LIBRARY

rise up against wealthy Gentiles. "All terror will emanate from us," pronounce the Elders. "Party conflict and paralysis in government will be orchestrated—there are no checks to limit the range of our activities."[14] Although a fake document, plagiarized from a pamphlet written by a Frenchman in the 1860s, right-wing extremist groups in the United States treated it as truth.

The Turner Diaries achieved a similar status. Authored in 1979 by William Pierce, a self-professed Nazi who obtained a physics degree at the University of Colorado and wrote under the pen name Andrew Macdonald, this novel portrays Earl Turner, the central character, as beset by gun control laws, urban riots, and Jewish-directed schemes in the 1990s. Turner puts together the Organization to overthrow the corrupt U.S. government and at one point blows up a federal building. The Organization gains control of North America and Europe and uses nuclear, biological, and chemical weapons to eliminate all nonwhites. This book found an audience with yet another far-right ideology expanding in the 1980s: Identity Christianity.

Identity Christianity, Aryan Nations, and Identity Survivalists

Identity Christianity actually had emerged as a full-blown ideology shortly after World War II, when Wesley Swift and William Potter Gale promoted it through the Christian Defense League, a religious group whose doctrine portrayed Jews as the devil's children, engaged in a conspiracy to take over the world. In the 1980s, several small Identity churches emerged similar to Swift's own Church of Jesus Christ Christian, claiming they "identified" (hence the name) with the Ten Lost Tribes that had been conquered in 722 B.C. and dispersed from Israel. According to Identity belief, these tribes had journeyed during an ancient period to England, where they had developed a superior culture, one divinely inspired, and one that made Americans, at least those descended from British civilization, the chosen people of God.

These Identity churches sometimes ignored the anti-Semitic emphasis in Swift's church; instead, they stressed the supremacy of the white race over "coloreds" or the "mud people" (as they called nonwhites), who had no right to equality with whites. A primary Aryan characteristic, Identity Christians asserted, was the ability to blush, or as they put it, show "blood in the face." The differences between anti-Semites and racists—Identity

Christians preferred the term "racialists"—proved slight, however, and in most Identity churches the concepts intermingled and became nearly indistinguishable. After all, Armageddon, the story had it, would in the end pit Aryans against both enemies, Jews and nonwhites.

Apocalyptic visions permeated Identity groups: They foresaw a showdown between Aryans and Jews (the latter representing Satan), at which time the U.S. government would collapse and a conflagration would begin, a necessary prerequisite to the Second Coming of Christ. Unlike fundamentalist Christians (criticized as too pro-Israel), Identity Christians believed no one would escape the impending battle; there would be no rapture, no dwelling with Christ prior to His Second Coming, not even for the righteous. Regardless of faith or piety the fight would ensue, and Aryans had to be mentally, physically, and morally prepared. One Identity group proclaimed, "We of the Nordic race who believe in Jesus Christ are determined this nation will remain ours."[15]

The Identity movement took an ominous turn in the 1980s, when Aryan Nations, a political arm of Identity Christianity founded by Richard Girnt Butler, a leader in the Christian Defense League, grew as a threatening force. Aryan Nations included Identity and non-Identity racists and considered itself engaged in a battle to protect and advance white power. One leader asserted, "We're racial brothers and sisters, struggling for the survival of the white race."[16] The organization was soon implicated in several plots to bomb businesses in Seattle. Meanwhile, Butler tried unsuccessfully to build a solid bond among Identity Christians, neo-Nazis, and the Ku Klux Klan and promoted the Northwest Territorial Imperative to make the Pacific Northwest a separate Aryan state, one in which only whites and Christians would be allowed to live. Butler portrayed it thus: "All hybrids called Jews are to be repatriated from the Republic's territory, and all their wealth be redistributed to restore our people...."[17]

At about the same time, several militant Identity survivalist groups emerged, determined to divorce themselves from mainstream society and prepare for the impending end of civilization. They built fortified camps and started paramilitary training, indicating a turn toward militia formation. In the 1980s, the Covenant, the Sword, and the Arm of the Lord (CSA) developed a heavily armed compound on 224 acres of land in the Arkansas Ozarks. The group's commando expert presented workshops on weaponry and conducted a military boot camp.

As these groups, movements, and ideas materialized, conspiracy theories abounded. According to Identity Christians, Jews controlled Hollywood ("Kosher Valley") with their power-perverted morals; the American Medical Association worked in league with Jewish leaders to poison Aryans through techniques such as chemotherapy; enemies of the white race were importing immigrants to contaminate the race with diseases; and foreign governments were using electromagnetic devices to alter weather patterns within the United States.

American Christian Ministries, America's Promise Ministries, Christ's Gospel Fellowship, the Christian Israel Covenant Church, Scriptures for America—these Christian Identity churches dotted the national landscape with small congregations that espoused racist and anti-Semitic hatred, or what they called "love for the white race." The group Scriptures for America used satellite television and shortwave radio to communicate its abhorrence for interracial marriages, while the Phineas Priesthood asserted that the highest calling from God was to murder Jews, blacks, and homosexuals. Taken together, Identity church membership totaled less than 40,000, but their influence among extremists exceeded this number. In the 1980s, Identity Christianity permeated a radical movement that had begun two decades earlier, but now attracted an audience in the economically hard-pressed Midwest: the Posse Comitatus.

Identity Christianity and the Posse Comitatus

Founded by Henry L. Beach, an Oregonian and retired dry-cleaning executive, the Posse Comitatus condemned liberal cultural changes and federal programs. A Posse-controlled radio station in Kansas intoned:

> [The Bible] didn't say you were going to vote them out—it said, "thus with violence shall the great city Babylon—that international Communist system—be thrown down and shall be found no more...." And all the disco bongo congo from the bongo is gonna' be gone. All the nigger jive and the tootsie wootsie is going to go.[18]

Posse ideology recognized no governmental authority higher than the county sheriff. Everything above that position lacked validity, for state and federal governments had usurped popular rights by taking power away from the local community. Consequently, Posse members refused to pay federal taxes—they refused even to purchase drivers' licenses and license plates for their cars. The Posse did not consider county sheriffs infallible, however; citizens in local communities had the ultimate power and responsibility to decide if the sheriffs were performing their duties properly. If the sheriff had failed, they were to bring him to the gallows and execute him in public at high noon, with his body remaining until sundown as an example to others who might subvert the law and defy the popular will.

The Posse cloaked itself in secrecy. Although it occasionally ran candidates for public office, it believed that publicity only invited federal oppression. The group refused to divulge membership numbers, but outsiders estimated that in the 1980s, 78 chapters existed in 23 states. In addition, the Posse often had close ties to other right-wing groups, including the Iowa Society of Education, the Montana Vigilantes, and the Christian Posse. One Posse leader publicly proclaimed that his organization had engaged in cooperative paramilitary training with members of the Ku Klux Klan and the Minutemen. On the other hand, Posse tactics often contributed to differences within the right-wing, as when the Birchers scorned the Posse as a bunch of crazies and the Posse responded by calling the Birchers weak.

Identity Christianity exerted a strong influence within the Posse. The group believed that a Jewish conspiracy existed, including one that involved the FBI and Central Intelligence Agency in league with the secret Jewish police. The Posse embraced Aryan supremacy and believed in an impending cataclysmic battle. Many in the Posse cherished *The Turner Diaries*, and some advocated a race war. In 1982, the Posse issued arrest warrants against a sheriff and his deputy in a small Kansas town. The attempt to capture the sheriff fizzled, but the event sent shock waves across the Midwestern countryside and showed the stridency within the Posse.

The most nationally recognized Posse incident involved Gordon Kahl, a farmer living in North Dakota who joined the Covenant, the Sword, and the Arm of the Lord and embraced Identity Christianity. He soon established his own church, the Gospel Divine Doctrine Church of Jesus Christ. When hard times struck the farm belt in the early 1980s (including his own farm), he spoke at rallies, portraying the federal government as Satan.

At the time, Kahl was on probation for having failed to pay his income taxes. (He had served one year in prison.) He still refused to file; and after he violated the terms of his probation, federal marshals, warrant in hand, tracked him down. Close to his farm near Medina, North Dakota, they set up a roadblock. Soon Kahl and several others—one of them his 23-year-old son—arrived in two cars. Kahl did not surrender, but stood his ground, rifle in hand. Then someone fired a shot, probably Kahl's son, and a bloody 30-second exchange followed. Amazingly, Kahl escaped, leaving behind two dead and four wounded marshals. Kahl took his wounded son to the local hospital, then fled.

He made his way to Arkansas, where it took several months for federal marshals to find him. In early 1983, they surrounded his hideout, a house made into a fortified bunker. After Kahl shot a local sheriff (who later died from his wounds), marshals fired into the bunker. They killed Kahl, but the episode made the Identity Christian a martyr, not only within the Posse Comitatus but also within the extreme right. To many radicals, Kahl's death reinforced their view that the federal government had become oppressive.

The New Right

The 1990s militia movement should not be seen as rooted only in those fringe groups discussed earlier that embrace Identity Christianity or other extreme racist and anti-Semitic ideas, for another wellspring is the widespread distrust of government that flowed through society in the 1980s. Such distrust reflected a strong conservative orientation with little tolerance for compromise. A New Right was born at this time, shaped considerably by political strategist Richard Viguerie. He thought that conservatives had previously compromised too much with liberals. Viguerie wanted to boost defense spending, dismantle social programs, and advance a traditional moral agenda in agreement with Christian fundamentalists. Toward this end, he linked the New Right to populist themes—the government bureaucracy stifled individuals, the media acted irresponsibly, academia condoned evil. One analyst claimed that the New Right, in this manifestation, was led by "passionate and angry men."[19]

Enter the 1990s: Government Assaults and Congressional Elections

Moving into the 1990s, this New Right made more possible the growth of militias, and nowhere more so than in the West, with a few exceptions an intensely conservative region. Here two additional developments intervened to build anger and hatred toward the federal government and convince the far right that liberty stood threatened: the showdown at Ruby Ridge, Idaho, and the conflagration at Waco, Texas. The anger affected more than the far right, however, and contributed to dramatic results in the 1994 congressional elections, sweeping conservatives and extremists from the West and other regions into power and advancing, at least for the time being, the New Right's drive to promote its agenda as national policy.

Ruby Ridge and Waco

Oppression appeared real at Ruby Ridge in 1992, when a controversial showdown occurred at a cabin owned by Randy Weaver and occupied by him, his wife, their children, and a friend. The federal government had begun pursuing Weaver shortly after he failed to show for a court hearing related to charges against him for having sold illegal shotguns to agents from the Bureau of Alcohol, Tobacco, and Firearms (BATF). Although the notice Weaver received to appear at the hearing had listed the wrong date, the government issued a warrant for his arrest and tracked him to his cabin. As federal marshals approached Weaver's primitive dwelling—it had no electricity or running water— shots rang out. Apparently, a surveillance team had encountered Weaver's 14-year-old son, Samuel; Weaver's friend, Kevin Harris; and the family dog. The gunfire erupted after a federal agent shot at the dog, and in the subsequent exchange, both Samuel and a surveillance team member were killed—Samuel from a shot in the back.

The FBI promptly dispatched a special Hostage Rescue Team to Ruby Ridge. One of its members, while aiming for Weaver, instead hit and killed Weaver's wife, Vicki, as she stood at the cabin door, holding her baby daughter. A 10-day siege ensued, during which Weaver and Harris, both wounded, remained in the cabin with Weaver's children (and his wife's dead body). The federal government brought in helicopters and armored personnel carriers. Weaver finally surrendered, and he and Harris were tried for the death of the federal agent. A jury acquitted them, and a government investigation subsequently found the FBI guilty of having violated long-standing rules of engagement—orders that shots be fired only at armed adults, and then only if life were endangered. The investigation concluded that Vicki Weaver's civil rights had been violated. After many denials and obstructions, including withholding crucial evidence, the Justice Department finally agreed in August 1995 to settle civil damage claims Weaver had filed against the federal government. Weaver's family received $3.1 million.

Many radicals believed government authorities had not only used excessive force but also persecuted Weaver for his beliefs: Identity Christianity and white separatism as espoused by Aryan Nations. The episode proved embarrassing to the FBI and served to reinforce conspiratorial fears among radicals. Ruby Ridge resulted, too, in Pete Peters and other leaders of the Christian Identity conducting a meeting in October 1992 in Colorado. There, they tried to forge unity within the far right, and formulated plans to organize militias. Although these leaders proved unsuccessful in establishing a central organization, their ideas resonated with extremists.

Oppression and conspiracy again seemed at work in 1994 at Mount Carmel, the Branch Davidian compound near Waco, Texas. Seven years earlier, David Koresh had become leader of the Branch Davidians, an offshoot of the Seventh Day Adventist Church. The Branch Davidians believed in Christ's second coming after an apocalypse. Critics labeled Koresh's group a cult, and one news report called the leader a "charismatic psychopath." Koresh declared himself the "father" of all the children, insisted on spartan conditions, armed the compound, and began daily paramilitary training. He did not intend to assault the government, but wrapped Mount Carmel in apocalyptic visions and insisted on defensive preparation.

The Bureau of Alcohol, Tobacco, and Firearms believed Koresh had stockpiled illegal weapons, and on 28 February 1993, agents raided the compound. They bungled what they intended to be a surprise attack. Koresh had stumbled across news of the impending assault after a reporter, tipped off about the raid, asked a stranger directions to the camp. The stranger turned out to be a Branch Davidian who ran to Koresh and told him of strange happenings. When the agents appeared, a gun battle ensued, leaving fatalities on both sides.

The government then surrounded the compound, with the FBI employing the same special unit that had been used at Ruby Ridge. The siege played right into Koresh's apocalyptic vision: The barbed wire, tanks, armored vehicles, helicopters, and recorded chants and animal screams blasted through loudspeakers by the federal agents, in an attempt to unnerve Koresh and his followers, simply fed his delusions.

After the siege had continued into mid-April, the government decided to end it. Tanks punched holes in the walls of the compound and pumped tear gas inside. This done, a fire erupted, and Mount Carmel burned to the ground, killing Koresh and 74 others, including more than 20 children. To this day, no one knows exactly how the fire started—whether the government or the Davidians purposefully set it, or whether it began accidentally, perhaps after a tank knocked over a lantern that, in turn, ignited a dry bale of hay. The latter is the story told by several survivors.

Irrespective of how the fire started, the U.S. government appeared to have erred substantially. To justify the original raid in February, federal officials had contrived stories about illegal drug production. Further, no credible evidence had existed to support the charges of child abuse made by the federal government during the siege, nor had the government recognized the emotionalism and irrationality behind Koresh's apocalyptic message. Added to this, the government had used tear gas dangerous to the children, had not prepared for the possibility of a fire, and had detained fire trucks answering a belated call for help. After the incident, the government failed to use an independent arson investigator, and according to a Treasury Department report, BATF agents lied and withheld evidence to make their position look good. *Commonwealth* magazine claimed that federal actions at Waco only helped "fanatics" who "ranted against the government."[20]

At an ensuing trial, 11 Branch Davidians, who pleaded self-defense, were acquitted of killing four agents during the February raid (although seven were found guilty of aiding and abetting the voluntary manslaughter of a federal agent). The *New York Times* called the verdict a "stunning defeat" for the BATF and Justice Department, and many right-wingers, and numerous people in society's mainstream, saw evidence of a police state out to crush liberty.[21]

The New Right in Congress

Americans elected a new Congress in 1994, one that reflected society's polarization and intolerance. Among the far-right members of the freshman class, none stood out more than Idaho representative Helen Chenoweth. She capitalized on the economic stagnation affecting her home state's First District (which stretches from the panhandle to the counties just west of Boise) and directed the voters' anger toward federal regulations and environmentalists. Her fiery rhetoric depicted a war underway, with the national government out to oppress citizens—as evident in laws that restricted property use, the designation by the United Nations of Yellowstone National Park as a world heritage site, and more spectacularly, in the violent assaults at Ruby Ridge and Waco. She expressed conspiratorial fears and warned of black helicopters flying mysteriously in the sky—some piloted by Federal Fish and Wildlife agents—instituting a police state intended to establish a New World Order.

Chenoweth obtained support from the religious right, the John Birch Society, and most particularly, militia groups. She proclaimed, "We have democracy when the government is afraid of the people."[22] After her election, she worked hard to destroy the environmental movement, which she thought evil. She also continued her attacks on federal regulations, despite the reliance of her district, and the entire West, on the national government for its economic survival; the government sponsored irrigation works, dam construction, and other similar programs. A year later, after the bombing at Oklahoma City, she insisted that the federal government should receive most of the blame for the catastrophe because the government had initiated oppressive acts inviting extremist reactions.

Chenoweth did not stand alone. A Republican representative from California, Robert Dornan, endorsed publications that linked President Clinton to political murders; and Congressman Steve Stockman, a Republican from Texas, supported the idea that federal agents would soon launch a raid on citizen militias as part of an expanding plan to oppress individual liberty.

Blood of the Heroes:
Contemporary Militias Organize

In late summer of 1994, the airwaves in Colorado Springs crackled with rage and chilling sounds. Chuck Baker was hosting his talk show on radio station KVOR, and callers were condemning the recent government actions at Ruby Ridge and Waco. Baker discussed with listeners forming small militia cells in urban and rural areas and provided his own sound effect—staccato clicking, replicating a firing pin in action. To the south, in Arizona, Bob Mohan, broadcasting on KFYI, ridiculed Sarah Brady, the wife of James Brady, former press secretary to President Ronald Reagan. Referring to her and to her husband, seriously wounded several years earlier when an assassin attempted to kill Reagan, he stated: "You know, she ought to be put down. A humane shot at a veterinarian's would be an easy way to do it....I wish she would just keep wheeling her husband around...wiping the saliva off his mouth once in a while—and leave the rest of us damn well alone."[23] Back east, in Washington, talk show host G. Gordon Liddy, a former campaign henchman for President Richard Nixon, told listeners how to shoot BATF agents: "Head shots, head shots," he urged. "Kill the sons of bitches!" This predatory hate talk personified the term that Jonathan Alter, a writer for *Newsweek*, has assigned to the 1990s: "Vulture Culture."[24]

In Noxon, Montana, a small town set against Huckleberry Mountain and approachable only by a one-lane bridge across a river gorge, the Militia of Montana organized, while another militia-affiliated group in the eastern part of the state, the Freemen, indoctrinated children in how to assassinate government officials. In Indiana, Linda Thompson declared herself adjutant general of the Unorganized Militia of the United States. At a pizza parlor in Goshen, New York, a farming town near the Catskills, Tony Russo met with his militia group, formally called the Orange County Committee. At a Michigan gun shop in tiny Alanson, men gathered to organize the Northern Michigan Regional Militia. In reference to Ruby Ridge and Waco, their leader, Norm Olson, declared, "The blood of the heroes is on the ground—people who died for freedom!"[25]

Other towns in other states entered the roster—anxious people, scared people, angry people—listening to talk radio and extremist politicians; watching government ineptitude and the passage of gun control laws; suffering economic stagnation or even decline; and hunkering down, gathering arms, forming militias. No one can be sure how many groups have organized or how many people have joined. Certainly only a small portion of the overall population—likely no more than 100,000—but with an influence that has bolstered the conservative political scene, particularly the extremists.

Witnesses who appeared before a hearing held by Senate Democrats in 1995 to investigate militia activity portrayed the armed organizations in forbidding tones. They told of threats directed at them for having opposed militia positions. One county official in California recounted how she angered a militiaman by insisting she did not have the power to remove a lien from his property. She later found a bomb planted in her car, gunshots were fired into her office, and she was physically attacked—slashed and beaten. Ellen Gray, an official with the

Pilchuck Audobon Society in Everett, Washington, told how, after she spoke in favor of a wetlands protection measure at a public meeting, a militia member said she had better watch out— or she would one day be found hanging from a tree. Martha Bethel, a city judge in Hamilton, Montana, revealed how militia members harassed her after she presided over a trial in which one militiaman was found guilty of not paying three traffic tickets. She received death threats.

Have militias obtained a sinister and insidious form? An answer to this question depends on which segment of the militia movement is studied. Prior to the Oklahoma City bombing in 1995, four organizations emerged as prominent: the Militia of Montana, the Michigan Militia, the American Justice Federation, and the United States Militia Association. Each has features common to the other, and each has its own particular leaders and ideas.

The Militia of Montana

Almost all analysts of right-wing extremism point to the Militia of Montana (MOM) as a leader in today's paramilitary upheaval. Within MOM's ideology we find conspiracy theories served up from earlier times, mixed with opposition to federal authority and the influence of Identity Christianity. The Weaver shoot-out at Ruby Ridge has deeply affected MOM's founder, John Trochmann, an auto parts distributor, who considers it evidence of government tyranny. Back in 1992, Trochmann had publicly renounced his U.S. citizenship and attacked violations of what he called the "organic Constitution," meaning the original Constitution with its first 10 amendments, considered to be a document divinely inspired. He participated in anti-government demonstrations held at Ruby Ridge during the siege and became close friends with Weaver. Then came the conflagration at Waco, which confirmed his fears and caused him, in January 1994, to found MOM. His wife, Carolyn, joined him in leading the organization, as did his brother David and David's son, Randy. Bob Fletcher soon emerged as spokesman for MOM, a position he held until the summer of 1995, when he left the organization.

John Trochmann declared that the time had come to pursue high moral values and gain control of the government from secular humanists and special interest groups, including private corporations. Fletcher reinforced these views. He asserted that constitutional rights were being eroded, with the Second Amendment particularly singled out, and that some federal officials intended moving the nation toward joining a One World government, or New World Order. Under this new government, national boundaries would become meaningless and a world-wide socialist government would rule. The United Nations, he insisted, had made this a goal to be completed by the year 2000. "The sooner people realize it and understand what it means," he said, "the better off everyone will be in America."[26]

Literature issued by MOM avoided explicit racism or anti-Semitism, and on more than one occasion Trochmann denied having any bigoted ideas. He claimed that he just happened to be born white and was not ashamed of his skin color. MOM's leader, however, had previously engaged in prayer meetings with Identity Christians and had visited the Aryan Nations compound in Idaho on several occasions—a compound replete with pictures of Adolph Hitler, swastikas, and a sign at its front entrance emblazoned: "Whites Only." Although in reaction to charges of racism Trochmann claimed he had minimal contact with Aryan Nations, the founder of this group, Richard Girnt Butler, disputed the Montanan's account, claiming Trochmann used to be a frequent guest, helping with Bible studies and advising members on a proper code of conduct.[27] At a militia rally in February 1995, MOM set up a table at which it sold videotapes, including one featuring Martin "Red" Beckman, considered by many observers to be anti-Semitic, and by the Coalition for Human Dignity in Portland, Oregon, to be extremely influential in the militia movement.

Although MOM likely has no more than 250 members, John Trochmann has led it to a high-profile position, providing guidance to other militias and distributing a mail-order catalog packed with videotapes and books about government conspiracies. He issues, too, his Blue Book, a loose-leaf binder filled with material to prove the conspiracy underway against liberty. To show a secret federal plan intended to divide America into occupied regions, the Blue Book once included a map reproduced from a box of Kix cereal, with markings added to it by MOM. When serving as MOM's spokesperson, Bob Fletcher loved to show the Blue Book at meetings with outside groups. He would point to the pages and proclaim: "Russian missiles! Russian trucks! Russian armored personnel carriers! On American soil.... Meanwhile, they're dumping three thousand U.S. tanks into the ocean so we can't defend ourselves. What kind of sense does *that* make, sports fans?"[28]

In addition to the Blue Book, MOM once issued what it called the *M.O.D. Training Manual,* a 200-page publication showing how to use explosives, engage in sabotage (to disrupt the economy), target government buildings (easy to attack), spread false rumors (to conduct a "war of nerves"), and raid armories (to gain weapons and ammunition). The manual states that "the placement of a bomb or fire explosion of great destructive power, which is capable of effecting irreparable loss against the enemy...is an action the urban guerrilla must execute with the greatest cold-bloodedness," and it recommends kidnapping prominent persons as a means to generate propaganda.[29] Claiming he neither knew what "M.O.D." stood for nor realized what the manuals contained, David Trochmann recently distanced MOM from them and ended their sale.

MOM has distributed other training manuals that clarify the meaning of militias, show how to take up arms within constitutional guidelines, and provide excerpts from *The Federalist*. And it publishes *Taking Aim*, a leading militia newsletter that presents the group's ideas, including the necessity of militias to prepare for war against federal forces in the near future. MOM insists that a governmental conspiracy is already underway to confiscate guns and move America toward authoritarian rule. According to John Trochmann, as with the Revolutionary period, wholesale injustices abound: The presidency became a dictatorship under George Bush, and Bill Clinton continues the practice, using executive orders to override Congress. Further, excessive taxes oppress the populace, the military has fallen under foreign control, and the government used brutal force at Ruby Ridge and Waco. Trochmann reminds people that in the 1780s, James Madison stressed the necessity of a militia to defend freedom—MOM and other patriot groups, he says, are simply following this advice.

Trochmann's critics, including the town historian of Noxon, Montana, accuse him of racism and greed, insisting Trochmann has on numerous occasions expressed his views that only whites are God's children and that women should not vote or own property. Trochmann used to work on old cars and relied on food stamps, reports the historian, but later, amid the hills that sometimes reverberated with automatic weapons fire, he began carrying bundles of catalogs to the post office for mailing, along with parcels containing books and videotapes ordered by people from around the nation. Thus, the historian believes, while Trochmann appears to be only concerned with principles, the militia has become a lucrative business important to his prosperity. Another long-time Noxon resident insists that John Trochmann has categorized Jews and nonwhites as inferior and that everyone in town knows it. On the other hand, Dennis Nichols, publisher of the local Noxon newspaper, calls Trochmann sincere in his disavowal of white supremacy.[30]

A strange incident occurred on 3 March 1995, between Trochmann and the law enforcement officers in Musselshell County, Montana. That evening, two vehicles containing five men entered the parking lot of the Musselshell County Sheriff's Department. The men intended to help two other men—in ways not clear, perhaps to escape—who had been arrested a short while before on charges of violating a concealed weapons law. Three of the men from the cars entered the sheriff's office and demanded that the two prisoners be released. The would-be rescuers, however, were themselves arrested for carrying concealed weapons. Deputies then arrested Trochmann and another man, both of whom had remained outside in a locked car, on a conspiracy charge. The arrests led to MOM orchestrating hundreds of phone calls and telegrams demanding Trochmann's release. Many who sent the messages expressed racist views and used threatening, fiery language. The authorities freed Trochmann because of insufficient evidence to prove the conspiracy charge. (See the testimony by John Bohlman in chapter 4.)

MOM's extremism has company in Montana. In fact, its actions occur within a context of local intolerance. Journalist Donald Voll says of the state: "This place is the motherlode not only of the militia movement but also of the deepest, most unsettling paranoia I've felt anywhere in my own country."[31] Racist and anti-Semitic groups, along with those opposed to federal jurisdiction, abound, perhaps encouraged by the state's spaciousness, which gives a sense of unrestricted activity; or by its largely white population; or by the difficulty law enforcement has in covering such a large area. There are so many groups, including Identity Christians, Christian Patriots, Constitutionalists, Aryan Nations, the Posse Comitatus, the White Students Union, the Church of Jesus Christ Christian, and others, that the Northwest Coalition Against Malicious Harassment warns about increased attacks directed at Jews, Indians, other ethnic minorities, and homosexuals. Stirred by economic problems and reinforced by mounting violence, hate crimes proliferate and involve vandalism and violent assaults on people. In the spirit of extremism, a representative in the Montana legislature recently introduced a bill that would have made it a crime for federal agents to make arrests, searches, or seizures in a locality without first getting the written permission of the county sheriff. The legislature passed it—only the governor's veto kept it from becoming law.

The Michigan Militia

Following MOM's example, a substantial militia organized in northern Michigan in April of 1994 and made its first public appearance at a playground. Amid swings and seesaws, men arrived in the town of Pellston, wearing battle fatigues and carrying guns. They caused a sensation and raised the hackles of many townspeople, who considered the militia's chosen practice area inappropriate. Led by Norm Olson and Ray Southwell, the Michigan Militia chose its venue and uniforms to gain attention, which it certainly did.

Olson, a Baptist pastor and owner of a gun store in Alanson, formed the Michigan Militia after Congress passed legislation restricting some guns and after the incidents at Ruby Ridge and Waco. At the time, he said these developments, plus the influence of Southwell, who had been talking about the evils of big government, convinced him of a threat to liberty. Citizens have the right to form militias, Olson insisted, since under the Tenth Amendment such power resides in the people. He considered it ridiculous to think that only the government could grant the right to organize, because conceivably, the oppressor would have in its hands the right to deny citizens the means needed to fight oppression. American independence came from an armed citizenry, Olson stated, and sometimes armed citizens must correct the government's course. Neither the president nor any legislature, he said, could outlaw the militia.

When he formed the Michigan Militia, Olson claimed that it rejected racism and anti-Semitism, and he condemned Skinheads, Nazis, and the Ku Klux Klan. He expressed constitutionalist views akin to those of the Posse Comitatus, insisting that whenever troubles arise, the local sheriff should deputize a militia, but that if the sheriff turns out to be corrupt, then the local citizens must strike out on their own against tyranny.

Despite his avowed rejection of racism and anti-Semitism, Olson stated his support for a "new confederacy," a favorite term among Identity Christians, since it means developing a theocratic government (in which ministers would rule according to "divine sanction") to replace a federal system considered too favorable to African-Americans. Another incident further called to question his rejection of bigotry: Late in 1994 he met clandestinely with a neo-Nazi leader from Germany. [32]

Under Olson's leadership, the Michigan Militia staged armed training exercises twice each month and claimed to have 12,000 recruits, with units in most of the state's 83 counties.

Southwell once likened this group to the militias of Revolutionary America and criticized Attorney General Janet Reno for forming a Cult Awareness Task Force that he claimed would further intrude on individual liberties. Olson complained that the Michigan Militia had come under intense government surveillance in the form of flyovers by mysterious helicopters and spying by suspicious-looking men who huddled outside meeting places and jotted down license plate numbers. This, Olson said, showed the government's intent to restrict liberty and chill dissent.

Yet extremists with connections to the Michigan Militia stoked government concerns. In January 1995, some of the group's militiamen plotted to bomb Camp Grayling, an Air National Guard base in northern Michigan. They claimed that Soviet tanks had been gathered there for an attack on American citizens. The authorities, however, discovered the militiamen's plot, and the bombing never occurred. Olson distanced himself from the entire scheme, but it seemed to be the work of Mark Koernke, a militia advocate who had a close relationship with Olson and a reputation for stirring discontent and gaining recruits through his speaking engagements and shortwave radio program. Koernke has since formed his own Michigan Militia-at-Large, an armed clandestine group, and Olson has since left the Michigan Militia, which continues to expand.

The American Justice Federation

Another group prominent in the militia movement is led by Linda Thompson, an attorney whose conspiracy views have complemented Olson's. Founded in 1994, Thompson's Indiana-based American Justice Federation (AJF) has not developed into a militia, but it promotes them. Thompson warns about the New World Order, calling it a beast made from money with its anatomy a structured financial system, its physiology greed, and its kinesiology enslavement. Any failure to defeat the beast, she says, will result in tyranny. She states the beast must be starved, and this means Americans must reject the international corporations that nourish it, companies such as Coca-Cola, Nabisco, General Mills, Exxon, and Reebok. To replace them, she advocates developing cottage industries.

In her concerns about liberty and conspiracy throughout America, Thompson complains that police in various localities have been using a little-known legal provision that allows them to pick up and confine to a hospital anyone they consider a danger to others. The confinement can be for 24 hours, or even 72, if hospital authorities declare the person mentally ill. This detention, duly registered, leaves the person with a record that makes legally buying a gun impossible. Thompson calls this a scam intended to reduce gun ownership and restrict the Second Amendment.[33]

Thompson's release of a videotape entitled *Waco: The Big Lie* excoriates the government for its actions against David Koresh, and claims to prove that federal agents committed numerous transgressions, including contributing to the fire that destroyed the Branch Davidian compound. Holes punched in the structure by tanks, she says, created air circulation that spread the flames.

In several statements Thompson has said that a disgruntled Branch Davidian, Mark Breault, circulated stories about wrongdoing at Mount Carmel in an attempt to get back at Koresh for having defeated him in a struggle to control the religious group. She insists that the FBI lied about Koresh putting people under his total control, and about child abuse and drug manufacturing at the compound. She has compared the putting out of false information about child molesting and weapons caches to the persecution of Jews by the Nazis, and has stated: "If you have a tank on the corner, it doesn't take much to get your compliance. Look at what they did in the Soviet Union. They kick one guy to smithereens, splatter his blood out in the neighborhood, terrorize everybody, and the rest of the neighbors whimper in the corner." Further, she says, using the army against private citizens, as in the case with the tanks employed at Waco, violated the nineteenth-century Posse Comitatus Act that prohibits the use of the military in such situations. She hopes the tragedy will motivate Americans: "So...we have cold-blooded killers running around our country. Isn't it about time you put down your beer, get up off the sofa, and do something about it?"[34]

Thompson's conspiracy theories range widely: reports about UN tanks shipped by rail into Portland, Oregon; highway signs displaying on their reverse sides stickers that serve as directions for the soon-to-be invading armies of the One World government; and internment camps set up by federal authorities to house dissidents. Her assertions and her call in 1994 for an armed march on Congress (later rescinded) earned her a rebuke from the John Birch Society. But, another instance seemed to vindicate some of her views: Many people laughed at her talk of black helicopters flying about and spying on Americans, until the U.S. Army admitted it had an unmarked helicopter unit stationed in Kentucky for its "counter-terrorism" campaign. At that point, some wondered if her extremism had a basis in fact.[35]

The United States Militia Association

A fourth group has stimulated the militia movement. Founded by Samuel Sherwood in 1991, the United States Militia Association (USMA) stands at odds with MOM. From his home in Idaho, Sherwood provides directions on how to form militia units, but expresses his preference for election campaigns and lobbying techniques over paramilitary exercises. He warns, though, of violence as an option, and has stated, "We want a bloodless revolution, but if the bureaucrats won't listen we'll give them a civil war to think about."[36]

Like other militia leaders, Sherwood considers government efforts to restrict gun ownership and the debacles at Ruby Ridge and Waco as grave threats to liberty. He pledges an aggressive effort to protect the people's right to form militias and traces that right back to the Revolutionary era and the Constitution. The independent militia, he argues, emanates from the people as a whole and serves as a bulwark against tyranny. Sherwood says the USMA will support and help create laws at the local and state levels for the formation of city, county, and state militia units. He warns about radicals who would break the laws, and insists that any militia needs to be recognized by the county government. In fact, official USMA policy prohibits militia units from participating in field training exercises where live ammunition is used and forbids them to form military-style units, wear camouflage clothing, or engage in paramilitary training. The policy restricts USMA units to live fire exercises only at official ranges and under the supervision of instructors. Lest militia members be unprepared, however, the USMA advertises in its newsletter essential items for sale: dress tans, Italian military backpacks, and field boots.[37]

Sherwood rejects conspiracy theories and calls *The Protocols of the Meetings of the Learned Elders of Zion* a hoax intended to encourage the persecution of Jews. Evil, he says, has taken hold of the world, but not because a small group of men have plotted to direct it; rather, it has resulted from a widespread decline in morality. He distances himself from white supremacists by rejecting policies based on racial factors, and he condemns *Spotlight*, the publication of the anti-Semitic Liberty Lobby. He says about John Trochmann, "I know [he's] a racist because he told me he is. He'd be happy to enlist that black man in the cause, and when the shooting starts, I guarantee he'll give him a front row seat...." [38] Unlike several other militia groups, especially in the West, the USMA rejects Identity Christianity. Yet Sherwood protects what he considers proper morals and has derided President Bill Clinton for supposedly promoting an ungodly homosexual agenda.

Sherwood's dislike for federal authority reveals itself in his declaration that the government does not have the right to own "federal lands," and he considers both the Democrats and Republicans to be socialists. The USMA wants the repeal of all gun control laws, the establishment of a national militia under the states, the bringing home of all American troops stationed overseas, and the elimination of the income tax and all "welfare programs," including Social Security. Sherwood reports that of late the USMA has grown considerably, with several hundred members in southeastern Idaho alone.[39]

Militias Across the Country

Militias have also organized in other states, brandishing weapons, distributing propaganda, and engaging in paramilitary exercises. In Virginia, the Blue Ridge Hunt Club, a militia begun by James Roy Mullins, planned to raid a National Guard armory at Pulaski—until authorities intervened and discovered that the group advocated an entire series of armed assaults against federal facilities. In Colorado, militias have appeared in Longmont, Boulder, Greeley, Lakewood, and Fort Collins, with the latter group led by a racist connected to Identity Christianity. In New Hampshire, Edward L. Brown has begun the Constitution Defense Militia in Plainsfield, tightly organized with just 15 members. Far to the south, in Florida, Robert Pummer of Stuart has issued the *Florida State Militia Handbook* in which he portrays Ruby Ridge and Waco as evidence of a government conspiracy to confiscate guns and destroy liberty. Pummer believes that Russian and UN troops have invaded American territory, and he recently sponsored an information fair and camp-out in St. Lucie County, attended by over 100 people. In Key Largo, the 1st Regiment Florida Militia has organized around the ideals of the American Revolution, asserting that the time has come to end bondage, much as the founding fathers once ended British rule.

In North Carolina, Albert Esposito leads the Citizens for the Reinstatement of Constitutional Government. He wants the Bible and the Constitution to rule the land, opposes the New

World Order, calls the Federal Reserve Bank part of a conspiracy, and claims that some federal employees have been implanted with microcomputer chips. Esposito urges his followers to stockpile "bibles, bullets, beans, and bandages."[40] Similarly, another North Carolinian, Nord Davis, Jr., claims to have organized Northpoint Teams, select combat units that have intervened in foreign engagements, including the Persian Gulf War. He insists that, if not stopped, a New World Order will soon take over the nation and merge it with other countries into a godless, socialistic system led by the United Nations with the active cooperation of prominent Americans. Toward this end, tyranny lurks. "The first time in this country that the government killed people in a Christian church was Waco," Davis observes. "And look at what's happened since—floods, hurricanes, earthquakes. This has never happened before. [God] won't come back here until we clean it up. The murderers at Waco have to be tried and executed to purify the land."[41] He identifies the main murderer as Attorney General Janet Reno.

In Missouri, the 51st Militia has named itself after the 51-day siege at Waco, which it considers similar to the Revolutionary-era confrontation at Lexington as a "shot heard 'round the world," awakening people to oppressive forces on the march. The 51st Militia fears a national takeover by the United Nations but advises people to accumulate weapons for defensive purposes only. In Texas, Jon Roland has founded the Militia Correspondence Committee in reaction to the events at Waco and to the 1994 Omnibus Violent Crime Control and Preventions Act, more popularly known as the Crime Bill, which bans 19 kinds of semi-automatic weapons. He warns that special-interest groups have caused Congress to pass laws unconstitutionally and instigate a "creeping tyranny" that few people recognize. As to organization, Roland promotes forming militias in rural areas and through neighborhood associations in the cities. In Graham County, Arizona, Sheriff Richard Mack openly declares his support for paramilitary groups, insisting that since, as a part of our history, Paul Revere called out the militia, he wouldn't hesitate to call one out against the federal government, should things get out of hand.[42]

Anti-abortion violence has become yet another part of the evolving militia movement. In May 1994, at a meeting in Wisconsin, the Free Militia distributed a booklet entitled *Principles Justifying the Arming and Organizing of a Militia,* in which it calls America a Christian nation and asserts that armed force may have to be used to uphold a crucial principle: the right to life. Another of the group's manuals, *Army of God,* lists 65 ways to destroy abortion clinics and provides instructions for making a fertilizer bomb from ammonium nitrate and fuel oil. Paul Hill, an anti-abortionist in prison for having gunned down an abortion doctor, told one newspaper, "I could envision a covert organization developing—something like a pro-life IRA [Irish Republican Army]."[43]

Added to this, militant Christian Reconstructionists favor a theocratic state. Toward this end, Reverend Jay Grimstead of the Coalition on Revival, a parent group to many Christian Reconstructionist organizations, promotes county militias to enforce God's law and stop the invasion of socialists from Mexico. Matthew Trewhella, a leading Reconstructionist, declares, "We should be founding militias, and there are people doing it across the nation....Churches can form militia days and teach their men how to fight."[44] For many in the far right, Christian Reconstructionism complements Identity Christianity as a means to build a godly, covenanted nation cleansed of evil elements. According to one report, 85 percent of all militias in America are either Identity Christian or Christian Reconstructionist.

Christian Reconstructionism finds support for a theocratic state in numerous writings, most notably a widely read book among extremists, Charles A. Weisman's *America: Free, White, and Christian,* published in 1989. Weisman portrays the pilgrims as having been guided by God and claims that the founding fathers had no intention of creating a pluralistic nation in terms of non-Christians. "In none of the colonial charters," Weisman says, "will one find the false and nonsensical ideas of religious pluralism where the colonists welcomed the followers of all religions of the world."[45]

Militia Themes

Although the militia movement lacks a centralized structure and militias bicker among themselves, certain themes have emerged common to all of the groups. One involves gun control. The Brady Bill, requiring a five-day waiting period for the purchase of handguns, has angered those who see an attack on the Second Amendment. This feeling has intensified with congressional passage of the 1994 Crime Bill, intended to make certain assault weapons illegal. Although both measures have received overwhelming public support, to the militias, gun control means people control, and thus tyranny. Randy Trochmann of MOM believes that the American people will band together to stop any effort at confiscating their guns.

As debate continues to surround gun control, the National Rifle Association (NRA), a powerful lobbying group with over three million members, has publicly refused to endorse the militia movement and has even expressed strong reservations about militia formation outside of state supervision, but nevertheless has developed close links to it. To some extent, the NRA has achieved this association by creating an atmosphere conducive to militia growth. One analyst, a supporter of gun control legislation, observes:

> The NRA has pushed an interpretation of the Second Amendment that...is ultimately about resistance to a tyrannical government. The militias and other groups are acting that out, engaging in dissent through armed force. The idea is that if you don't like abortion clinics, shoot doctors. If you don't like the [B]ATF, blow up a building. Obviously, the NRA will not say this in such blunt terms, but it's the logical extension to what they've been saying for years."[46]

More directly, several NRA board members have allied themselves with the militias as part of a move begun in 1991 by a militant core within the organization that wants to guide it in a radical, strident direction.

Another militia theme involves the United Nations. Many people in addition to Linda Thompson believe a plot exists; in fact, the idea of such a plot permeates extremist literature. According to the story, the international body, in cooperation with treasonous American leaders, both within government and within the corporate and financial communities, is working to end America's independence and merge the nation with others to create a socialist New World Order or a One World government.

A third militia theme emphasizes an intrusive federal government that has violated the Constitution and, with it, personal liberty. The accusations revolve around numerous supposed transgressions, including excessive taxes, wasteful welfare programs, and environmental regulations. The latter has blossomed as a big issue in the West and functions in tandem with the Wise Use Movement, consisting of activists dedicated to dismantling all environmental controls (and, ironically, backed by many of the same corporations often criticized by the militias). Ranchers, loggers, miners, businessmen, and small landowners complain about restrictions on property development. They claim, for example, that the Endangered Species Act protects owls over human beings and, as a result, has put many people out of work. Federal officials have reported threats, and even actual attacks, against their persons and also against property such as forest service offices. John Trochmann, among others, has taken advantage of this discontent and the vehemence stirred by Wise Use, speaking at several Western venues to raise support for militias. At an appearance in Okanogan County, Washington, he verbally attacked environmentalists and discussed the threat posed by Soviet-made cargo planes and vehicles supposedly massing in the Montana back woods.

Some militias accuse the Federal Emergency Management Administration (FEMA) of putting together plans that will destroy American independence. FEMA, the accusations go, controls street gangs, Nepalese Gurkhas, and the Hong Kong police, all of which will soon be integrated into an effective unit within the United States to oppress Americans. Whatever the specific focus in militia ideas, the main thrust involves scapegoating, conspiracy theories, and fears of a secular humanist liberal conspiracy manifesting itself in tyrannical tax and spending policies, gun control, internationalism, environmentalism, and more: sex education, feminism, progressive educational practices, abortion, and the acceptance of homosexuals.

A pamphlet prepared by the right-wing group Constitution Society equates militias with the people and urges every adult to carry firearms. Anyone can call up the militia, the Constitution Society says; hence, the general populace can assemble and do it themselves. Militia action is needed, it insists, for two main reasons: abuses committed by public officials and a conspiracy eating at liberty and national independence, a conspiracy led by industry, the military, the media, financiers, and intelligence agencies. Fascism, it says, is alive, well, and running the United States.[47]

Beneath these themes, stagnation in the economy works its influence. Despite recent economic growth, many middle-class Americans feel squeezed. Average wages have not kept pace with inflation, and unemployment and displacement have occurred with industries relocating overseas or downsizing with the use of new technology. Added to this, certain areas of the nation have not fully recovered from the recession of the early 1990s. In short, many Americans feel opportunity has evaporated, and militias attract those frustrated with these developments. As a writer in the *London Review of Books* says, "One does not have to be a historian...to recognize the connection between what the economy is doing to most Americans and the increasingly intolerant climate of contemporary American life."[48] The Committee to Restore the Constitution, located in Fort Collins, Colorado, has hit a nerve with its declaration: "Americans have been reduced to economic serfs in the land that was once theirs. A secret government of monetary power, employing perverted mass media and the authority of a captured Bureaucratic Civil Service, is forcing us into a 'New World Order' of 'Liberty, Fraternity, Equality.' To liquidate this threat to life and property, Americans must first accept the fact that the [Constitution] upon which they erroneously rely to preserve the Republic no longer exists."[49]

The Oklahoma City Bombing and the Militia Movement

On 19 April 1995, a tremendous explosion ripped through the Alfred P. Murrah Federal Building in Oklahoma City, Oklahoma. The blast left a large portion of the nine-story structure a tangled, shattered mess of glass, concrete, metal support rods, and human bodies. Workers, visitors, and children in a daycare center were injured; 167 people died. The explosion came from a bomb made of ammonium nitrate fertilizer planted in a vacant van near the entrance to the building. (The target, type of bomb, and time of explosion—around 9:00 A.M.—corresponded with a plan dramatized in *The Turner Diaries*.)

Within days, federal authorities arrested Timothy McVeigh, a 26-year-old Army infantry veteran from New York who had fought in the Persian Gulf War, and newspapers linked the ex-soldier to the militia movement. They claimed that McVeigh had associated with the Michigan Militia and navigated a subterranean world of armed malcontents who lived in areas such as Kingman, Arizona, a desert center of anti-government extremism. In fact, McVeigh had imbibed the words of Mark Koernke, listening avidly to his shortwave radio broadcasts; associated with members of the Arizona Patriots, a militia group dating from the 1980s; studied material published by Bo Gritz; watched videotapes produced by Linda Thompson about the Waco incident; and read and re-read *The Turner Diaries*. Yet as the year came to an end, no solid evidence existed to show that the terrorist act had been perpetrated by a militia. Did the connection not exist? Or had the perpetrator or perpetrators followed a tactic to make discovery impossible?[50]

Whatever the case, the bombing unleashed a media and government investigation of militias and put the entire militia movement on the defensive, casting it in a negative light. Militia supporters, meanwhile, accused federal officials of using the Oklahoma City tragedy as a bogeyman by which to discredit them. To a certain extent they have a point—the government and media have portrayed the bombing as an outgrowth of militia extremism and have lumped all militias together as racist, anti-Semitic, and terrorist. The point, though, becomes lost in the rash of comments offered by some prominent militia leaders and their supporters shortly after the catastrophe. Bo Gritz likened the bombing to a work by Rembrandt, a masterpiece of art and science. Norm Olson claimed the Japanese had exploded the bomb in retaliation for the United States supposedly having committed a terrorist act in 1995 by detonating poison gas on a Tokyo subway. This assertion earned Olson a reprimand from the command council of the Michigan Militia, which removed him from his leadership position. (He has since reappeared as leader of his own militia.) In addition to these comments, the New Jersey Militia called it strange that no one in the BATF offices on the ninth floor of the Murrah Building was killed. Some reports, said the militia, indicated that the BATF workers were given the option to take the day off. The New Jersey Militia wondered, too, why no children of BATF agents were in the daycare center. This assertion implies that the federal agency had been warned in advance about the bombing. [51]

Other militiamen told of mysterious black helicopters circling the Murrah Building before the blast and charged that the federal government had exploded the bomb to launch an offensive to eliminate militias. Linda Thompson claimed, "I definitely believe the government did the bombing. I mean, who's got a track record of killing children?"[52] Frank Smith, head of the Georgia Militia, blamed the federal government, too. "We expected them to do something drastic," he said. "We didn't expect it to be that drastic."[53] Vernon Weckner, leader of the Unorganized Militia of El Dorado County, California, pointed a finger at the CIA as the real culprit in the Oklahoma City bombing, and Mark Koernke claimed the federal government placed Timothy McVeigh, the man arrested for the bombing, in bright orange prison garb so he would be an easy target for an assassin.[54]

Several militia leaders chastised President Clinton for handling the event in a partisan manner meant to benefit him politically and enhance his power; they compared his actions to those of Adolph Hitler after the burning of the Reichstag. Randy Trochmann, a member of MOM, insinuated the president may have planned the bombing as a way to build support for his proposed Comprehensive Terrorism Protection Act and gun control legislation. MOM asserted a mysterious second explosion had occurred shortly after the first one, indications that the government wasn't telling the entire story, perhaps because of its own involvement in the attack.[55]

Militias: Perspectives and Activities After Oklahoma City

The close scrutiny of militias that has occurred in the wake of the bombing has not cooled the movement's ardor. If anything, the explosion has reinforced a picture militia members embrace of America in decline—socially, politically, and economically. Archibald Roberts, leader of the Committee to Restore the Constitution, declares: "America need not become a land of 'yesterday's people.'" All it takes to regain the freedoms lost is the courage to face today's political reality, and to implement successful techniques and procedures to reverse the mindless march toward [a] new feudalism."[56] In his view, the Constitution, the courts, and representative government—all ostensibly protectors of individual liberty—have given way to totalitarian decision making.

Militias remain active. In Florida, they have organized in several counties and maintain contact through fax machines and cellular phones. A militia in Pensacola has developed arms caches and claims 150 members. One leader there considers assault weapons a necessity to fight any possible attack the army might make on liberty. Pastor Chuck Baldwin of the local Crossroad Baptist Church agrees with this, adding that guns contribute to much-needed masculinity and that after Waco no church can feel secure, for the government can crush any of them.

Near Atlanta, a militia group has conducted paramilitary exercises on a 38-acre tract, and Linda Thompson showed her continuing appeal when she addressed 800 people at a rally. In New York, militias have been most evident near the Pennsylvania border, and a group in Chemung County has held training exercises. Active militias have appeared in Orange and Dutchess Counties, as well. In Texas, the Constitutional Militia has allied with the North Texas Constitutional Militia in Richardson, near Dallas. The Militia of Wisconsin claims it is preparing for battle. MOM reports that mysterious-looking trucks in Biloxi, Mississippi, are being prepared by the United Nations to further the One World government. In California, Bo Gritz and Mark Koernke have stirred militia activism. In Arizona, William Cooper of St. Johns broadcasts a program on shortwave radio to encourage militia formation. In Alabama, several militias have expanded, including the Sons of Liberty Southern Command, the Gadsden Minutemen, the Mobile Regulators, the Committee of Seventy-Six, the Sand Mountain Militia Company, and the Shelby County Citizen's Militia. Some of these recently formed a coalition.

In Michigan, militias have developed a new tactic: packing township meetings in an attempt to take them over, or at least to disrupt their proceedings. This strategy has pitted neighbor against neighbor in Wellston, where militia supporters have protested all attempts to regulate property use, including zoning regulations, and militia opponents see over outside agitators who have infiltrated their town. (In fact, several militia leaders in Wellston hail from well beyond the township borders.) Militia members argue that a group of voters posting notice of a meeting can hold one and enact regulations. These militiamen warn that attempts by town officials to prohibit this practice reflects cooperation with the perceived ongoing conspiracy to establish a One World government.

The Anti-Defamation League (ADL) has found that some militias in the national movement might be following the advice of white supremacists Tom Metzger and Louis Beam, and the recommendations found in a widely circulated handbook released by the Wisconsin Free Militia. These extremist sources call for militias to use leaderless resistance and divide into small cells of no more than six to eight members, each cell with its own leader, staging area, and standing orders, so as to make detection more difficult and, in case of infiltration, prevent the discovery of any connections to leaders and members outside the group. Militias, the ADL claims, have organized in 40 states and show no signs of abatement. California alone has 30 of them.

The Southern Poverty Law Center has reported that 224 militias exist in 39 states, with 45 of these groups having ties to neo-Nazi and white supremacist movements. Although most militias are not racist, the Law Center says, many are susceptible to white supremacist takeover, and the more extreme militias are conveying apocalyptic messages, stockpiling weapons, and preparing for Armageddon. The Law Center has rejected new, intrusive anti-terrorist legislation and instead calls for enforcing the paramilitary laws on the books in 41 states.

This report has brought a reaction from the New Jersey Militia. The group accuses the Law Center of receiving money from the federal government under an executive order signed in the 1980s by President Ronald Reagan, whereby intelligence agencies can contract secretly with private concerns. Meanwhile, in its publication *Spotlight*, the Liberty Lobby has charged Morris Dees, head of the Law Center, with leading a smear campaign to portray the militia movement as racist.

Militia activities have encountered local opposition, as evident in a dispute involving residents of Hamilton, Montana. In 1995, some militia members rejected their social security numbers and even refused to use zip codes, claiming these meant relinquishing individual rights to the national government. Amid this controversy, a federal facility in town received two bomb threats, as did the county courthouse, and because some militiamen refused to get driver's licenses or even identify themselves when stopped for traffic violations, jury trials had to be held, bogging down residents in hearings and jamming the legal system. Cal Greenup led this radical resistance while serving as coordinator in Montana for the North American Volunteer Militia. In reaction, many townspeople backed their sheriff and government officials. One resident even circulated a petition signed by 800 Hamiltonians, proclaiming their denouncement of violence and their support for the town's elected representatives.

In Washington, shortly after the Oklahoma City bombing, Senator Arlen Specter, a Republican from Pennsylvania and chair of the Judiciary Subcommittee on Terrorism and Government Information, held hearings into the militia movement. Supporters and critics of the militias testified. Norm Olson, for example, defended the militias, as did an African-American militiaman from Massachusetts who called the BATF, CIA, and Internal Revenue Service tyrannical. In response, Senator Specter told of militia groups connected to violent acts against law enforcement officials. Senator Max Baucus, a Democrat from

Montana, discussed the relationship between John Trochmann and Aryan Nations. He considered the main factors in the growth of the militia movement to be anger over the stagnant economy and intrusive federal regulations, along with racism and anti-Semitism, and said the formation of militias in Montana was tied to an increase in violence against Jewish properties. Yet, he reported, the militias in his home state had only a small following: some 500 members with 25 to 30 hard-core leaders.

As charges flew back and forth and circulated widely in the media, critics of militias circulated their own exaggerations. Several newspaper accounts, for example, portrayed Samuel Sherwood, the leader of the USMA, as out of control, alleging that he told a public meeting that everyone there should get a good look at their local legislators because they might some day be shooting them in the face. The Idaho legislature reacted to Sherwood's statement by condemning such threats. Whether Sherwood said what he was purported to have said remains, however, a matter of dispute. A reliable eyewitness later contradicted the version presented in the media and wrote that Sherman had merely told his listeners to get a good look at their local legislators because they, too, were fathers, mothers, husbands, and wives. To this day, Sherwood insists he actually inveighed against violence, telling "hotheads" in the audience they should not blame local legislators for any problems related to a global conspiracy, that it is foolish to talk about physically attacking these people when they are not to blame. At a March 1995 gathering in Idaho, Sherwood, in fact, urged electoral action and lobbying, not violence, and in none of his publications has he advocated the use of armed force.[57]

The media have usually failed to draw distinctions among the different types of armed protesters: racists and tax resistors, survivalists, racial separatists, and religious zealots, loners, and political activists concerned about specific policies threatening liberty. By and large, militias do not hold training sessions, but conduct meetings devoted to discussion. Most militia members do not itch for a fight; rather, they want to discourage government oppression. Most believe that the Holocaust did occur and that prevention of another one necessitates an armed citizenry. Most promote battle readiness as a defensive measure, not an offensive one.

Groups such as the Sons of Liberty insist that militia strategy should include stockpiling arms and that each militiaman must have the courage to use guns. The Sons, however, want arms-gathering to occur within legal boundaries and state weapons should be used as a last resort, only if political access becomes closed. The best protest, the group advises, occurs through the election system and in the courts, although other actions, such as destroying files in BATF offices, may certainly be warranted in light of that agency's assaults on liberty.

Even some leftist commentators admit that militias have legitimate grievances, for both Democrats and Republicans have violated rights in everything from the war on drugs to the war against terrorism. Property has been seized for minor drug offenses and without trials, and searches have been conducted under flimsy pretenses. Militia complaints thus should not be lightly dismissed, the argument goes, although the militias should realize their real enemy is not the United Nations, but the multinational corporations; not liberalism, but corporate authoritarianism.

A legal scholar has reminded militia critics that individual rights do not come from the government. Rather, the founding fathers "designed the Bill of Rights to prohibit our government from infringing rights and liberties presumed to be preexisting."[58] These include the right to bear arms and form a militia, for back in the eighteenth century revolutionaries such as Samuel Adams remembered well the British seizure of the colonists' weapons. The debate over protection of arms figured prominently in the Constitutional ratification process, and on one issue the framers, supporters, and opponents of the Constitution stood in agreement: the importance of an armed populace in protecting liberty. The Second Amendment, then, is meant to apply to the general public as a right protected from government intrusion.

Yet, in reaction to this scholarly assertion, it should be noted that the formation of militias in this nation has always been greeted with ambivalence. Indeed, events in the early years of the United States, namely Shays' Rebellion in the mid-1780s and the Whiskey Rebellion in the early 1790s, display what can happen when largely private citizen militias take the law into their own hands. In the former case, angry farmers in western Massachusetts, supported by local militiamen, disrupted foreclosure proceedings at courthouses and threatened to march on the state legislature. The Massachusetts state militia eventually quashed the uprising, but the threat to disorder won the condemnation of George Washington, Alexander Hamilton, and other leaders and propelled those concerned with weaknesses under the existing governing document, the Articles of Confederation, to call a convention that resulted in the writing of the Constitution.

Although this document, which replaced and superseded the Articles, eventually had the Second Amendment and the entire Bill of Rights attached to it, the intent of the Constitution in its totality was to shift power from the states to the national government, not to exterminate state power (despite the desire of Hamilton to largely do so) or to eliminate any variation over the years in the distribution of power between the central government and the states, but clearly to create a pecking order in which the central government would rank first. Later, the Civil War effaced the pretenses of state primacy that lingered in ideologies such as nullification and secession. What numerous militias have recently advocated with their interpretation of the federal government's proper sphere of activity means nothing less than a return to the Articles of Confederation, despite their pronounced sympathies for the Constitution "as originally written," a highly debatable phrase given the uncertainty of what the founding fathers intended and the intervention of 200 years of development that have created economic and social changes the founders would find difficult to recognize.

In the 1790s, George Washington, recently elected president, faced the Whiskey Rebellion, a challenge to the national government's power. Once again farmers protested; this time, mainly those from western Pennsylvania. They refused to pay the newly enacted excise tax on whiskey, an important commodity for them, a form of exchange similar to money. They threatened revenue collectors and, consequently, the authority of the national government to levy taxes and enforce laws. Alexander Hamilton, then Washington's secretary of the treasury, insisted that the president amass troops to exert federal authority. Any failure to crush the rebellion, he believed, would make the Constitution a mere piece of paper. Washington agreed; subsequently, he and Hamilton led a large force into the Pennsylvania mountains, and the rebellion quickly collapsed. Neither Washington nor Hamilton expressed remorse about disbanding a militia, for in this instance, they believed, the militia had amounted to no more than an unruly mob opposed to legitimate governmental authority.

In 1995, Daniel Levitas, former director of the liberal Center for Democratic Renewal, said that when far-right groups glorify violent confrontation with the government, an Oklahoma City is bound to occur. Such glorification has certainly been the hallmark of some modern militias. Ironically, in pursuit of "the enemy"—government and leftist tyranny—militias sometimes copy the enemy's practices: infiltration, intimidation, threats, and violence aimed at those who disagree; and secret organizations to fight secret organizations, such as the cells advocated by Louis Beam. Perhaps pursuing enemies gives the pursuers an opportunity to engage in the behavior they condemn. Christian Identity militias, in particular, seek to impose on Jews and African-Americans an oppression, a relegation to inferior status that they, as white citizens, claim haunts them.

Conclusion

In today's militia movement paranoia runs deep. When, in June 1995, police stopped a militia leader in southeastern Ohio and then shot and killed him after he exited from his car with gun drawn and his body in a stance as if ready to fire, several militias labeled it part of a conspiracy to wipe them out. Indeed, contemporary militia activities fit the American predilection for paranoia and society's infatuation with conspiracy theories. As Richard Hofstadter described it 30 years ago, the paranoid person in politics emphasizes slights against the nation and the overall deterioration of society, critical elements in the 1990s world view. Militias, like other paranoid entities, consider intellectuals, socialists, and assorted liberals the primary traducers of religion, mainstream culture . . . the entire correct way of life.

Political analyst Seymour Martin Lipset once explained that right-wing extremism always arises amid social change in which certain groups feel strongly threatened or suffer displacement, a development that in turn disorganizes the major political parties. Thus, the right-wing manta: both Democrats and Republicans have failed the nation; those who lead important institutions act unpatriotically and even treasonably; liberal economic and social programs have destroyed society and in the process created a bureaucratic monolith that benefits the political, labor, business, and media elite; conspiracies prevail and work a mighty force; and direct action—perhaps even violence—must be used to destroy the conspirators.

In 1995, one analyst compiled a psychological profile of the typical militia member as a paranoid person who believes in an impending apocalypse, feels alienated from mainstream society, demonizes the government, and displays an obsession with guns. Informational inbreeding produced by adherence to an alternative media that presents extremist world views deepens the estrangement of militias. Interestingly, though, Scott Stevens, head of the White Mountain Militia Information Service, based in New Hampshire, counters talk of paranoia by saying of militia members, "We're like libertarians on steroids, but we're not nuts. We're totally against overthrowing the federal government."[59]

Overall, the current paranoia—if that is the proper description—exudes a particular character created by historical developments not evident when Hofstadter and Lipset wrote, developments from the counterculture, the Vietnam War, Watergate, and the Iran-Contra scandal. The 1960s counterculture has unleashed challenges to traditional values that many conservatives still find disconcerting. For its part, the Vietnam War has damaged American credibility and called into question the nation's sense of mission, the belief that with its moral, political, and economic superiority, America should direct world affairs. As a result, today's militias often advocate bringing all American troops home—in effect, complete military disengagement.

Along with the counterculture and Vietnam War, Watergate and the Iran-Contra scandal have produced a sense of political and moral decay, a belief that government cannot be trusted and that the federal government engages in conspiracies to subvert liberty. Somewhat contradictorily, given supposed government ineptitude, those immersed in conspiracy theories refuse to admit that perhaps no one is in control, that many developments are beyond human correction.

The publication *Operation Vampire Killer 2000* circulates widely within today's militia movement. This 75-page book, issued by the American Citizens and Lawmen Association in Arizona, a group headed by former Phoenix police officer Jack McLamb, purports to provide evidence of treasonous activities by prominent Americans who intend to end national independence and crush liberty by promoting a socialist One World government. If the plotters get their way, the book says, they will accomplish their goal in the year 2000. *Operation Vampire* goes on to claim that Republicans and Democrats alike have joined the plot, as has independent presidential hopeful Ross Perot, and that the proof of the treasonous crime underway resides in the very words of the nation's political and business leaders. The author asserts, "Like [sic] the legendary Vampire Dracula lays claim to his victims, the Globalist slowly drains the essence of life and liberty from our Land."[60]

The vampires include banker David Rockefeller, betrayed by his statement, "The world is now more sophisticated and prepared to march towards a world government. The supranational sovereignty of an intellectual elite and world bankers is surely preferable to the national autodetermination practiced in past centuries."[61] The vampires include media moguls, such as former CBS News president Richard Salant, who once proclaimed, "Our job is to give people not what they want, but what WE decide they ought to have."[62] The vampires include former president George Bush, who sold out to the United Nations, as evident in his statement, "It is the sacred principles enshrined in the UN Charter to which we will hence forth pledge our allegiance."[63]

Vampires of the New World Order, the book argues, seek to encourage race war and similar strife to make Americans desire martial law. Thus, "hate must be kept flowing to prevent the various races in America from finding out the truth."[64] The vampires will admit no limits in circulating stories to scare the nation and will not stop until Americans accept nothing less than their tyrannous domination as the only way to restore tranquillity.

Many militias feed on these paranoid views, as do many people outside the militia movement, evident in 1996 by the actions of Republican presidential candidate Patrick Buchanan, who loudly criticized the elite for selling out America to the New World Order and who, through such talk, invited charges that he was racist and anti-Semitic. Buchanan's affinity for militias, or at least their mentality, revealed itself in his appointment of Larry Pratt as his campaign co-chairman. Pratt, the executive director of Gun Owners of America, an extremist group that endorses militia formation, has on several occasions addressed militias and white supremacist groups. (As the presidential campaign intensified, media exposure of his background forced him to step down from Buchanan's campaign.)

Paranoia and conspiracy theories have also appeared among the Freemen, a group on the edge of the extremist fringe. (See the testimony by John Bohlman and Max Baucus in chapter 4.) In March 1996, FBI agents surrounded the Freemen at their ranch near Jordan, Montana, beginning a long showdown. The Freemen had adopted convoluted theories, closest in content to Identity Christians and the Posse Comitatus. They fear a New

World Order, disavow the validity of the Constitution beyond the first ten amendments, and believe that the current national government has violated this document through policies that favor Zionists and nonwhites. The Freemen thus conclude they do not have to abide by federal laws or pay income tax. Nor do they recognize state governments, which they believe have become corrupted by the federal system. Under their leader LeRoy Schweitzer, the Freemen reached the point of separating themselves from society at large, retreating to their ranch, which they proclaimed to be independent Justus Township.

Schweitzer and other Freemen, however, had printed and circulated checks and money orders, passing them off as valid when in fact they were fraudulent. In all, they defrauded some $1.8 million from banks and businesses. And they threatened the life of a U.S. District Court judge. Thus the federal agents surrounded their ranch, and when the Freemen refused to surrender, the FBI decided to implement what it called a "soft siege," to avoid the bloodshed that had occurred at Ruby Ridge and Waco.

As the siege continued, nearly all militias shied away from the Freemen, even MOM, whose leader, John Trochmann, had previously associated with them. MOM officially called for militias to "stand down" and not rush to the Freemen's assistance. On the other hand, MOM called the government confrontation with the Freemen part of a plot to cause divisions within the militia movement. "The controllers of America have now decided that the militia/patriot movement can be no more," MOM declared in its publication *Taking Aim*. [65]

The siege lasted several weeks, with the FBI worried about the Freemen's stockpile of rifles, handguns, shotguns, and 11,000 rounds of ammunition, along with the presence of several children in the group of 20 people on the ranch. Local residents, meanwhile, urged action, expressed their disgust with the Freemen, and said they did not want militias to come in and help the extremists.

At times it appeared the standoff would result in violence, such as when efforts by Bo Gritz and other far-right leaders to negotiate a compromise failed. Early in June, however, the FBI increased its pressure by cutting off electricity to the ranch and blocking the Freemen's cellular phones. The Freemen finally surrendered on 13 June 1996.

Despite newspaper headlines to the contrary, the Freemen had acted not as a militia, but as an isolated armed group, hunkered down, dangerous, and engaged in criminal scams. Nevertheless, they share many views with the militia movement, and their actions reinforce widely held beliefs that militias have become obsessed with conspiracy theories and overwhelmed by paranoia.

Further evidence of this obsession came when, on 1 July 1996, federal agents arrested 12 members of the Vipers, an Arizona militia. The agents confiscated 90 high-powered rifles, over 11,000 rounds of ammunition, and hundreds of pounds of bomb-making compound found in a house near Phoenix. An observer called the raid one of the largest hits ever on a militia.

The Vipers have sworn to fight enemies who oppose the United States Constitution and to kill any informers who infiltrate their group. Federal agents portray them as a serious threat, an urban terrorist cell, and claim the group has put together a training videotape that shows government buildings in the Phoenix area and provides advice on how they can be destroyed. Some, however, doubt the government's story. One Arizonan affiliated with the Libertarian Party said the Vipers have no malicious intentions—they only like to go into the desert, shoot their guns, and blow up rocks. Whatever their true desires, the Vipers, like other militias, oppose any type of gun control and harbor fears about a socialistic New World Order and creeping tyranny.

In embracing paranoia, militias have reputable company, and that makes any assessment of these groups difficult. The American Revolution, after all, was not only violent, it made violence acceptable—if used for the good of the cause in a good cause (whatever that may be). While it is true the American Revolution expressed its ideology through the rational writings of John Locke, as incorporated into the Declaration of Independence, it expressed itself as well, and perhaps more extensively, through widely supported irrational beliefs in conspiracy—a conspiracy intended to eradicate liberty in America and make the colonies mere servants of a distant, unresponsive government. Many at the time who opposed these views called them paranoid; today we hail them as harbingers of freedom.

Nevertheless, there is little doubt that armed militias are today operating outside of Constitutional provisions. Militias are to be under joint federal and state direction, primarily the latter. Ohio State University historian Mark Pitcavage believes that the Constitution is clear on this point and provides information at his Internet site to support his view (see the World Wide Web sources in chapter 7). He states that people who think they are forming militias actually are not, at least not in a Constitutional sense. Even the National Rifle Association recognizes this with its statement that any organized citizen militia must be created under the Constitution itself or the laws of a state.

Further, militias are likely acting illegally, since most states prohibit their formation, paramilitary training, or both, and the courts have never recognized the Second Amendment as granting protection for militia operations outside the established network of governmental control. Individuals may, of course, meet in groups and discuss any issues they desire; such is the Constitutional protection under freedom of assembly and speech. But private groups engaging in armed training falls outside this protection and enters a realm defined as insurrection.

While this answers the legal question concerning armed citizens operating privately, outside of wider community control, it does not, however, answer the moral one of whether insurrection should be pursued. A concern with order and open discourse free of intimidation would insist these activities be ended; but revolution is not conducive to either order or openness, and liberty is often not preserved if its defense relies on going through legal channels. If a person adopts the position that a higher moral calling is at stake, however, then it must be called what it is: a revolutionary advocacy perhaps necessitating the overthrow of the government. If revolution is the course militias wish to follow, they should recognize it as such and not try to assert convoluted arguments about statuary laws and Constitutional provisions. Revolution, though, entails reaction by the authorities to crush it; such was the action undertaken by Britain and its supporters in 1776, an action that for them failed not because a few Americans banded together in private armed groups but because a crucial number acted in concert with the larger community and within long-prescribed guidelines to achieve independence and advance republican ideals.

Notes

1. Louis Birnbaum, *Red Dawn at Lexington* (Boston: Houghton Mifflin, 1986), 178.

2. Richard Brown, *Strain of Violence: Historical Studies of American Violence and Vigilantism* (New York: Oxford University Press, 1975), 97.

3. Robert E. Shalhope, "The Ideological Origins of the Second Amendment." In Robert J. Cottrol, ed., *Gun Control and the Constitution: Sources and Explorations on the Second Amendment* (New York: Garland Publishing, 1993), 87.

4. David Brion Davis, *The Fear of Conspiracy: Images of Un-American Subversion from the Revolution to the Present* (Ithaca, NY: Cornell University Press, 1971), xiii.

5. *Ibid.*, 333.

6. Dan Smoot, *The Invisible Government* (Boston: Western Islands, 1962), xi, 77.

7. Benjamin R. Epstein and Arnold Foster, *The Radical Right: Report on the John Birch Society and Its Allies* (New York: Vintage Books, 1967), 110.

8. Richard Hofstadter, *The Paranoid Style in American Politics and Other Essays* (Chicago: University of Chicago Press, 1965), 45.

9. Harry J. Jones, Jr., *The Minutemen* (Garden City, NY: Doubleday, 1968), 20.

10. *Ibid.*, 108, 65.

11. James Ridgeway, *Blood in the Face: The Ku Klux Klan, Aryan Nations, Nazi Skinheads, and the Rise of a New White Culture* (New York: Thunder's Mouth Press, 1990), 62.

12. Elizabeth A. Rickey, "The Nazi and the Republicans: An Insider View of the Response of the Louisiana Republican Party to David Duke." In Douglas D. Rose, ed., *The Emergence of David Duke and the Politics of Race* (Chapel Hill: University of North Carolina Press, 1992), 59-63.

13. Sergiei Aleksandrovich Nilus, *The Protocols of the Learned Elders of Zion*, trans. Victor E. Marsden (Houston: Pyramid Book Shop, 1934), 19.

14. *Ibid.*, 14.

15. Michael Barkun, *Religion and the Racist Right: The Origins of the Christian Identity Movement* (Chapel Hill: University of North Carolina Press, 1994), 110.

16. Ridgeway, *Blood in the Face*, 102.

17. Robert Crawford, S. L. Gardner, Jonathan Mozzochi, and R. L. Taylor, *The Northwest Imperative: Documenting a Decade of Hate* (Portland, OR: Coalition for Human Dignity, 1994), 1.17.

18. Ridgeway, *Blood in the Face*, 113.

19. David H. Bennett, *The Party of Fear: From Nativist Movement to the New Right in American History* (Chapel Hill: University of North Carolina Press, 1988), 400.

20. "Enforcing the Law: Consider the Bill of Rights," *Commonwealth*, 21 May 1993, 5.

21. "11 In Texas Sect Are Acquitted of Key Charges," *New York Times*, 27 Feb 1994.

22. Sydney Blumenthal, "Her Own Private Idaho," *New Yorker*, 10 July 1995, 28.

23. Report by Leslie Jorgensen, accessed on August 1995 at http://paul.spu.edu/~sinnfein/fair.html

24. "The Plot," *Newsweek*, 8 May 1995, 44.

25. Don Hazen, Larry Smith, and Christine Triano, eds., *Militias In America* (San Francisco: Institute for Alternative Journalism, 1995), 14.

26. National Public Radio, *Morning Edition*, 12 May 1995.

27. Anti-Defamation League, *Beyond the Bombing: The Militia Menace Grows* (New York: Anti-Defamation League, 1995), 21-22.

28. Michael Kelly, "The Road to Paranoia," *New Yorker*, 19 June 1995, 61.

29. "Manual for Terrorists Extols 'Greatest Coldbloodedness'," *New York Times*, 29 April 1995.

30. Mona Vanek, "Statement to the Senate Judiciary Committee on Terrorism," 24 May 1995 (submitted to the author); Michael Kelly, "The Road to Paranoia," 75.

31. Daniel Voll, "The Right to Bear Sorrow," *Esquire*, March 1995, 81.

32. Tom Burghardt, "Leaderless Resistance and the Oklahoma City Bombing," (San Francisco: Bay Area for Reproductive Rights, 1995), 6 (version acquired via Internet); Hazen, et al., eds., *Militias in America* 7, 13, 39-43.

33. Adam Parfrey, and Jim Redden, "Patriot Games," *Village Voice*, 11 October 1994, 26-30; Anti-Defamation League, *Armed and Dangerous: Militias Take Aim at the Federal Government* (New York: Anti-Defamation League, 1994), 6 (version acquired via Internet).

34. Parfrey and Redden, "Patriot Games," 27; Internet message posted 22 April 1993.

35. *Ibid.*, 26–30.

36. Anti-Defamation League, *Beyond the Bombing*, 13.

37. M. Samuel Sherwood, *Establishing an Independent Militia in the United States* (Blackfoot, ID: Founders Press Publishing, 1995), vii,1, 13,17; for militia supplies see the advertisements, for example, in *Aide-de-Camp*, March 1995.

38. Statement confirmed by Samuel Sherwood in a telephone conversation with the author, 13 June 1996.

39. Sherwood, *Establishing an Independent Militia*, 35.

40. Kenneth S. Stern, *A Force Upon the Plain: The American Militia Movement and the Politics of Hate* (New York: Simon and Schuster, 1996), 135.

41. Susan Ladd, and Stan Swofford, "On the Brink of Doom," *Greensboro News-Leader* 25 and 27 June 1995 (version acquired via Internet).

42. Stern, *A Force Upon the Plain*, 64; untitled Internet document accessed 14 August 1994.

43. Laura Flanders, "Far Right Militias and Anti-Abortion Violence," *Extra!*, July/August 1995, 12.

44. Tom Burghardt, "God, Guns, and Terror," (San Francisco: Bay Area for Reproductive Rights, 1994), 17 (version acquired via Internet).

45. Charles A. Weisman, *America: Free, White and Christian* (Burnsville, MN: Charles A. Weisman, 1989), 113.

46. Charles M. Sennott, "NRA Becomes Militias' Beacon," *Boston Globe*, 13 August 1995.

47. Hazen, et al., *Militias In America*, 31-33; Stern, *A Force Upon the Plain*, 119-132, 187-194; Dees, Morris, *Gathering Storm: America's Militia Threat* (New York: Harper Collins, 1996), 85; Question-and-answer posting on the Internet accessed August 1995.

48. "America's Angry White Males," *World Press Review*, July 1995, 28.

49. *Bulletin: Committee to Restore the Constitution*, March 1995, 1.

50. *Los Angeles Times*, 22 April 1995; Dees, *Gathering Storm*, 155-156.

51. Stern, *A Force Upon the Plains*, 204-205; *New Jersey Militia Newsletter*, September 1995.

52. Anti-Defamation League, *Beyond the Bombing*, 15.

53. *Ibid.*, 12.

54. *San Francisco Examiner*, 24 April 1995.

55. Stern, *A Force Upon the Plain*, 208; Dees, *Gathering Storm*, 175.

56. *Bulletin: Committee to Restore the Constitution*, 1.

57. *Idaho Falls Register*, 12 March 1995; Mack Tanner, "Extreme Prejudice: How the Media Misrepresent the Militia Movement," *Reason*, July 1995, 45.

58. Stephen P. Halbrook, "The Right of the People or The Power of the States: Bearing Arms, Arming Militias, and the Second Amendment," *Valparaiso University Law Review*, 26 (1991): 147.

59. "New Hampshire Talking," *Village Voice*, 6 February 1996, 21.

60. American Citizens and Lawmen Association. *Operation Vampire Killer 2000* (Phoenix: Police Against the New World Order, 1992), 9.

61. *Ibid.*, 13.

62. *Ibid.*, 19.

63. *Ibid.*, 21.

64. *Ibid.*, 34.

65. "The Heat Is On: A Covert Attempt to Split Militia," *Taking Aim*, April 1996, 1.

Chronology 2

The history of militias in America dates back to the colonial period, but modern origins rest in the cold war that immediately followed World War II. Given this, the following chronology focuses primarily on the 1940s and later. The dates indicate the emergence of leaders and ideas important to militias, along with events that stimulated the militia movement.

Early History

The 1600s   Massachusetts Bay organizes a militia and places it first under the governor's council and later under a council of war. Militias appear in all the British North American colonies founded during this century. These militias are ready for military action, when deemed necessary, against Indians and foreign nations.

The 1700s   Prior to the American Revolution, militias are generally involved in less and less fighting as colonists turn to armies manned by full-time soldiers.

1774   As tension mounts with Britain, the Massachusetts
             Provincial Congress orders the formation of
             minutemen units.

1775   On 19 April the first military battles of the Ameri-
             can Revolution occur with engagements between
             British troops and colonial militias at Lexington
             and Concord. By the end of the next day, 20,000
             militia men converge on Boston to face the enemy.
             Two centuries later, in the 1980s and 1990s, many
             militias consider 19 April a sacred date, remem-
             bered for the time when citizen patriots bravely
             took up arms and rebelled against British tyranny.

1786   Farmers in western Massachusetts arm themselves
             to protest harsh economic conditions and oppres-
             sive policies established by the state legislature.
             This paramilitary action, under Daniel Shays, so
             alarms many Americans that support increases for
             revising or replacing the new nation's governing
             document, the Articles of Confederation, with one
             establishing a federal system that can effectively
             regulate militias.

1789   Under the guidance of James Madison, Congress
             passes and agrees to send to the states 10 amend-
             ments to the recently adopted Constitution. These
             include the Second Amendment, which protects the
             right to bear arms as part of maintaining a well-
             regulated militia. Grounded in European political
             thought, the amendment is based on republican
             ideology that a militia is important in protecting
             liberty and property from a possibly tyrannical
             government.

Recent History

1945   World War II ends and the cold war begins, con-
             tributing in America to a fear of communism that
             feeds conspiracy theories underlying militia organi-
             zations that form in the following two decades.

1946   The Red Scare begins with hearings held in Holly-
             wood and elsewhere by the House Un-American

Activities Committee. The search for Communists continues unabated into the early 1950s when Senator Joseph McCarthy holds Senate hearings on what he calls a conspiracy. The atmosphere lends itself to militia activities.

1948   Francis Parker Yockey writes *Imperium*, a book that extols Nazi ideas and warns of a conspiracy by Jews wedded to humanism and determined to create a One World government. Civilization, he insists, stands imperiled. Yockey's work feeds the hysteria by right-wing extremists amid the cold war and later serves as an ideological foundation for those militias that adopt anti-Semitism and white supremacy.

1954   The Supreme Court decision in *Brown v. The Board of Education* mandates the desegregation of public schools. The recently dormant Ku Klux Klan revives to fight this decision and to oppose civil rights activists. In the process it forms paramilitary units in some states.

1957   Willis Carto begins the Liberty Lobby, a racist and anti-Semitic right-wing organization that fuels conspiratorial fears among extremists. *Spotlight*, the organization's main publication, later gains a substantial readership.

1958   Businessman Robert Welch founds the ultra-right John Birch Society, which belives that a Communist conspiracy exists in the United States to establish totalitarianism. The Birchers do not advocate militias, but the group's ideology stimulates conspiratorial fears and raises the specter of a One World government, an important component of militia ideology.

1960   Wesley Swift and William Potter Gale found the Christian Defense League (CDL), whose doctrine considers Jews to be lower than human beings. The CDL develops paramilitary training (with Gale organizing the California Rangers) and conceives a plot to kill Martin Luther King, Jr. (considered to be an agent of the Jews). Under Gale, this ideology

1960
cont.

soon coalesces into the Christian Identity movement, a largely, but not exclusively, militant group.
These militants sometimes refer to themselves as
Christian Patriots. Most Identity Christians embrace the *Protocols of the Meetings of the Learned
Elders of Zion*, an anti-Semitic tract written in
the early 1900s, outlining a supposed Jewish
conspiracy to take over the world.

1961

The fears concerning Communist conspiracies and
a One World government lead Robert DePugh, a
Missouri businessman, to organize a militia group,
the Minutemen. Small in size, it nevertheless stock-
piles arms and ammunition and holds paramilitary
exercises.

1967

The Black Panthers are founded in Oakland,
California, by Huey Newton and Bobby Seale.
The Panthers promote black community and black
pride, but also militancy to advance a leftist political agenda. The group forms armed urban patrols
and militias to end police brutality and to advance
the Panthers' political program.

1969

Weatherman organizes as a breakaway group from
the leftist Students for a Democratic Society and
engages in terrorist activities, such as the bombing
of public buildings, to advance its radical agenda.
One leader, Bernardine Dohrn, organizes a small
women's militia.

The Posse Comitatus emerges as a secretive group
under the leadership of Henry L. Beach, an Oregonian. Beach and his followers condemn liberal
cultural changes and federal programs, and assert
that the highest law and governmental authority in
any locality is that of the county sheriff, who is
responsible to the citizenry. Because of their beliefs,
Posse members refuse to pay federal taxes or even
obtain drivers' licenses.

Robert DePugh is sentenced to prison for jumping
bond and violating federal gun control laws.
Following this, the Minutemen deteriorate as
an organization.

1973 Lyndon LaRouche, the founder of the National Caucus of Labor Committees, forms a short-lived paramilitary structure of ghetto youths to politicize them.

    Richard Girnt Butler organizes Aryan Nations. Based in Idaho, this group consists of racists who believe in a violent struggle to protect and advance white power.

1974 Samuel Sherwood founds the Constitutional Militia Association in Idaho, a research group intended to protect constitutional rights.

1978 Using the pen name Andrew Macdonald, William Pierce, a member of the National Socialist White People's Party (formerly the American Nazi Party), writes *The Turner Diaries,* which becomes a revelation of fact to some militias. This book, a novel, portrays a time when America is besieged by gun-control laws, urban riots, and Jewish plots. The main character, presented as a true hero, saves the nation through his organization, which uses nuclear, biological, and chemical weapons against nonwhites.

1979 In October, armed Ku Klux Klan (KKK) members affiliated with recent militia activity fire into an anti-Klan rally in Greensboro, North Carolina, killing five leftist demonstrators.

1980 Tom Metzger founds the White American Political Association, which soon changes its name to White Aryan Resistance—WAR. An organization of rightist Skinheads, WAR attack Jews, blacks, and homosexuals. WAR's activities include paramilitary training.

1981 The KKK and other right-wing extremists engage in military training exercises in California's Sierra Nevada Mountains and operate a paramilitary camp near Birmingham, Alabama.

1982 Gordon Kahl, a member of the Posse Comitatus and an Identity Christian, is wanted by federal agents for failing to pay his income taxes and for

1982 cont.	violating parole. In February, a shoot-out occurs near Kahl's farm in Medina, Iowa, but he escapes. Two federal marshals are killed.

In March, the Posse Comitatus holds militia training exercises in Weskan, Kansas.

1983	In September, authorities track Gordon Kahl to a cabin in Arkansas. After he wounds a local sheriff, he is shot and killed. Kahl's case becomes a cause celebre in the militia movement and strengthens the extreme rightists who believe government tyranny is expanding.

Also in September, the Silent Brotherhood, commonly called the Order, is organized in Metaline Falls, Idaho, by Robert Matthews. The group plots to overthrow the U.S. government, or what it calls ZOG, the Zionist Occupation Government.

1984	The Order issues a "declaration of war" against the U.S. government. The group robs a Brinks armored truck in April and another in July, and in June murders Alan Berg, a liberal Jewish radio talk show host in Denver. In December, the FBI tracks Robert Matthews down and kills him at Whidbey Island in Washington, and within two years the Order dissolves.
1985	In December, 10 members of the Order are convicted on charges of arson, counterfeiting, and murder; 12 others plead guilty.
1986	Glenn Miller and Stephen Miller, the leaders of the White Patriot Party, a racist North Carolina militia organization, are found guilty of contempt of court for violating an earlier agreement not to engage in paramilitary training.

William Pierce, the author of *The Turner Diaries*, moves to a farm near Mill Point, West Virginia, where he establishes the Cosmotheist Community, which is dedicated to recruiting fighters opposed to so-called Jewish power.

Aryan Nations detonates bombs at a federal building, a priest's home, and two businesses in Idaho.

William Potter Gale, one of the founders of Christian Identity, is arrested for conspiring to assassinate a federal judge and IRS officials in Nevada. One year later, a federal jury convicts Gale and several associates of the crime.

1989   In December, David Duke, former grand wizard of the Louisiana Knights of the Ku Klux Klan, wins a seat in the state legislature as a Republican. His attachment to racism and anti-Semitism, including using his legislative office to sell books such as *Hitler Was My Friend*, fuels the idea that right-wing extremism has a legitimate place in American politics and encourages groups, militias and otherwise, dedicated to such an agenda.

1991   Sam Sherwood organizes the United States Militia Association to provide instructions on forming citizen militias, while at the same time promoting lobbying techniques and engaging in election campaigns. Like other militia leaders, Sherwood criticizes government efforts to restrict gun ownership. He rejects Identity Christianity and anti-Semitic tracts such as the *Protocols of the Meetings of the Learned Elders of Zion* and publicly distances himself from white supremacists while expressing distrust of anything other than local, community authority.

1992   Federal agents surround a cabin at Ruby Ridge, Idaho, that is occupied by Randy Weaver, his wife, their children, and a family friend. Weaver, an Identity Christian and supporter of Aryan Nations, is wanted for possible violation of firearms laws. At one point the agents kill Weaver's 13-year-old son; at another, they fire into the cabin and kill Weaver's wife. Within the militia movement, the incident is considered a prime example of excessive governmental power—an attempt to persecute Weaver for his beliefs and his ownership of guns. A later investigation of the confrontation finds the FBI had violated its own rules of engagement and falsified evidence to hide its transgressions. (In 1995, the federal government reached an out-of-court settlement with Weaver, awarding his family over three million dollars.)

1992
cont.

In order to reduce the possibility of infiltration and exposure, Louis Beam, a white supremacist and militia advocate, proposes the use of leaderless resistance as a tactic whereby militia units will be no larger than six or eight people.

1993

In February, white supremacist Bo Gritz travels the nation promoting his program, Specially Prepared Individuals for Key Events (SPIKE). Through SPIKE, he teaches paramilitary techniques and instructs Christian Patriots in Oregon, Washington, Idaho, California, and elsewhere.

The same month, Mark Koernke, one of the most influential people in recruiting for the militia movement, releases *America in Peril*, a videotape that calls upon Americans to defend themselves against a New World Order that will bring oppressive rule through the United Nations.

Also in February, agents from the Bureau of Alcohol, Tobacco and Firearms (BATF) attack Mount Carmel, a Branch Davidian compound located near Waco, Texas, and under the leadership of David Koresh. The agents had suspected Koresh and his followers of possessing illegal weapons. A shootout occurs, after which the federal government orders in tanks, helicopters, and armored vehicles to surround the compound. A long siege ensues, accompanied by charges the Davidians are a cult and that Koresh abuses children (the latter never proved). The end comes when tanks puncture holes in the compound and inject gas to force the Davidians to flee. A fire erupts, however, and Koresh and most of the Davidians, including children, burn to death. As with Ruby Ridge, militias consider this a show of excessive government power and of tyranny, and many Americans agree with them. The conflagration obtains added significance because it occurs on 19 April, a date considered special by militias because of its link to the American Revolution—when shots rang out at Lexington and Concord.

In November, Congress passes the Brady Bill, requiring a nationwide five-day waiting period prior to handgun purchases. Many militias consider the bill an example of federal tyranny.

1994   In January, John Trochmann, along with David Trochmann, his brother, and Randy Trochmann, his nephew, organize the Militia of Montana (MOM). This organization quickly obtains a high profile, offering through its catalog a training manual and numerous books and videotapes depicting conspiratorial efforts by political, financial, and business leaders to incorporate the United States into a One World government. Critics accuse MOM of anti-Semitism and racism, particularly because of the close relations between John Trochmann and Aryan Nations.

Encouraged by MOM's example, the Michigan Militia organizes in April. Norm Olson and Ray Southwell emerge as its leaders and claim they reject racism and anti-Semitism. Within a year, the Michigan Militia grows to approximately 6,000 members.

Linda Thompson begins the American Justice Federation (AJF) in Indianapolis. She seeks to alert the public about a conspiracy to form a tyrannical One World government. The AJF releases *Waco: The Big Lie*, a videotape that purportedly shows numerous errors by the federal government in the conflagration at the Branch Davidian compound and raises the specter of conspiracy. Her call in September for an armed march on Congress by militias earns her a rebuke from the John Birch Society, which considers her a loose cannon.

Mark Koernke, known as Mark from Michigan, broadcasts nationally on a shortwave radio network, attacking the federal government and gaining additional recruits for militias.

In July, Congress passes a federal crime bill that bans some types of assault weapons. Militias see this as the growth of tyranny.

1994
cont.

In October, Morris Dees, head of the Southern Poverty Law Center, writes U. S. Attorney General Janet Reno to warn of the growing threat from militias connected to racist agendas. That same month, the Anti-Defamation League issues a report detailing militia activity in 13 states and characterizes much of the paramilitary activity as linked to racism and anti-Semitism.

Also in October, six militias in New Mexico meet at Raton to form a combined militia, but they fail to reach any agreement.

Republican Helen Chenoweth wins a November election to Congress from Idaho's First District. Her victory comes with the help of militia groups, and she proclaims that democracy exists when government is afraid of the people. Part of a conservative landslide in national elections, the Chenoweth campaign and others similar to it signify the widespread frustration and discontent many Americans have toward government—a feeling that reflects the decade's expanding militia activity and that provides fertile ground for continued militia growth.

Mark Koernke—Mark from Michigan—travels to several states, including California, Montana, and Louisiana, late in the year (and early the following year), where he addresses hundreds of people.

In December, militia groups rally in Florida at a Patriot Alert Rally in Brevard County, where literature is distributed detailing the conspiracy to establish a One World government. In Gainesville, militia activists protest the flying of the United Nations flag at the city hall.

In an active year for organization, several new militias and their support groups appear, including the Constitution Defense Militia in New Hampshire, the 1st Regiment Florida Militia in Key Largo, the 51st Militia in Missouri, the Texas Militia Correspondence Committee, the New Jersey Militia, and the Committee to Restore the Constitution in Fort Collins, Colorado.

1995   In January, members connected to the Michigan Militia plot to bomb Camp Grayling, an Air National Guard base in the northern part of the state. They claim that Soviet tanks were gathered there in preparation for an attack on American citizens as part of an effort to create a One World government. Authorities discover the plot and thwart the attack.

In February, James Roy Mullins, founder of the Blue Ridge Hunt Club, a militia in Virginia, pleads guilty to violating federal firearms laws. In May, he is sentenced to a five-year prison term.

Talk show host G. Gordon Liddy tells his listeners how to shoot agents of the Bureau of Alcohol, Tobacco, and Firearms. His show, along with dozens like it across the nation, sharpens the political atmosphere and encourages militia activity.

More than 2,000 people gather in Meadville, Pennsylvania, to hear militia recruiter Mark Koernke discuss what Americans must do to stop the New World Order.

In March, Republican Congressman Steve Stockman, from the Ninth District in Texas, accuses the federal government of preparing a military assault on militias.

Also in March, Militia of Montana co-founder John Trochmann is arrested on charges of conspiring to obstruct justice in a case involving a prisoner being held by the sheriff in Musselshell County, Montana. The charges are dropped due to insufficient evidence.

On 19 April, an explosion demolishes the Alfred P. Murrah Federal Building in Oklahoma City, killing more than 100 people, including children in a day-care center. One or more terrorists had planted a bomb made of ammonium nitrate fertilizer in a parked van near the entrance to the building. Within days, Timothy McVeigh is arrested by federal agents and charged with the crime. In August, he

1995
cont.

and Terry Nichols are indicted for conspiring to blow up the federal building. McVeigh had attended meetings of the Michigan Militia, but by year's end no evidence surfaces to indicate the attack was planned by a militia group, although some observers point out the connection to the all-important date, 19 April. Despite the lack of a clear link on to a militia, the tragedy draws media and public attention to militia groups and raises questions as to the nature and goals of extremists who inhabit the movement.

Several militia leaders accuse the federal government of involvement in the bombing at Oklahoma City. Linda Thompson declares the federal government did the bombing; Bo Gritz calls the bombing a "true Rembrandt"; and Norm Olson claims it was done by the Japanese in retaliation for a gas attack on the Tokyo subway system supposedly staged by American agents. Because of this comment, the Michigan Militia decides to remove Olson from his command.

A fundraising letter distributed by the National Rifle Association calls federal agents "jack-booted government thugs" in "Nazi bucket helmets" who have the authority to harass and murder citizens.

Senate Democrats proceed with an informal inquiry into the militia movement. Witnesses appear who tell of threats and actual physical attacks.

In another active year for militias, a group in Pensacola, Florida, develops arms caches. A militia holds paramilitary exercises near Atlanta, while in New York, another militia holds training exercises in Chemung County; the Militia of Wisconsin declares it is preparing for battle; and in Alabama, the Sons of Liberty distribute pamphlets urging citizen action.

In June, police in southeastern Ohio stop a local militia leader, then shoot and kill him after he exits from his car with gun drawn and his body in a stance as if ready to fire. Several militias label the killing part of a conspiracy to wipe them out.

Also in June, the U.S. Senate Judiciary Subcommittee on Terrorism, Technology, and Government Information holds public hearings into the militia movement. The sessions, led by Chairman Arlen Specter (Republican, Pennsylvania), arouse opposition from militias, which consider it a witch hunt, and criticism from militia-monitoring groups, which call the investigation weak and perfunctory.

During the summer, the Anti-Defamation League warns that some militias might be following the advice of white supremacists Tom Metzger and Louis Beam by using leaderless resistance, meaning dividing into small, self-contained cells of six to eight members each to avoid detection. The Anti-Defamation League reports that militias are operating in at least 40 states and calls their existence a "menace."

The Southern Poverty Law Center reports that 224 militias exist in 39 states and claims that 45 of them have ties to neo-Nazi and white supremacist organizations. The Law Center rejects anti-terrorist legislation and calls instead for enforcing existing state laws against paramilitary activities.

The New Jersey Militia charges the Southern Poverty Law Center with receiving secret funding from the federal government under an executive order signed years earlier by President Ronald Reagan.

Residents of Hamilton, Montana, circulate a petition (which acquires 800 signatures) proclaiming their denouncement of those who advocate violence and their support for elected officials amid threats made by some local militiamen against federal and county facilities.

In Arizona, former Phoenix policeman Jack McLamb circulates *Operation Vampire Killer 2000*,

1995
cont.

a tract purporting to show conspiratorial actions by national leaders to advance a One World socialist government. McLamb seeks to recruit law enforcement officers around the nation to fight the conspiracy.

At the Patriot Archives site on the Internet, 19 April is declared national militia day, "a day on which all able-bodied citizens will be called up for formations of their local militias for training and discussion." The announcement expresses the militia view that the right to bear arms and assemble to protect the republic must be preserved.

Militias in Wellston, Michigan, gain attention late in the summer for disrupting town meetings and attempting to prohibit all government regulations concerning property, including zoning laws.

1996

In March, a standoff begins at a ranch near Jordan, Montana, between radical Freemen and the FBI. Although not a militia, the Freemen adhere to views held by some in the militia movement, especially ideas promoted by Identity Christians and the Posse Comitatus. The FBI implements a tactic called "soft seige" to avoid the bloodshed that occurred at Ruby Ridge and Waco.

In June, the Freemen surrender to the FBI after federal agents cut off electricity to the ranch where the extremists had barricaded themselves. At least five Freemen face federal charges of fraud and making threats against a U.S. District Court judge.

On 1 July, federal agents raid a house near Phoenix, Arizona, and arrest 12 members of a militia called the Vipers. The agents claim they uncovered high-powered rifles, ammunition, and bomb-making materials and that the militia may have intended to blow up government buildings.

Biographical Sketches

Little public information exists about most of the leaders involved in the 1990s militia movement, hence the following biographies are sketches at best, and in more than one instance rely on interviews conducted by the author. Wherever possible, places of birth and dates of birth (and, where applicable, death dates) have been included—along with other biographical facts not directly related to extremist politics, such as education and employment. The focus, however, is on involvement in the militia movement.

Henry L. Beach (1903–?)

Henry L. Beach founded the Posse Comitatus. In the 1930s, he joined and served as a recruiter for the Silver Shirts, a group that supported Adolph Hitler. Sometime after World War II, he began his own company in Portland, Oregon, called Beach Cleaning Machinery and Equipment. Beach retired from his business in 1969 and at that time organized the Posse Comitatus, a Latin name meaning "power of the county." The Posse Comitatus believes that all power resides in the county sheriff—not the

Constitution—and that other levels of government have usurped popular authority and trampled individual rights.

Opposed to all but minimal governmental authority, members of Posse Comitatus refuse to pay federal taxes or even purchase state license tags and drivers' licenses. The group acts secretively, generally rejecting traditional politics, such as campaigning for office, in favor of violent attacks and paramilitary activities. The Posse Comitatus is closely aligned with the Christian Identity movement. Thus, the Posse considers Jews to be leaders of a conspiracy to seize all power and crush liberty. The Federal Reserve system, for example, is condemned as an illegal private operation directed by Jews.

Beach served as national leader of the Posse until 1974 and denied it had any racist agenda or connection with neo-Nazis. He denied, too, numerous reports about Posse members engaging in paramilitary activities. At its height around 1980, the Posse likely had chapters in 23 states with a national membership in the tens of thousands.

By the 1980s, Beach had numerous differences with Posse members and criticized those who had been involved in notorious attacks over land disputes and other similar matters. He called the members of Aryan Nations and the Order "knot heads," and said, "I don't have any use for 'em. These neo-Nazis should go someplace else....A lot of those guys [are] extreme radicals. I don't know what you could do for 'em. Any time they take Hitler for their king, I've got no use for them. I'm strictly a law-abiding citizen."

Beach proclaimed his complete retirement from political activities in 1985 and died shortly thereafter. By this time, the Posse had declined considerably. Although most militias in the 1990s are not part of the Posse, they often reflect its opposition to governmental authority and its conspiratorial world views. The Posse has both represented and contributed to the distrust of government widespread in contemporary American society.

Louis Beam (b. 1947)

Louis Beam, a leader within the Knights of the Ku Klux Klan (KKKK) and the militia movement, grew up in Lake Jackson, Texas, a town near Houston. In the 1960s, he fought in the Vietnam War and joined the Ku Klux Klan when he returned to the United States. In 1976, he joined with the KKKK, newly organized under Louisianian David Duke. Beam held the office of Grand Titan and led a drive to recruit soldiers from Fort Hood, Texas.

With his military background, Beam served the KKKK by instructing its members in guerrilla warfare. In the early 1980s, he trained men to fight against Vietnamese immigrants who were operating fishing boats in and near Galveston Bay. The Vietnamese, however, filed suit against the KKKK and gained a federal court order shutting down the paramilitary training camps. Beam did not totally cease his activities, however, and he was soon arrested and convicted on a charge of using federal land to train militias.

Beam shortly thereafter left the Klan and emerged as a major figure in Aryan Nations, a militant white-supremacist organization based in Idaho. He established a computer network for the group, then entered a relationship with the Order, an offshoot of Aryan Nations dedicated to violently overthrowing the federal government, which it called the Zionist Occupation Government (ZOG). In 1987, he was indicted for this activity and charged with sedition; he then fled to Mexico. Authorities there, however, captured Beam, and extradited him to the United States. In April 1988 a jury acquitted him, a decision he called a great blow to ZOG.

Beam continued his affiliation with Aryan Nations. In 1992, in his newsletter *The Seditionist*, he advocated a new tactic called leaderless resistance. This meant that ZOG must be fought through small militia groups, no more than six or eight members in each, subject to broad central orders, but independent in their specific actions so that if one group, or cell, should be exposed, the others would remain untouched. In this way, terrorist activities could be conducted successfully and appear as if they were linked to only one or two individuals. In 1995, Beam spoke at the Aryan Nations World Congress. Some observers speculated he might soon emerge as the organization's overall leader.

Richard Girnt Butler (b. 1918)

Richard Girnt Butler is the founder of Aryan Nations. Before moving to the Northwest, Butler lived in California, where he worked as an engineer for Lockheed. He was heavily influenced by William Potter Gale, who promoted a Christian Identity ideology. In 1973, Butler moved from California to Coeur d'Alene, Idaho, and soon thereafter founded the Church of Jesus Christ

Christian at nearby Hayden Lake. This church followed Gale's Christian Identity teachings and as such considered Jews to be Satanic and nonwhites to be inferior "mud people."

Butler developed a political arm to his church, called Aryan Nations. This organization consisted of Identity Christians and others who supported white supremacy and anti-Semitism. He sponsored an Aryan Nations Congress at his Hayden Lake compound (an event still held annually), and leading speakers from racist organizations appeared, including neo-Nazis. Over the years, Butler advocated the establishment of a "whites only" nation in the Pacific Northwest and promoted his Christian Identity ministry in the nation's prisons through his newsletter, *Calling Our Nation.*

In 1987, a federal grand jury in Fort Smith, Arkansas, indicted Butler for his role in plotting to overthrow the U.S. government. He was acquitted the following year. At about the same time, he underwent heart bypass surgery, and his role in Aryan Nations diminished. Yet his influence in the militia movement continues, not so much as a founder of militias, but as a promoter of Identity Christianity. To those militias that have adopted this ideology—a small minority—Butler remains a hero.

Robert DePugh (b. 1923)

Robert DePugh, founder of the Minutemen militia, was born in Independence, Missouri, where his father served as deputy sheriff. He graduated from high school in 1941 and a year later enlisted in the Army, although he opposed the U.S. entry into World War II, criticizing it for abetting communist Russia. DePugh's stint in the military did not last long; in 1944 he was dismissed for chronic nervousness and depression. In 1946, he enrolled at Kansas State University, but stayed there for only 18 months. He then held various jobs from 1947 until 1953, the year he founded the Biolab Corporation in Independence. Biolab produced, most prominently, a dog food supplement. The company went out of business just three years later, and DePugh enrolled at Washburn University in Topeka, Kansas.

In 1959, DePugh reactivated Biolab in the small town of Norborne, Missouri. The following year, in part because of his disgust with the rise of Fidel Castro to power in Cuba and the failure of an effective American response, and in part because of reading literature issued by the right-wing John Birch Society and the House Un-American Activities Committee, he founded the Minutemen. He described the group as a patriotic organization dedicated to stopping the enemies within the United States who sought to advance communism. At the same time, he was a member of the Birch Society.

DePugh considered the Minutemen a diverse group: a guerrilla warfare outfit ready to fight communists, a nationwide spy network reporting on treasonous activity, and a propaganda group distributing literature about the international socialist conspiracy and showing how to make bombs and ammunition. He said that he wanted to provoke the federal government—which he considered dominated by communist sympathizers—into repressive measures that would, in turn, provoke the people against it. He edited the Minutemen newsletter, *Taking Aim*, which in 1964 advised its readers: "If you are ever going to buy a gun, buy it now."

That same year, he held a paramilitary training camp in California that attracted 50 Minutemen out of a total membership numbering several hundred. While involved in this, he broke with the John Birch Society after its leaders accused him of trying to take over the organization. In 1966, he founded the Patriotic Party, a political wing of the Minutemen, intended to be a public, high-profile organization running candidates for office. By and large, though, the Minutemen operated in great secrecy, decentralized and divided into small groups. Members of the Minutemen stockpiled weapons, including rifles, submachine guns, and mortars.

In his 1966 book, *Blueprint for Victory*, DePugh urged the privatization of government activities to reduce the budget deficit, claimed there must be a broad resistance movement to oppose socialists, charged that labor unions had been infiltrated by an internationalist socialist movement, insisted that bureaucracy would soon destroy states' rights, and urged Americans to regain their freedom through a counterrevolution—violent or otherwise. That same year, authorities arrested him for violating federal firearms laws. He was convicted in November 1966 and resigned as head of the Minutemen in 1967 (although he continued as its unofficial leader). In 1968, while free on appeal, a grand jury indicted him for conspiring to rob several banks in Washington state. DePugh fled, but FBI agents captured him in New Mexico in July 1969. He served nearly four years of an 11-year prison sentence before receiving parole in February 1973.

Without DePugh, the Minutemen faded into obscurity. In the 1980s, he reentered the radical picture by adopting Identity

Christianity, and published a survivalist book with recommendations on how to handle the catastrophe that would occur when, he predicted, the Federal Reserve recalled all paper money. He had another encounter with the law in 1991 and was arrested and later convicted on a morals and pornography charge involving an underage girl. In 1992 he was convicted on three counts of federal firearms violations.

The Minutemen have recently revived without DePugh's leadership. DePugh has professed disgust with all politics and has retired from the scene. However, his legacy remains—one of taking up arms to fight One World socialism and those within the United States who would promote it, a leading concern in the contemporary militia movement.

William Potter Gale (1917–1988)

William Potter Gale served during World War II on the staff of General Douglas MacArthur and directed guerrilla operations in the Philippine Islands against the Japanese. Soon after the war, he retired from the military and began selling securities in California. In 1956, he started his own securities brokerage business. At the same time, he emerged as an outspoken critic of President Dwight D. Eisenhower and the Supreme Court justices, claiming they should be impeached for having made decisions leading to the desegregation of public schools. In 1958, he ran for governor of California as the candidate of the Constitution Party but received only a small vote.

Two years later, Gale founded the California Rangers, a paramilitary group linked to the Christian Identity church begun by Wesley Swift. Gale warned that Jews had better not attack him or his supporters, for if they did "every rabbi in Los Angeles will be dead within 24 hours." The Rangers did not last long; the group disbanded several months later, after the state attorney general exposed and condemned them.

Gale, however, continued his extremist activities. With Henry Ward Beach, he founded the Posse Comitatus, a group that considered the county sheriff to be the highest level of governmental authority. Many in Posse Comitatus adhered to Identity Christianity. In 1982, Gale conducted paramilitary training in Kansas, and in 1984 he founded the Committee of the States, an organization that protested the federal income tax as unconstitutional. In 1987, a federal grand jury convicted Gale of obstructing the Internal Revenue Service and threatening the lives of IRS agents. A judge sentenced him in January 1988 to a one-year prison term, but Gale died a few weeks later, on 28 April. The political ideas he expressed remain a part of the militia world view, and some militias embrace his Identity Christianity.

James "Bo" Gritz (?–)

James "Bo" Gritz has been an important activist in promoting paramilitary training. A former Green Beret in the Vietnam War who returned to southeast Asia several times in attempting to find missing American prisoners of war, Gritz gained notoriety in 1988 when he ran for vice president of the United States on the Populist Party ticket, the same one that presented former Ku Klux Klan leader David Duke for president. This party was founded by Willis Carto, a leader in the anti-Semitic Liberty Lobby, and attracted many white supremacists. Gritz disclaimed any bigotry, but his ideology included a belief that Jews controlled the federal government and that a conspiracy existed to deprive Americans of gun ownership and other constitutional rights. He charged that eight Jewish families ruled America by controlling the Federal Reserve.

After the election, Gritz continued to express conspiratorial views, including that the federal government promoted the outbreak of AIDS (acquired immune deficiency syndrome) as a form of population control, and that mysterious black helicopters flew across America as part of a program to spy on people. He spoke at meetings of Christian Identity supporters and in 1992 again joined the Populist Party ticket, this time as its presidential candidate.

The following year, he figured prominently in the showdown at Ruby Ridge in Idaho between Randy Weaver and federal agents. He volunteered to intervene and subsequently negotiated an end to the crisis. After the incident, Gritz organized Specially Prepared Individuals for Key Events (SPIKE). This program, which he presented around the nation, emphasized survivalist techniques and paramilitary training. He also developed a plan to establish Christian covenanted communities in central Idaho to be armed for protection against federal agents. Gritz founded the Center for Action in Mesa, Arizona, through which he sells conspiracy tapes and anti-Semitic literature. Gritz refuses to condemn the tragic bombing in 1995 at Oklahoma City and has called it "a Rembrandt—a masterpiece of art and science." In 1996, he tried unsuccessfully to negotiate an end to a standoff between extremists in Montana (the Freemen) and federal authorities.

Gordon Kahl (1920–1983)

Gordon Kahl, at one time a farmer in North Dakota, became a martyr within the Posse Comitatus. In the 1970s, the state experienced substantial economic hardship. In part motivated by this suffering, which included financial difficulties with his own farm, Kahl joined the Posse Comitatus, dedicated to an extreme doctrine in believing that the county sheriff, not the Constitution, was the highest level of governmental authority. Kahl served in Texas as statewide coordinator for the Posse in 1974 and appeared on television to recruit members. In agreement with Posse ideology, Kahl refused to pay his income taxes or even to obtain a driver's license. In 1977, the federal government charged him with income tax evasion, and later that year he was found guilty and sentenced to one year in prison and five years' probation.

Kahl embraced a conspiratorial view prevalent within the Posse and believed that Jews and Masons (members of a secretive, fraternal order) were secretly working to take over the federal government. He established his own church, the Gospel Divine Doctrine Church of Jesus Christ, and through it he espoused a Christian Identity ideology.

Kahl's problems with the law worsened in 1981 when he failed to report to his probation officer. Consequently, the authorities issued a warrant for his arrest. When they tried to serve him with it as he left an anti-tax meeting in Medina, North Dakota, a shoot-out ensued. Kahl escaped, but not until after he and his associates had killed a federal marshal and a deputy marshal. The Medina shoot-out made Kahl a hero to the Posse Comitatus.

For months, authorities could not uncover Kahl's whereabouts, but in June 1983 they finally tracked him down to a farm tucked in the hills near Smithville, Arkansas. When they tried to arrest him, Kahl opened fire, wounding a local sheriff, who later died. Kahl was killed in the ensuing exchange, which lasted about two hours. In death he became a martyr within the Posse Comitatus and to some extremists within the militia movement who praised his stand against the federal government.

Mark Koernke (b. 1958)

Mark Koernke is a prominent militia broadcaster and recruiter. During the late 1970s and into the mid-1980s, he served in the Army Reserves. In 1984, he was arrested in Detroit, Michigan, for carrying a concealed weapon and given a one-year deferred sentence. Koernke emerged in the 1990s as a leading recruiter within the militia movement. He describes himself as a former U.S. Army Intelligence Officer and a Counterintelligence Analyst. Whatever the case, in the 1990s he worked as a janitor at the University of Michigan in Ann Arbor. From 1994 until spring 1995, he hosted a widely listened-to show on a shortwave radio station. The show, however, was pulled from the air after "Mark from Michigan," as he was known, implied that the federal government had masterminded the 1995 bombing at Oklahoma City. Koernke asserted also that a plot existed, again on the part of the federal government, to have Timothy McVeigh, the main suspect in the bombing, assassinated.

Koernke, who in 1994 organized the clandestine and heavily armed Michigan Militia-at-Large, remains highly active in the militia movement, maintaining close ties with the Militia of Montana, traveling around the nation, encouraging people to join the movement and promoting his conspiracy theories. For example, in 1995 he warned of a coup d'etat soon to occur against the American government as part of a nefarious plan by bankers, elite politicians, and those who desired a One World system. In addition to his speaking engagements, Koernke produces videotapes effective in recruiting for the militias.

William Pierce (b. 1935)

William Pierce, author of the racist and anti-Semitic *The Turner Diaries*, grew up in Atlanta, Georgia. In 1952, he obtained a doctorate in physics from the University of Colorado at Boulder and then worked as a science laboratory researcher. In 1962, he became an assistant physics professor at Oregon State University. He left that position three years later and moved to Connecticut, where he worked in a private science lab. He quit, however, in 1966 to devote his energies to the American Nazi Party. The following year, he became one of the main leaders in the organization, renamed the National Socialist White People's Party.

In 1970, Pierce began the National Alliance, which made an appeal to young people to protect the white race against Jews and what he called other "undesirables." This organization produced racist and anti-Semitic works and considered itself a promoter of Adolph Hitler's ideology. In 1978, Pierce wrote *The Turner Diaries* (under the pen name Andrew Macdonald), a novel that was intended to transmit his ideology. Steeped in anti-Semitism and racism, the book tells of a world ruined by a Jewish conspiracy, then saved by a fearless fighter who leads "the Organization," dedicated to killing Jews and nonwhites. *The Turner Diaries* gained a wide audience within the far right, perhaps selling over 200,000 copies, and exerted considerable influence among militia leaders. Even those who rejected its anti-Semitism and racism could relate to the vision of a deteriorating society under the control of a conspiratorial elite. Most Americans, however, never heard of *The Turner Diaries* until after the 1995 bombing at Oklahoma City, when observers pointed out the similarity between the explosion that leveled the federal office building there and a tactic used by the main character in Pierce's fictional story. The perpetrator of the attack in Oklahoma City may have followed the scene from the book.

Pierce purchased a farm in 1985, nearly 400 acres located in West Virginia. There he continues to write his extremist literature and provides what he calls a training ground for his followers to prepare for the great fight to save white civilization.

Samuel Sherwood (b. 1951)

Samuel Sherwood, founder and leader of the United States Militia Association (USMA), was born Mason Stanley Sherwood in Berkeley, California. He grew up in San Francisco and Los Angeles and served in both the U.S. Army and Navy. He earned a bachelor's degree in communications from Brigham Young University, followed by a master's degree in international relations. He lived for two years in Israel, where he worked on a kibbutz, and today serves as headmaster of a private school, Navoo Academy in Idaho.

Sherwood's interest in politics led him in 1975 to form the Constitutional Militia Association, a research group dedicated to protecting constitutional rights. From this organization he founded the USMA in 1994, after incidents at Ruby Ridge and elsewhere reinforced his view that a too-powerful federal government was a threat to liberty. Today, Sherwood believes the

Second Amendment is under assault as part of a conspiracy aimed at weakening individual rights and creating a One World political system.

Sherwood condemns racists and anti-Semites; he considers books such as *The Protocols of the Meetings of the Learned Elders of Zion* hate-mongering propaganda. Similarly, he rejects Identity Christianity and refuses membership to neo-Nazis and Skinheads. Sherwood views the USMA as primarily educating Americans about threats to their liberty. Although he supports the formation of militias and claims to have units in 12 states, he believes militia activity must be in accordance with all laws and with the permission of local governments.

In 1994, the USMA campaigned for Anne Fox, who won election as Idaho Superintendent of Education. Sherwood's effort probably helped Fox, and she returned the favor by making him part of her transition team. She has since spoken favorably about the militia movement. Sherwood foresees the USMA engaging in other campaigns in the near future.

Linda Thompson (?–)

In a personal interview with this author, Linda Thompson, a lawyer and advocate for the militia movement through the Indiana-based American Justice Federation, refused to divulge any but the sparsest of personal information about herself, asserting she was not about to assist the Anti-Defamation League, which she claimed had for years been trying to discover her birth date and activities in her youth. She has refused a biographical listing in the leading publication for lawyers in the United States and did not list her date or place of birth on papers filed when she ran for public office in 1996.

Thompson says she experienced a political change after observing a federal government that she believes is out of control. She says she developed serious misgivings about the government when, in the 1980s, she saw local police forces becoming increasingly "federalized" and authorities imprisoning people on the flimsiest of pretenses, usually African-Americans collared for drug crimes. She particularly disliked the mandatory sentencing that gave judges little leeway in determining prison terms and resulted in people serving more time for minor drug offenses than for serious felonies. She and her husband subsequently began a computer bulletin board service and received more and more reports about government raids that violated Second Amendment rights and other liberties.

Thompson began reading literature published by right-wing protest groups, much of which she rejected because it sounded like stories of "Elvis meeting aliens." But then the shoot-out at Ruby Ridge occurred, and soon after that the tragedy at Waco. In 1994, she founded the American Justice Federation (AJF) in Indianapolis not as a militia per se, but as a support group for militia development. Through the AJF she condemned the Trilateral Commission (an international association of leading politicians and businessmen) and the Council on Foreign Relations (a foreign policy think tank in New York City) as promoters of a New World Order dedicated to an international socialist government. She claimed an elite conspiracy existed to use the U.S. Army against the people and shape a public school agenda that would indoctrinate students with views supporting the socialistic New World Order. Thompson criticized the younger generation for shirking its responsibilities to freedom and community, and she tried to alert people of all ages through literature and videotapes issued by the AJF. Her videotapes *Waco the Big Lie* and *Waco II—The Big Lie Continues*, depict in dramatic fashion what she calls the deceit of the federal government at Waco. She blames the government for having started the fire at the Branch Davidian compound.

In 1994, Thompson called on militia groups to unite and march in uniform, weapons in hand, to the nation's capital. Once there, she expected to get the Fourteenth, Sixteenth, and Seventeenth Amendments to the Constitution repealed (the latter two she especially disliked for establishing the federal income tax and direct election of U.S. Senators), along with the Brady Bill (which created a waiting period for the purchase of handguns), and the North Atlantic Free Trade Agreement. She threatened to arrest several Congressmen guilty of "treasonous activities." The march, however, never occurred as most in the militia movement ignored her, and the far-right John Birch Society ridiculed her, implying she was unstable.

She has since blamed the federal government for the bombing at Oklahoma City in 1995, saying the nation's leaders are known for killing children. Although the fiasco surrounding her proposal to march on Washington and, to a lesser extent, her comment regarding Oklahoma City have damaged her standing, Thompson remains a vocal leader within the militia movement. In 1996 she ran for Marion County (Indiana) Superior Court Judge but suffered a resounding defeat.

David Trochmann (b. 1945)

Born near Newfolden, Minnesota, David Trochmann, a founder of the Militia of Montana (MOM), grew up on his family's farm. He graduated from Newfolden Community High School and began to race cars in the 1960s. Along with his brother John, he soon operated a snowmobile accessories manufacturing company.

Trochmann's interest in politics extended back to high school, when he followed the Cuban Missile Crisis in 1962 and suspected the U.S. government had lied to the American people when it claimed that all Soviet missiles had been removed from the island. Trochmann says that ever since the 1970s he has been trying to warn the public about an attempt by a political and business elite to establish a One World government and crush liberty.

Trochmann moved to Montana around 1984 and in succeeding years grew more discontent with the federal government, which he believes is too bureaucratic and has trampled individual rights—most evident at Ruby Ridge and Waco. He joined with his brother John and son Randy to form MOM early in 1994, an organization he today describes as mainly educative and informational. Trochmann denies charges that MOM has links to Aryan Nations or is a white supremacist, anti-Semitic organization. Like his brother John, he complains that the Anti-Defamation League (ADL) and other "watchdog" groups have failed to contact anyone within MOM to learn what the group is all about. He recently called the ADL a sham organization, run not by Jews, as it purports, but by British intelligence.

John Trochmann (b. 1943)

John Trochmann, born near Newfolden in northwestern Minnesota, is a founder and the most prominent leader of the Militia of Montana (MOM), grew up as a farm boy on the Minnesota plains. At age 17, after dropping out of high school, he joined the Naval Air Force and worked first as an engine mechanic and later as a flight engineer.

His military service took him to Iceland and Puerto Rico, and he participated in reconnaissance flyovers during the 1962 Cuban Missile Crisis. He took photographs of Soviet ships as part of an attempt to confirm that Russian missiles were being removed from Cuba. To this day, he believes this was not done and that American leaders deceived the public into thinking the Soviets had been forced to back down. In the 1960s, after he left the military, Trochmann developed an auto repair and race car business in Delano, Minnesota, that diversified into work on snowmobiles.

After his brother David relocated to Montana, Trochmann became attracted to that state's wide-open spaces and moved there in 1988. He had a long-standing interest in politics, in what he has called a constant effort trying to warn the American people about threats to their liberty. In 1990, he appeared at the national Aryan Nations Congress meeting in Idaho and spoke in support of that group's white-supremacist activities. He later denied any affinity for Aryan Nations, but Aryan Nations founder Richard Girnt Butler revealed a supportive relationship between his group and Trochmann.

As with many in the militia movement, events at Ruby Ridge and Waco convinced Trochmann that the federal government intended to crush liberty. He felt frustrated that most Americans did not recognize this, and consequently traveled to Alaska and planned to live there permanently. Then, however, he saw more and more Americans criticizing the media and raising questions about their government, and this rebelliousness convinced him to return to Montana and form a political organization. In January 1994, he, along with wife Carolyn, brother David, and nephew Randy, organized MOM, which he claims emphasizes education over everything else, with the name "militia" chosen simply to signify strength.

Many observers consider MOM to have stimulated by example and promotion the formation of militia groups around the nation. John Trochmann, in particular, traveled to other states and encouraged people to establish militias. MOM produced a storm of controversy with the literature and videotapes it made or sold. Many observers labeled the organization racist and anti-Semitic. Both the Anti-Defamation League and the Montana Human Rights Commission have portrayed Trochmann as a white supremacist. He denies this charge and criticizes both groups for failing to contact him or investigate the situation thoroughly.

Trochmann remained at the center of controversy when, in the spring of 1995, authorities in Musselshell County, Montana, arrested him and charged him with conspiring to interfere with justice. Trochmann apparently supported and sympathized with a prisoner, a member of the radical Freemen, in the county jail, but it is unclear as to what Trochmann's intentions were— whether he was trying to help the prisoner escape or force some other type of confrontation with the authorities. In any event, Trochmann did not go to trial because the state's attorney believed the case lacked sufficient evidence.

Later in 1995, Trochmann took part in a debate at Yale University on the militia movement and by his own account convinced many in the audience as to the correctness of his views, stressing a government conspiracy to crush liberty. Trochmann is viewed by some as an opportunist taking advantage of the militia movement and extremist political scene to make money selling videotapes, audiotapes, books, and other literature. Whatever the case concerning this and his views, and despite numerous instances of disagreement with other militias, Trochmann's influence remains substantial.

Randy Trochmann (b. 1967)

Randy Trochmann, the cofounder of the Militia of Montana (MOM) was born in rural northwestern Minnesota, where he graduated from Warren High School. About 1984, he moved with his father, David, to Montana and worked in the logging industry. Always interested in politics, he became incensed over the federal government's actions at Ruby Ridge and Waco. To him, the Second Amendment appeared under attack as part of a wide-ranging assault on liberty and a conspiracy by the nation's elite to make the United States part of a One World government.

Trochmann joined his father and his uncle, John, in forming MOM early in 1994. The organization quickly became the most high-profile of the contemporary militias and earned the wrath of the Anti-Defamation League and the Montana Human Rights Commission for its supposed racism and anti-Semitism. Indeed, MOM sells many materials through a catalog it issues, several of which items champion the positions of racists. Trochmann, however, denies any bigotry and any emphasis on violence—he sees MOM as primarily informational, alerting Americans to the threat against individual freedom. He believes the organization, or at least many within it, will in the near future become more involved in traditional-style political campaigning. In 1996, he announced plans to head the Educational Economic Abuse Foundation, intended to expose the alleged New World Order conspiracy.

Primary Documents

4

The following primary material is presented in several sections. The federal statute providing for a national militia appears in section one, followed by a relevant passage from the U.S. Constitution and an example from one of several state laws regulating militias. Section two includes observations from early American history to complement that part of the overview essay that discusses colonial and Revolutionary-era America.

Section three presents a variety of material from militias themselves, or material that many if not all militias find expressive of the truth about American society. Most of these come from the Internet or newsletters. The intent here is to expose the reader to a wide range of militia ideas and fears—the broad content of which are discussed in the overview. These include racist and anti-Semitic ideas, as well as ideas about conspiracies by the government and reactions to developments that have stimulated militia formation, such as the events in Waco, Texas, and Oklahoma City, Oklahoma. Brief excerpts from *The Protocols of the Meetings of the Learned Elders of Zion* and *The Turner Diaries* are also found in this section.

The final section provides material from the Center for Democratic Renewal and the American Jewish Committee, both of which monitor militias, and testimony from a 1995 investigation into militias by a subcommittee in the U.S. Senate.

A list of paramilitary training sites is appended to the primary material.

With the exception of a few minor corrections to spelling and punctuation, the primary material is worded as it originally appeared.

Militias: National and State Regulations

The National Statute

The national statute that provides for a militia—Title 10, United States Code, Section 311—reads as follows:

311. MILITIA: COMPOSITION AND CLASSES

(a) The militia of the United States consists of all able-bodied males at least 17 years of age and, except as provided in section 313 of title 32, under 45 years of age who are, or who have made a declaration of intention to become, citizens of the United States and of female citizens of the United States who are members of the National Guard.

(b) The classes of the militia are—
   (1) the organized militia, which consists of the National Guard and the Naval Militia; and
   (2) the unorganized militia, which consists of the members of the militia who are not members of the National Guard or the Naval Militia.

The Constitutional Provision

The Constitution refers to militias in what is known as the War Powers Clause. Article I, Section 8 clearly stipulates that control over the militias is shared by the federal and state governments, with the former exerting its authority for the most part only when it calls militias into service. The clause states that Congress shall have the following power:

To provide for calling forth the Militia to execute the Laws of the Union, suppress Insurrections, and repel Invasions;

To provide for organizing, arming, and disciplining the Militia, and for governing such Part of them that may be employed in Service to the United States, reserving to the States respectively, the

Appointment of the Officers, and the Authority of training the Militia according to the discipline prescribed by Congress.

State Regulation

Many states today regulate militia activity. Although New Hampshire prohibits unauthorized paramilitary training, it designates those individuals who belong to the unorganized militia as follows:

I.   The militia shall consist of all able-bodied residents of the state who shall be more than 17 years of age and not more than 45 years of age...

II. The militia shall be divided into 2 classes, namely, the organized militia, which shall be the national guard, and the unorganized militia.

III. The national guard shall consist of the army national guard, an air national guard, and an inactive national guard....

IV. The unorganized militia shall be composed of those classes of persons described in paragraph I of this section who are not members of the organized militia, provided, however, that those persons who are lawfully carried upon the state reserve list or the state retired list shall not be deemed to be a part of the unorganized militia....

Source: Mark Pitcavage at http://www.greyware.com/authors/pitman/militia.htm (accessed 7 January 1996).

Militias: Observations from Early American Society

In the late eighteenth century, views concerning militias, a standing army, and liberty were expressed frequently as Americans battled Britain in the Revolution and struggled to develop a national government. Presented here are statements about militias from the Articles of Confederation *(the first national governing document, ratified in 1781),* The Federalist, *and prominent Virginian Richard Henry Lee.*

From the Articles of Confederation:

Here the emphasis is on militias subject to supervision by the individual state governments:

No vessels of war shall be kept up in time of peace by any State, except such number only, as shall be deemed necessary by the United States in Congress assembled, for the defense of such State, or its trade; nor shall any body of forces be kept up by any state, in time of peace, except such number only, as the judgment of the United States in

Congress assembled, shall be deemed requisite to garrison the forts necessary for the defense of such State; but every State shall always keep up a well-regulated and disciplined militia, sufficiently armed and accoutered ....

Source: George Brown Tindall, *America: A Narrative History* (New York: W.W. Norton, 1988), A7.

From The Federalist:

America's founding fathers, like most of those who supported the Revolution, worried that a large standing army could crush liberty. In The Federalist, *a compendium of articles written in 1787 to support the ratification of the Constitution, Alexander Hamilton offered his view regarding militias. This particular article, known as "The Federalist: No. 29," appeared in New York City's* The Independent Journal *on 9 January 1788, the following day in* The Daily Advertiser, *and the next two days in* The New-York Packet *and* The New-York Journal, *respectively. In this article, Hamilton parries the arguments of those who object to the Constitution because of the possibility that a federal government will both create a permanent standing army and dominate the militias. Hamilton—long distrustful of popular power—believed the militias should be under federal regulation and, in times of crisis, under federal direction. He saw this not as crushing liberty but as making the threat to liberty less likely:*

CONCERNING THE MILITIA
To the People of the State of New York:

The power of regulating the militia, and of commanding its services in times of insurrection and invasion are natural incidents to the duties of superintending the common defence and of watching over the internal peace of the Confederacy.

It requires no skill in the science of war to discern that uniformity in the organization and discipline of the militia would be attended with the most beneficial effects, whenever they were called into service for the public defence. It would enable them to discharge the duties of the camp and of the field with mutual intelligence and concert—an advantage of peculiar moment in the operations of an army; and it would fit them much sooner to acquire the degree of proficiency in military functions which would be essential to their usefulness. This desirable uniformity can only be accomplished by confiding the regulation of the militia to the direction of the national authority. It is, therefore, with the most evident propriety, that the plan of the convention proposes to empower the Union "to provide for organizing, arming, and disciplining the militia, and for governing such part of them as may be employed in the service of the United States, *reserving to the States respectively the appointment of the officers, and the authority of training the militia according to the discipline prescribed by Congress."*

Of the different grounds which have been taken in opposition to the plan of the convention, there is none that was so little to have been expected, or is so untenable in itself, as the one from which this particular provision has been attacked. If a well-regulated militia be the most natural defence of a free country, it ought certainly to be under the regulation and at the disposal of that body which is constituted the guardian of the national security. If standing armies are dangerous to liberty, an efficacious power over the militia, in the body to whose care the protection of the State is committed, ought, as far as possible, to take away the inducement and the pretext to such unfriendly institutions. If the federal government can command the aid of the militia in those emergencies which call for the military arm in support of the civil magistrate, it can the better dispense with the employment of a different kind of force. If it cannot avail itself of the former, it will be obliged to recur to the latter. To render an army unnecessary, it will be a more certain method of preventing its existence than a thousand prohibitions upon paper.

In order to cast an odium upon the power of calling forth the militia to execute the laws of the Union, it has been remarked that there is nowhere any provision in the proposed Constitution for calling out the POSSE COMITATUS to assist the magistrate in the execution of his duty; whence it has been inferred, that military force was intended to be his only auxiliary. There is a striking incoherence in the objections which have appeared, and sometimes even from the same quarter, not much calculated to inspire a very favorable opinion of the sincerity or fair dealing of their authors. The same persons who tell us in one breath, that the powers of the federal government will be despotic and unlimited, inform us in the next, that it has not authority sufficient even to call the POSSE COMITATUS. The latter, fortunately, is as short of the truth as the former exceeds it. It would be as absurd to doubt, that a right to pass all laws necessary and proper to execute its declared powers would include that of requiring the assistance of the citizens to the officers who may be entrusted with the execution of those laws, as it would be to believe, that a right to enact laws necessary and proper for the imposition and collection of taxes would involve that of varying the rules of descent and of the alienation of landed property, or of abolishing the trial by jury in cases relating to it. It being therefore evident that the supposition of a want of power to require the aid of the POSSE COMITATUS is entirely destitute of color, it will follow, that the conclusion which has been drawn from it, in its application to the authority of the federal government over the militia, is as uncandid as it is illogical. What reason could there be to infer, that force was intended to be the sole instrument of authority, merely because there is a power to make use of it when necessary? What shall we think of the motives which could induce men of sense to reason in this manner? How shall we prevent a conflict between charity and judgment?

By a curious refinement upon the spirit of republican jealousy, we are even taught to apprehend danger from the militia itself, in the hands of the federal government. It is observed that select corps may be formed, composed of the young and ardent, who may be rendered subservient to the views of arbitrary power. What plan for the regulation of the militia may be pursued by the national government, is impossible to be foreseen. But so far from viewing the matter in the same light with those who object to select corps as dangerous, were the Constitution ratified, and were I to deliver my sentiments to a member of the federal legislature from this state on the subject of a militia establishment, I should hold to him, in substance, the following discourse:

"The project of disciplining all the militia of the United States is as futile as it would be injurious, if it were capable of being carried into execution. A tolerable expertness in military movements is a business that requires time and practice. It is not a day, or even a week, that will suffice for the attainment of it. To oblige the great body of the yeomanry, and of classes of citizens, to be under arms for the purpose of going through military exercises and evolutions, as often as might be necessary to acquire the degree of perfection which would entitle them to the character of a well-regulated militia would be a real grievance to the people, and a serious inconvenience and loss. It would form an annual deduction from the productive labor of the country, to an amount which, calculating upon the present numbers of the people would not fall far short of the whole expense of the civil establishments of all the States. To attempt a thing would abridge the mass of labor and industry to so considerable an extent, would be unwise: and the experiment, if made, could not succeed, because it would not long endure. Little more can reasonably be aimed at, with the people at large, than to have them properly equipped; and in order to see that this be not neglected, it will be necessary to assemble them once or twice in the course of a year.

"But though the scheme of disciplining the whole nation must be abandoned as mischievous or impracticable; yet it is a matter of the utmost importance that a well-digested plan should, as soon as possible, be adopted for the proper establishment of the militia. The attention of the government ought particularly to be directed to the formation of a select corps of moderate extent, upon such principles as will really fit them for service in case of need. By thus circumscribing the plan, it will be possible to have an excellent body of trained militia, ready to take the field whenever the defense of the State shall require it. This will not only lessen the call for military establishments, but if circumstances should any time oblige the government to form an army of any magnitude that army can never be formidable to the liberties of the people while there is a large body of citizens, little, if at all, inferior to them in discipline and the use of arms, who stand ready to defend their own rights and those of their fellow-citizens. This appears to me the only substitute that can be devised for a standing army, and the best possible security against it, if it should exist."

Thus differently from the adversaries of the proposed Constitution should I reason on the same subject, deducing arguments of safety from the very sources which they represent as fraught with danger and perdition. But how the national legislature may reason on the point, is a thing which neither they nor I can foresee.

There is something so far-fetched and so extravagant in the idea of danger to liberty from the militia, that one is at a loss whether to treat it with gravity or with raillery; whether to consider it as a mere trial of skill, like the paradoxes of rhetoricians; as a disingenuous artifice to instill prejudices at any price; or as the serious offspring of political fanaticism. Where, in the name of common-sense, are our fears to end if we may not trust our sons, our brothers, our neighbors, our fellow-citizens? What shadow of danger can there be from men who are daily mingling with the rest of their countrymen, and who participate with them in the same feelings, sentiments, habits, and interests! What reasonable cause of apprehension can be inferred from a power in the Union to prescribe regulations for the militia, and to command its services when necessary, while the particular States are to have the *sole and exclusive appointment of the officers*? If it were possible seriously to indulge a jealousy of the militia upon any conceivable establishment under the federal government, the circumstance of the officers being in the appointment of the States ought at once to extinguish it. There can be no doubt that this circumstance will always secure to them a preponderating influence over the militia.

In reading many of the publications against the Constitution, a man is apt to imagine that he is perusing some ill-written tale of romance, which, instead of natural and agreeable images, exhibits to the mind nothing but frightful and distorted shapes—Gorgons, hydras, and chimeras dire—discoloring and disfiguring whatever it represents, and transforming every thing it touches into a monster.

A sample of this is to be observed in the exaggerated and improbable suggestions which have taken place respecting the power of calling for the services of the militia. That of New Hampshire is to be marched to Georgia, of Georgia to New Hampshire, of New York to Kentucky, and of Kentucky to Lake Champlain. Nay, the debts due to the French and Dutch are to be paid in militiamen instead of louis d'or and ducats. At one moment there is to be a large army to lay prostrate the liberties of the people; at another moment the militia of Virginia are to be dragged from their homes five or six hundred miles, to tame the republican contumacy of Massachusetts; and that of Massachusetts is to be transported an equal distance to subdue the refractory haughtiness of the aristocratic Virginians. Do the persons who rave at this rate imagine that their art or their eloquence can impose any conceits or absurdities upon the people of America for infallible truths?

If there should be an army to be made use of as the engine of despotism, what need of the militia? If there should be no army, whither would the militia, irritated by being called upon to undertake a distant and hopeless expedition, for the purpose of riveting the chains of slavery upon a part of their countrymen, direct their course, but to the seat of the tyrants, who had meditated so foolish as well as so wicked a project, to crush them in their imagined intrenchments of power, and to make them an example of the just vengeance of an abused and incensed people? Is this the way in which usurpers stride to dominion over a numerous and enlightened nation? Do they begin by exciting the detestation of the very instruments of their intended usurpations? Do they usually commence their career by wanton and disgustful acts of power, calculated to answer no end, but to draw upon themselves universal hatred and execration? Are suppositions of this sort the sober admonitions of discerning patriots to a discerning people? Or are they the inflammatory ravings of incendiaries or distempered enthusiasts? If we were even to suppose the national rulers actuated by the most ungovernable ambition, it is impossible to believe that they would employ such preposterous means to accomplish their designs.

In times of insurrection, or invasion, it would be natural and proper that the militia of a neighboring State should be marched into another, to resist a common enemy, or to guard the republic against the violence of faction or sedition. This was frequently the case, in respect to the first object, in the course of the late war; and this mutual succor is, indeed, a principal end of our political association. If the power of affording it be placed under the direction of the Union, there will be no danger of a supine and listless inattention to the dangers of a neighbor, till its near approach had superadded the incitements of self-preservation to the too feeble impulses of duty and sympathy.

Source: Jacob E. Cooke, ed., *The Federalist* (Hanover, NH: Wesleyan University Press, 1961), 181–187.

Richard Henry Lee

Despite the preceding argument, in Letters from a Federal Farmer, *Richard Henry Lee, who feared the intrusion of the Constitution on states' rights and eventually proposed the Tenth Amendment that reserved to the states those powers not delegated to the national government, saw little difference between a standing federal army and a select militia:*

Should one fifth or one eighth part of the men capable of bearing arms, be made a select militia, as has been proposed, and those be the young and ardent part of the community, possessed of but little or no property, and all the others put upon a plan that will render them of no importance, the former will answer all the purposes of an army while the latter will be defenseless. The state must train the militia in such form and according to such systems and rules as congress shall prescribe: and the only actual influence the respective states will have respecting the militia will be in appointing its officers.

Source: Walter Hartwell Bennett, ed., *Letters from the Federal Farmer to the Republican* (University of Alabama Press, 1978), 21–22.

Militias: Views from Their Supporters

The Ultimate Questions

Andrew Molchan, publisher of American Firearms Industry, *a trade publication, expresses the opinion held by many in the militia movement concerning guns and recent efforts to control them:*

The ultimate questions are these: How is the government going to "take" 200 million firearms away from 80 million people when the people have already made it very clear that they ARE NOT going to give them up? Is Congress going to declare war on the American people? Is Congress, like the Nazis, going to start raiding homes, torturing people, sending them to concentration camps? Are there a lot more Wacos in the future? If the answer is "NO," then gun control against honest citizens is a dead issue. Any time spent on such a project by Congress, Clinton or America's journalists is a criminal waste of time, and profoundly un-American.

Most of America's journalists have failed in their duty to protect the Bill of Rights. If the 2nd Amendment is "meaningless," that makes everything meaningless, and those who control the police can do anything they want, and take anything they want.

Source: Andrew Molchan, "The Failure of American Journalists," *The Firearms Sentinel*, January 1995, 9.

Maintaining a Healthy Militia

From the pages of Soldier of Fortune, *Carl D. Haggard offers several guidelines to those who might be forming a militia:*

It is presumed militias will conduct themselves lawfully. A few suggestions to citizens who choose to organize into a militia unit include:

Know the laws of God and obey them. God will not bless His people with victory over the godless, one-world-order federalists if His laws are not obeyed to begin with . . . .

Know the law of the land and obey it. This doesn't mean that you won't be harassed or arrested, but don't give the government an argument that can be used against you. If you don't like the law, work to change it . . . .

Control your unit and each other. Under the law, commanders must be (and will be) held responsible for the conduct of the members of a unit.

Avoid agent provocateurs. They are easy to spot—they are always trying to get you to do something illegal. Kick them out of your unit and alert others.... Militias are purely defensive, so don't let any well-intentioned but misguided individual back you into illegal conduct.

Avoid agent saboteurs. They are also easy to spot—they are always trying to subvert a perfectly good militia unit into a political action committee. The first and foremost reason for a militia is to collectively exercise a fundamental right: to keep and bear arms. The goal is to be prepared to assist local law enforcement officials in time of an emergency, disaster or other crisis. Do not allow your militia unit to go political; it will degenerate into internal fights and squabbles that will destroy unit cohesion and effectiveness....

Protect the land owner. Sign a third-party lease. You know the drill—don't ask, don't tell.

Source: Carl D. Haggard and Nancy E. Haggard, "A Well-Regulated and Legal Militia," *Soldier of Fortune*, May 1995, 47.

America Returning to Its Roots as a Militia Nation

In fall 1995, Aide-de-Camp, *the official newsletter of the United States Militia Association, championed the rise of contemporary militias in an article written by Gabriel Taylor, headquarters staff assistant:*

The trouble with maintaining a large and powerful army is that we invariably seem to find some excuse for using it.

The current budget cuts advocated by the American public, coupled with the revived interest in the militia concept indicate Americans may be reawakening to the basic concepts of self-defense that has been the bedrock of our philosophy for over 350 years.

After the Boston Massacre, Samuel Adams began to organize the traditional citizen-militia won at Runneymeade and immortalized in the Magna Charta. The American colonists were coming to a distrust of the "standing army of the crown" and began arming and training themselves. Among their acts was the pilfering of Crown armories of canon, musket & balls and powder, including: the loss of two cannons from the Boston armory....

As all despots have learned, the citizen soldier makes a terrible soldier for conquest, though a magnificent soldier in the defense of his own liberties, family, nation and religion. The citizen soldier is also very independent lacking the constraints of regimentation shared with his professional cousin.

Source: Gabriel Taylor, "America Returning to Its Roots as a Militia Nation," *Aide-de-Camp*, Fall 1995, 1.

Excerpts from the Militia Day Proclamation

The following proclamation, originally carried over the Patriots Network on the Internet, displays the reverence accorded the date 19 April. Militias often link the American Revolutionary period with the catastrophe in 1994 at Waco:

TO: ALL CITIZENS OF THE UNITED STATES AND ITS TERRITORIES:

April 19th of this and each year hereafter is declared to be Militia Day. All able-bodied citizens are to assemble with their arms to celebrate their right to keep and bear arms and to assemble as militias in defense of the Republic, as recognized in the Second Amendment to the Constitution of the United States. The order of the day shall be to sign up the members, organize them into squads of approximately 20 persons each, and spend the morning in training in the military arts and the safe and effective handling of arms, and instruction in their rights and duties under the U.S. and state laws. This should include learning to recite at least the First, Second, Fourth, Fifth, and Tenth Amendments of the U.S. Constitution from memory.

The order of march shall be to begin after lunch to march two abreast across the city to a site on the opposite side, where speeches shall be given and the militia dismissed. Each squad should be equipped with one video camera to record the events and any resistance to them which may be encountered. Each squad should have a plan to secure the video tapes and have copies of them made and distributed before they can be seized by any hostile parties. The press should be kept informed and encouraged to provide coverage of the event prior and during its occurrence.

Women and children are urged to participate, as are citizens of all creeds, and religions. It is suggested that children hold the protest signs....

Militias must avoid allowing any persons to become indispensable leaders, so that the Militia Movement could be suppressed by attacking its leaders. The Militia must be, to the extent possible, "leaderless" and spontaneous. We must also work together to get April 19 declared a national holiday, Militia Day. Not a "right to keep and bear arms" day, because every day is a right to keep and bear arms day. Militia Day shall be a day on which all able-bodied citizens will be called up for formations of their local militias, for training and discussion.

Source: Institute for Alternative Journalism, *Militias in America, 1995* (San Francisco, 1995), 21.

Blueprint for Victory

In the mid-1960s, Robert DePugh, the Minutemen founder, wrote his book Blueprint for Victory, *in which he presented ideas that still resonate with the militia movement 30 years later. After a tumultuous political career that at one point found him in prison, he retired from politics in the 1990s. This is what he said three decades earlier:*

Our nation has reached a point of no return—a point beyond which the American people can no longer defend their freedom by the traditional means of politics and public opinion. Our next task is both obvious and urgent: we must find new and more effective means by which the enemies of freedom can be resisted and ultimately defeated. If we fail in this task, then future Americans for generations to come will live in slavery.

American patriots must act quickly. We must stop supporting the U.S. Postal Service with plaintive letters to disinterested congressmen. We must stop wasting time on routine rallies and speaking tours. We must stop wasting money on fancy headquarters and elaborate offices. We must stop the petty competition that now exists between conservative organizations.

We must develop a coordinated plan of action. We must know what we are fighting for as well as that which we are fighting against. We must build a firm philosophical basis for our actions and beliefs. We must call on the best minds available to examine man's proper relationship to government. Only from a sound philosophical base can we find the necessary courage to continue a battle against seemingly impossible odds.

We must have the wisdom to avoid wishful thinking and find courage to face the facts—somber as they are. Our nation has been occupied by the enemy. Today the chains of slavery lay lightly on our people, but with every passing day the chains become stronger and the American people are more tightly bound. We must either break these chains soon while they are yet weak or else we must face an uncertain future, frightful to behold.

Never in all of recorded history has a people saved themselves from tyranny through political means alone. We must study past resistance movements to learn which tactics are successful and avoid those that are futile. We must study the methods which our enemies are using against us and we must use their own strategies against them. We must investigate every opportunity and seize on every possible advantage. Nothing short of total resistance can hope to succeed.

Source: Robert B. DePugh, *Blueprint for Victory* (Norborne, MO: Robert B. DePugh, 1966), 1–2.

Reaction to Oklahoma City

On 19 April 1995, a massive bomb explosion destroyed the Alfred P. Murrah Federal Building in Oklahoma City. Militia leaders and their supporters reacted with controversial observations, sometimes blaming the national government for the catastrophe. Some of their reactions:

Norm Olson, former Michigan Militia commander:
"When a tyrant's brutality is not reined in by justice, you will have somebody out there who takes it upon himself, deranged though he may be, to balance the scales of justice."

William Pierce, author of *The Turner Diaries:*
"We'll see some terrorism—planned, organized terrorism—before too long. I suspect that a growing number of exasperated, fed up Americans will begin engaging in terrorism on a scale that the world has never seen before."

Dennis Mahon of White Aryan Resistance, a California-based white supremacist group:
"The bombing was a fine thing. I hate the federal government with a perfect hatred.... I'm surprised that this hasn't happened all over the country."

Tom Metzger, founder of White Aryan Resistance:
"I have told people for years... that the government of this country—what we call the criminals—had better start listening to the dispossessed white people, the dispossessed majority. There was a hot war in the 1980s... and now things are heating up again."

Ray Southwell, former Michigan Militia chief of staff:
"There is one last hope to avoid armed confrontation, and that's if our state governments rise up and tell our federal government to back off. If the state does not rise up... the American people will."

Linda Thompson, Indianapolis lawyer and militia proponent:
"I mean, [regarding the federal government] who's got a track record of killing children?"

Source: *Klanwatch Intelligence Report*, June 1995, 13.

Establishing an Independent Militia in the United States

In 1975, Samuel Sherwood founded the Constitutional Militia Association. Twenty years later, it emerged as the United States Militia Association with units in 12 states. In 1994, he published Establishing an Independent Militia in the United States *in which he discussed the importance of the Second Amendment and the intentions of America's founding fathers, and provided guidelines for establishing a militia. The following excerpt from his book presents ideas about the nature of the militias and why they should be formed:*

The militia, being the body of the whole of the people, has always owed its allegiance to the constitution of the United States, the constitution of the states in which they resided, and the people. In modern-day

America, we see that a new loyalty has been created for the National Guard which takes an oath of loyalty to "the President of the United States."

This would have been considered elevating the President to the status of a king in the Constitutional debates. There is no officer of government who takes an oath to "the President of the United States." There is no judge, no cabinet post, no department head, no governor, no senator, or congressman; there is no under-secretary, or secretary of any kind, who takes the oath of office to be loyal to the President of the United States. Why then is the National Guard doing so?

When the Chancellor of the Weimer Republic put forward an oath to the Chancellor in 1935, we later, in 1945–1947, sent men to prison, and death, for taking and upholding that oath. It was to Adolph Hitler as "the Leader," der Führer of the Republic of Germany. Have we forgotten everything in 50 years? Did we not mortally wound that beast in the head deadly enough?

The very fact that an oath exists for our National Guardsmen, and may exist for other federal employees, to swear allegiance to the president of the United States, shows us how far we have come to implement the German example within our own nation, a tragedy yet waiting to happen. That we now desert the Constitution and swear all allegiance to the personality of the president is deplorable and reprehensible in the least, and probably traitorous in execution. Our attitude as citizens must certainly be that any soldier at any level who executes an order of the president which is unconstitutional will be held to the same level of accountability as was the German soldiers who blindly followed Adolph Hitler.

And this should be a warning too. That any government official, any soldier, airman, or sailor who holds to such an oath contrary to the supreme law of this land, the Constitution, shall certainly be held to such earthly tribunal and just penalty duly executed as per our very just and noble laws. Let it be said by every patriot of American law, that we shall not let our nation devolve into a nation served and mastered by a personality cult figure no matter how high and lofty his position. And likewise, we shall not bow in fear and trembling to any such lackey of such cult figure, no matter how much brass he has.

We must come to a realization that it is us, "the people" who make up the body of the whole of the people. And that we are the ones responsible for the protection of our government, including protection from those who are serving in some of its offices. The National Guard will not do that as they blindly follow the orders given them, just as they did at Ruby Ridge, and Kent State University. If we do not want our "National Guard" becoming the tool of the president and becoming in effect the brown shirts ... revisited, from Hitler's Germany, we must do more than we are doing.

We have to educate and convert our fellow Americans in this effort. Among the "minutemen" who stood at Lexington and Concord it is estimated that 30% of them were either then, or had previously, served in the Colonial Militia, the equivalent of our National Guard.

But, in the siege of Boston with 20,000 militia standing watch over the "regulars," it is estimated that 60% of them were Colonial Militia or Crown Militia. Among the leadership of those men were former Regular officers, and men who had served a whole career for the crown. We must have the same impact in recruiting the same men who love freedom today as these men did in the time of the revolution.

If we will allow tyrants to rule over us, we deserve tyranny. If we maintain just rulers we shall thereby enjoy justice and peace. It is our responsibility to look back in history and understand just what the militia is, and what it did for us, and what we, as "the whole body of the people," have the duty to do. May we ever thank the Father of our Glorious Revolution from tyranny and oppression, Samuel Adams, for giving us not only the Revolution, but the nation from whence its loins proceeded, and the "independent militia" of the body of the whole of all of the people....

Why do we need a militia?....

No other nation in the world has as many people in jail as does the U.S., per capita. The fact is that the government has become the oppressor, and we have more to fear from government than the burglar. The burglar in his whole life will only be able to rob three or four people a day, whereas the government robs everybody in the nation everyday. People are being resistive to oppressive laws that the government won't change; if they won't change those laws to make us free again, why won't they, what is their motive? And, why do they fear us so much?

Why can't we own automatic weapons like we did prior to 1934 or 1968? Why can't we own a semi-automatic hand gun—we did for over 90 years and there was no big problem. Who and what is the government afraid of, and why?...

Source: Samuel Sherwood, *Establishing an Independent Militia in the United States* (Blackfoot, Idaho: Founders Press Publications, 1995), vii–viii, 17.

How to Hide Your Guns

This article appeared in the August/September 1995 issue of Taking Aim, *the newsletter published by the high-profile Militia of Montana. In it, David Trochmann outlines his views about the New World Order and recent attempts to place restrictions on the acquisition of guns. The concern with the Second Amendment runs as a nearly constant theme in militia literature:*

The New World Order gun grab is escalating at lightning speed in America. Since the Oklahoma bombing, the liberals' anti-gun measures are now proceeding under the guise of "Anti-Terrorism" bills. It's another step in the insidious ploy to get your guns.

Here are just a few examples of bills on the floor of Congress right now:

H.R. 174 makes gun manufacturers liable for criminal behavior. The cost of guns will skyrocket, and guns will be harder to get. Their increased value will make them much more appealing to thieves.

H.R. 915 gives vast new powers to the BATF to control gun ownership and sales.

H.R. 169 forces national registration of all handguns and imposes new penalties on gun owners.

H.R. 250 criminalizes possession or transfer of "non-sporting" handguns.

S. 118 bans .25 caliber, .32 caliber, and 9mm ammunition.

H.R. 221, 120, 433, and 200 bans more ammo, including plastic ammo and allows the feds to tax it to the sky....

The UN manipulators are, undoubtedly, thrilled. Our naive do-gooder Congressmen who vote for such measures are just plain stupid. They simply don't understand why America is still free....

There are 300 million guns in private hands in this country, and they are the sole power keeping the UN at bay. Without these guns, the populace would be helpless—and we would all be enslaved. Just think about it. Almost all of the NWO [New World Order] goals have been fulfilled over the last 40 years—except for the elimination of private guns....

If you haven't already done so, it's time to hide your extra guns for future use. But hiding guns presents some unique challenges.

Where do you hide them?

How do you keep them ready and dry?

The deeper and more remote you bury them, the safer they are—but the less ready access you have.

What good are your guns if you can't get to them quickly?...

Source: David Trochmann, "How to Hide Your Guns," *Taking Aim*, August/September 1995, 27–28.

Militia Day 1995

Many militias consider 19 April to be Militia Day. An advertisement issued by the Sons of Liberty expressed this view:

APRIL 19, 1775:

"Stand your ground. Don't fire unless fired upon. But if they mean to have a war, let it begin here."

—Capt. John Parker, Lexington Militia Co.

APRIL 19, 1995:

"Today's Redcoats wear black uniforms and ski masks and call themselves Federal Police. They prey on the innocent, the isolated, the weak. If they want our liberty, they must take our guns first. Let them try..."

Source: Sons of Liberty poster, 1995.

The Minutemen

A flyer released in August 1992 advertised a new Minutemen militia based in Sepulveda, California. This group, like that of Robert DePugh's original organization, expressed the desire to promote resistance to oppressive government measures through an underground organization:

Dear American Patriot,

I represent a group in America known as the MINUTEMEN. We are a patriotic group that deals mainly with political interest. We are paramilitary, patriotic, and survivalistic oriented. Our group has been growing for some time now and we wish to expand and grow. As an American of similar interests, you know of the troubled times that lay ahead. If people of our country do not join together as one group or voice then we are sure to perish! Generally the Minutemen do things by the law. However, we are willing to do whatever it takes to restore our country to the great nation it once was.

By 1993 the enemies of freedom must be challenged by a strong experienced political party. That party, if it is to succeed, cannot stand alone. It must be the political arm of the true American people.

Along with the political party, the MINUTEMEN (True Americans) must develop into a complete resistance movement, including a well trained underground organization....

Here are just a few items and projects we are currently working on: Prepare for civil war, provide protection for Pro-White candidates, educate and train in survival techniques, provide weapons and paramilitary training, intelligence gathering, network with other people and groups, educate and inform White people of their culture and heritage....

Sign up now and join the many other people who have decided to become part of the solution.... FIGHT AND NO SURRENDER!

Source: Minutemen flyer, August 1995, 1.

Conspiracy? What Conspiracy?

In September 1995 the New Jersey Militia criticized right-wing commentator Rush Limbaugh for trying to deny that a New World Order conspiracy existed. Many in the militias consider Limbaugh little more than a bombastic showman who sold out to the Republican Party, which they consider no better than the Democrats:

Rush Limbaugh on his daily radio show has on occasion ridiculed the idea of a New World Order, claiming it only exists in the overactive imaginations of conspiracy "wackos" or "nutty militia types." It is difficult to understand why Limbaugh maintains this position considering the fact that former President George Bush made references to a "New World Order" in at least two speeches....

The New World Order (NWO) is simply this: all nations that have nuclear weapons will turn them over to UN control, thus making the UN the supreme military power on earth; and no nation, including the U.S., would have the military might to wage war. United States sovereignty, along with the sovereignty of other nations, will come to an end.

Source: "Conspiracy? What Conspiracy?" *New Jersey Newsletter*, September 1995, 1.

The Turner Diaries

William Pierce of Mill Point, West Virginia, wrote The Turner Diaries *in 1978 under the pen name Andrew Macdonald as a novel intended to transmit racist and anti-Semitic ideas. Some militias embrace the book wholeheartedly; others reject its bigotry but accept its vision of an oppressive government and a world gone awry. Some analysts claim that right-wing radicals have been influenced by the novel's account of attacks on federal buildings. For example, the 1995 bombing at Oklahoma City resembled an attack that unfolded in the novel. The following excerpt comes from* The Turner Diaries*:*

Today it finally began! After all these years of talking—and nothing but talking—we have finally taken our first action. We are at war with the System, and it is no longer a war of words....

We Americans...regarded—correctly—all...non-Whites as mere herds of animals and were not surprised that they behaved as they did. But we regarded ourselves—incorrectly—as something better.

There was a time when we were better—and we are fighting to insure that there will be such a time again—but for now we are merely a herd, being manipulated through our basest instincts by a pack of clever aliens. We have sunk to the point where we no longer hate our oppressors or try to fight them; we merely fear them and attempt to curry favor with them.

So be it. We will suffer grievously for having allowed ourselves to fall under the Jewish spell....

If the white nations of the world had not allowed themselves to become subject to the Jew, to Jewish ideas, to the Jewish spirit, this war would not be necessary. We can hardly consider ourselves blameless. We can hardly say we had no choice, no chance to avoid the Jew's snare. We can hardly say we were not warned....

We had chance after chance to save ourselves—most recently 52 years ago, when the Germans and Jews were locked in struggle for the mastery of central and eastern Europe.

We ended up on the Jewish side in that struggle, primarily because we had chosen corrupt men as our leaders....We ignored the really important issues in our national life and gave free rein to a criminal System to conduct the affairs of our nation as it saw fit, so long as it kept us moderately well-supplied with bread and circuses.

Source: Macdonald, Andrew, *The Turner Diaries* (1978), pp. 1, 102, 195–196.

Random Thoughts on the Second American Revolution: Advice to Prospective Sons of Liberty

Recently, a writer using the name Samuel Adams II (presumably a pen name dating back to the American Revolution) issued this advice to Americans as Congress debated a crime bill he considered oppressive:

The "Crime Bill" has passed but not yet been signed. It is August 28th, two minutes past midnight. I have been to a gun show today, an event characterized by frantic buying, much loud damnation of politicians in general and Bill Clinton in particular, and in the back aisles of the hall otherwise sober men quietly plotted revolution. In voices that rose and fell in direct proportion to the nearness of strangers, they reminded me of the desperate characters in Rick's Cafe American in "Casablanca." Fear was clearly blended with their defiance, and they were careful not to be overheard by the representatives of local and federal law enforcement. Americans, it seems, no longer feel free to speak their minds on the subject of the Second Amendment and what they can do to protect their liberties from an increasingly oppressive central government. Observing this, I wanted to scream "BUT THIS IS AMERICA, WHERE ALL MAY SPEAK FREELY!" At the same moment I realized how utterly foolish that thought was, for when the "Coward in Chief" puts his pen to this odious act in a few days the die will be cast, the Rubicon crossed, and the United States government will put itself on a collision course with the fundamental liberties of its own citizens....

Some particularly outrageous items from recent newspaper articles are indicative of the gulf between the fought-and died-for principles of the founding fathers and the present "Brave New World" Meets "1984" administration:

Property seizures under the Endangered Species Act and the federal drug laws are reaching new highs under the Clinton administration. Citizens are being falsely accused, and in some cases killed, for property.

Federal wiretaps during the first year of the Clinton administration are up more than 150%, and that's just the ones they bothered to get a court order for. The National Security Agency is reported to be conducting illegal phone surveillance in the name of "anti-terrorism operations...."

Freedom is dying today from a thousand tiny cuts. We are bleeding out our liberties every time a government database is cross-referenced, every time we cannot go where we wish from fear of crime, every time the tax man comes back for more and more, every time a prayer cannot be uttered in public nor a "politically-incorrect" thought be debated on campus....

Militias are forming, but I would suggest that what we rather need are more clandestine Sons of Liberty clubs. ("Clubs" sounds too fraternal but "cells", while more descriptive, sounds too left-wing. "Teams" sounds too small. Perhaps "Club" is the right term, for what we are attempting calls for the most implicit trust in our fellow revolutionaries.)....

Our task as Sons of Liberty is, in the utmost secrecy, to prepare the framework for the resistance to the anti-Constitutional forces who have usurped our government for their own purposes. This includes, but is not limited to:

Stockpiling of arms and ammunition for future use by the forces of freedom.

The clandestine aid of the political forces representing liberty, either by staging events that publicize the oppressive nature of the current government or by sabotaging the campaigns of the enemies of liberty....

Stage radicalizing, but non-violent, attacks on the bureaucracy itself. As in instead of a Tea Party, throw a 4473 party at your local gun store. Seize the files and dump them into a shredder, manure pile, or bonfire. Break into the BATF computer files and destroy the data, sending out a press release announcing that you have done so after the fact. Stink bomb the local BATF office. Spray paint their cars "Gun Gestapo." Post signs in their front yards. (No, boys, no crosses. We've got to keep this strictly political. There's no place for racism in it. We are ALL Americans. We have ALL fought and, if need be, died to keep this country free. Remember that the first American killed in the Revolution was Crispus Attucks, a black man shot down during the Boston Massacre of 1770. If you've got too much hate in your belly that you can't see past it, don't join the Sons of Liberty; go join the Sons of Adolph or something.)....

Stand ready to begin military operations if the situation is irretrievable by political means. The Sons should consider themselves, in 20th Century parlance, to be urban guerrillas when the conflict breaks out....

Most of all you must think through your level of commitment. If you are not willing to say now with Patrick Henry, "Give me Liberty, or give me death!", then don't commit to something you will not follow through. If you have not the courage to use your guns now, bury them for the time when your courage will be forced upon you by the choice of slavery or death....

Source: Samuel Adams II, "Random Thoughts on the Second American Revolution," n.d., 1995?, passim.

The True Purpose of the Second Amendment

As part of its promotional literature, the Militia of Montana issued what they called an "information and networking manual." In it, the group presented a history of militias in America and measures for organizing them. The manual included a defense of the Second Amendment as a bulwark to individual liberty:

There was much discussion during the constitutional convention as to how the states would secure their sovereignty and liberties from a national government. They were afraid that sooner or later there would come a time that this nation might be attacked or that the government would turn into a monarchy. They established the three branches of government with the separation of powers. To further ensure that this nation could not be subverted from within, they protected the right of the militia of the several states to keep and bear arms through the second amendment.

The majority of Americans today believe the reason that our forefathers wanted the people to have the right to keep and bear arms was for the purpose of self defense against criminals, hunting, etc. This is not the primary reason for the enactment of the 2nd Amendment. Let's let Thomas Jefferson explain:

"The strongest reason for the people to retain the right to keep and bear arms is, as a last resort, to protect themselves against tyranny in government."

Thomas Jefferson also understood that those who would attempt to take away the liberty of the citizens of this nation must first disarm them. He knew what their argument for infringing on the second amendment would be and what their argument would be for abusing it. We are all familiar with the anti-gun advocates' argument, that if we take away the guns of the people, we will lower the crime rate. But this argument was dealt with by Thomas Jefferson when he copied in his Commonplace Book the words of the Italian philosopher Cesare Beccaria in 1775:

"False is the idea of utility . . . that would take fire from men because it burns and water because one may drown in it; that has no remedy for evils except destruction (of liberty). The laws that forbid the carrying of arms are laws of such nature. They disarm only those who are neither inclined nor determined to commit crimes; such laws serve rather to encourage than to prevent homicides for an unarmed man may be attacked with greater confidence than an armed man."

Source: *Militia of Montana Information and Networking Manual,* n.d., 1994?, 2.

Militia Update

In August 1995 a militia group in Alabama circulated the following flyer with its references to the involvement of the Bureau of Alcohol,

Tobacco, and Firearms at Waco, Texas, and recent congressional investigations into that confrontation:

LOST AND FOUND DEPARTMENT ———

FOUND: ONE LEG, WEARING TWO SOCKS AND BLACK COMBAT BOOT, AT FORMER SITE OF MURRAH FEDERAL BUILDING, OKLAHOMA CITY, OK. OWNER, OR NEXT OF KIN, SHOULD APPLY TO FBI HQ, WASHINGTON, DC, FOR RETURN OF SAME. YOU MAY HAVE TO ANSWER A FEW QUESTIONS.

LOST: ONE EMMY AWARD FOR BEST DRAMATIC PERFORMANCE IN A DAYTIME CONGRESSIONAL HEARING. PLEASE RETURN TO JAMES CAVANAUGH, ATF, 2121 BLDG. DOWNTOWN BIRMINGHAM, ALABAMA....

Source: Militia Update flyer, August 1995.

National Freedom Day

In 1995, a call went out from a militia group for Americans to protest actions, past and present, by a duplicitous federal government. The notice read as follows:

NATIONAL FREEDOM DAY
(CREATIVE ANARCHY DAY)
A CALL TO INFORM DEMOCRACY

Wednesday November 22, 1995 at 12:30 PM CST (1:30 PM EST)
Purpose: A CALL TO ACTION. TO ALL CONCERNED CITIZENS.

To show displeasure and dissatisfaction against the nullification of our democratic system 32 years ago by a Secret Government of The National Security State, and in commemoration of the anniversary of the murder of our 35th President, John F. Kennedy, on Nov. 22, 1963, by conspiratorial forces of the CIA, US Military Intelligence, the FBI, the Secret Service and other Federal, State and local law enforcement agencies, and the same's complicity in the murders of Robert F. Kennedy and Dr. Martin Luther King, Jr. (and other assassinations, as well), and TO PROTEST the subsequent decades-long cover-up by the above mentioned government agencies. A CALL TO END THE LIES served to the AMERICAN PEOPLE and promulgated by the Congress, the Executive branch, the Injustice Department, the US Military Establishment, all government law enforcement agencies, and the Media.

Plan of Action: To vote by protest on Nov. 22, 1995 at 12:30 PM CST (1:30 PM EST)— the time that President John F. Kennedy was murdered—by stepping-out of your workplace or home, and going out into the street; or, if you are in a motor vehicle, in traffic, by parking (or stalling) your vehicle, and honking your horn, ringing a bell, blowing a whistle or horn (bring one to work that day); by stepping outside of your home (or sticking your head outside of your door or a window), and banging a pot, singing or whistling, chanting or shouting ('Freedom",

JFK, RFK, MLK); or by acting out any other form of creative nonviolent expression or protest that may suit your individual, or group mood or temperament, FOR A DURATION OF AT LEAST 1O OR 15 MINUTES, A HALF HOUR, OR LONGER (whatever suits you)....

Source: patriots@kaiwan.com (accessed 14 November 1995).

The Newstates Constitution

To some militias a plot is underway to destroy the U.S. Constitution, and they see the machinations in the proposal for a Newstates Constitution. Militias often label it a secret document, but the Newstates Constitution, as formulated by the Center for the Study of Democratic Institutions, has been widely circulated and presented pub-licly by one of its authors, Rexford G. Tugwell, a former adviser to President Franklin D. Roosevelt. The complete text appears in his book, The Emerging Constitution, *published in 1974. Tugwell emphasizes that the document is meant to encourage discussion—and not be treated as a definite solution—with the goal of replacing the Con-stitution, considered by him and others to be outdated in many respects. The Newstates Constitution stresses a more centralized government with emphasis on planning and minimizing the unexpected impact from technological change. The document's interesting and controver-sial proposals include a national planning agency, a single term of nine-years for the president with the chief executive subject to recall, two vice-presidents, senators elected for life, a National Watchkeeper to review the operations of government agencies for their integrity and usefulness, an Overseer to regulate political parties, and an alteration of existing state boundaries. Presented below are two of the more contro-versial articles in the Newstates Constitution, from the standpoint of the militias:*

PREAMBLE

So that we may join in common endeavors, welcome the future in good order, and create an adequate and self-repairing government—we, the people, do establish the Newstates of America, herein provided to be ours, and do ordain this Constitution whose supreme law it shall be until the time prescribed for it shall have run.

The first article protects many of the liberties Americans are accus-tomed to, but the section labeled "responsibilities" limits gun owner-ship—a move militias consider anathema:

ARTICLE I
Rights and Responsibilities

A. Rights

Section 1. Freedom of expression, of communication, of movement, of assembly, or of petition shall not be abridged except in declared emergency.

Section 2. Access to information possessed by governmental agencies shall not be denied except in the interest of national security; but communications among officials necessary to decision making shall be privileged.

Section 3. Public communicators may decline to reveal sources of information, but shall be responsible for hurtful disclosures.

Section 4. The privacy of individuals shall be respected; searches and seizures shall be made only on judicial warrant; persons shall be pursued or questioned only for the prevention of crime or the apprehension of suspected criminals, and only according to rules established under law.

Section 5. There shall be no discrimination because of race, creed, color, origin, or sex. The Court of Rights and Responsibilities may determine whether selection for various occupations has been discriminatory.

Section 6. All persons shall have equal protection of the laws, and in all electoral procedures the vote of every eligible citizen shall count equally with others.

Section 7. It shall be public policy to promote discussion of public issues and to encourage peaceful public gatherings for this purpose. Permission to hold such gatherings shall not be denied, nor shall they be interrupted, except in declared emergency or on a showing of imminent danger to public order and on judicial warrant.

Section 8. The practice of religion shall be privileged; but no religion shall be imposed by some on others, and none shall have public support.

Section 9. Any citizen may purchase, sell, lease, hold, convey, and inherit real and personal property, and shall benefit equally from all laws for security in such transactions.

Section 10. Those who cannot contribute to productivity shall be entitled to a share of the national product; but distribution shall be fair and the total may not exceed the amount for this purpose held in the National Sharing Fund.

Section 11. Education shall be provided at public expense for those who meet appropriate tests of eligibility.

Section 12. No person shall be deprived of life, liberty, or property without due process of law. No property shall be taken without compensation.

Section 13. Legislatures shall define crimes and conditions requiring restraint, but confinement shall not be for punishment; and, when possible, there shall be preparation for return to freedom.

Section 14. No person shall be placed twice in jeopardy for the same offense.

Section 15. Writs of habeas corpus shall not be suspended except in declared emergency.

Section 16. Accused persons shall be informed of charges against them, shall have a speedy trial, shall have reasonable bail, shall be allowed to confront witnesses or to call others, and shall not be compelled to testify against themselves; at the time of arrest they shall be informed of their right to be silent and to have counsel, provided, if necessary, at public expense; and courts shall consider the contention that prosecution may be under an invalid or unjust statute.

B. Responsibilities

Section 1. Each freedom of the citizen shall prescribe a corresponding responsibility not to diminish that of others: of speech, communication, assembly, and petition, to grant the same freedom to others; of religion, to respect that of others; of privacy, not to invade that of others; of the holding and disposal of property, the obligation to extend the same privilege to others.

Section 2. Individuals and enterprises holding themselves out to serve the public shall serve all equally and without intention to misrepresent, conforming to such standards as may improve health and welfare.

Section 3. Protection of the law shall be repaid by assistance in its enforcement; this shall include respect for the procedures of justice, apprehension of lawbreakers, and testimony at trial.

Section 4. Each citizen shall participate in the processes of democracy, assisting in the selection of officials and in the monitoring of their conduct in office.

Section 5. Each shall render such services to the nation as may be uniformly required by law, objection by reason of conscience being adjudicated as hereinafter provided; and none shall expect or may receive special privileges unless they be for a public purpose defined by law.

Section 6. Each shall pay whatever share of governmental costs is consistent with fairness to all.

Section 7. Each shall refuse awards or titles from other nations or their representatives except as they be authorized by law.

Section 8. There shall be a responsibility to avoid violence and to keep the peace; for this reason the bearing of arms or the possession of lethal weapons shall be confined to the police, members of the armed forces, and those licensed under law.

Section 9. Each shall assist in preserving the endowments of nature and enlarging the inheritance of future generations.

Section 10. Those granted the use of public lands, the air, or waters shall have a responsibility for using these resources so that, if irreplaceable, they are conserved and, if replaceable, they are put back as they were.

Section 11. Retired officers of the armed forces, of the senior civil service, and of the Senate shall regard their service as a permanent obligation and shall not engage in enterprise seeking profit from the government.

Section 12. The devising or controlling of devices for management or technology shall establish responsibility for resulting costs.

Section 13. All rights and responsibilities defined herein shall extend to such associations of citizens as may be authorized by law.

The following article holds out the possibility of changing the existing state boundaries. To militias, this enhances the prospect of greater governmental centralization:

ARTICLE II

The Newstates

Section 1. There shall be Newstates, each comprising no less than 5 percent of the whole population. Existing states may continue and may have the status of Newstates if the Boundary Commission, hereinafter provided, shall so decide. The Commission shall be guided in its recommendations by the probability of accommodation to the conditions for effective government. States electing by referendum to continue if the Commission recommends otherwise shall nevertheless accept all Newstate obligations.

Section 2. The Newstates shall have constitutions formulated and adopted by processes hereinafter prescribed.

Section 3. They shall have Governors, legislatures, and planning, administrative, and judicial systems.

Section 4. Their political procedures shall be organized and supervised by electoral Overseers; but their elections shall not be in years of presidential election.

Section 5. The electoral apparatus of the Newstates of America shall be available to them, and they may be allotted funds under rules agreed to by the national Overseer; but expenditures may not be made by or for any candidate except they be approved by the Overseer; and requirements of residence in a voting district shall be no longer than thirty days.

Section 6. They may charter subsidiary governments, urban or rural, and may delegate to them powers appropriate to their responsibilities.

Section 7. They may lay, or may delegate the laying of, taxes; but these shall conform to the restraints stated hereinafter for the Newstates or America.

Section 8. They may not tax exports, may not tax with intent to prevent imports, and may not impose any tax forbidden by laws of the Newstates of America; but the objects appropriate for taxation shall be clearly designated.

Section 9. Taxes on land may be at higher rates than those on its improvements.

Section 10. They shall be responsible for the administration of public services not reserved to the government of the Newstates of America, such activities being concerted with those of corresponding national agencies, where these exist, under arrangements common to all.

Section 11. The rights and responsibilities prescribed in this Constitution shall be effective in the Newstates and shall be suspended only in emergency when declared by Governors and not disapproved by the Senate of the Newstates of America.

Section 12. Police powers of the Newstates shall extend to all matters not reserved to the Newstates of America; but preempted powers shall not be impaired.

Section 13. Newstates may not enter into any treaty, alliance, confederation, or agreement unless approved by the Boundary Commission hereinafter provided. They may not coin money, provide for the payment of debts in any but legal tender, or make any charge for inter-Newstate services. They may not enact ex post facto laws or ones impairing the obligation of contracts.

Section 14. Newstates may not impose barriers to imports from other jurisdictions or impose any hindrance to citizens' freedom of movement.

Section 15. If governments of the Newstates fail to carry out fully their constitutional duties, their officials shall be warned and may be required by the Senate, on the recommendation of the Watchkeeper, to forfeit revenues from the Newstates of America.

Source: Rexford G. Tugwell, *The Emerging Constitution* (New York: Harper's Magazine Press, 1974), 595–621.

Suspicious Deaths in the Butte County Jail

A militia group in California reported suspicious events at the Butte County Jail in late 1995. The report reflects the militia's view of itself as a protector of liberties and displays a deep distrust of government in general:

One of the largest news stories is transpiring in Butte County California, and it is being met with outright silence and blatant censorship. In the middle of this story, the Sovereign Patriot Group, a Constitutional Organizational trust, was called in by the family to help.

The story starts at the Butte County Jail. For the second time in less than a month, two people have mysteriously died in this jail. On September 16th, 1995, 26-year-old Sareena Lynn Mills, a healthy young . . . woman with no previous history of illness, suddenly died. The subsequent Coroner's report stated that Ms. Mills died of a blood-clot located in her lung.

Following Ms. Mills' death, in October, a young 20-year-old man, Mr. Brady-Davis Cumbuss, died three hours after being booked into the Butte County Jail. Again, the government's response as to the cause of the death stated that Mr. Brady-Davis Cumbuss died of "natural causes" due to an apparent seizure. This autopsy, performed by an "outside agency" of the Sacramento Coroner's office, stated that Brady-Davis Cumbuss apparently had "shunts" located in his head to relieve pressure, and this apparently contributed to the young man's death. Both Ms. Mills and Mr. Cumbuss were Black.

Mr. Robert Cumbuss, the father of the young man, refuted such charges concerning his son's health. "My son never suffered an attack or seizure of any type in his life...." This apparent disparity could be written off as circumstantial, if it were not for Brady-Davis Cumbuss' twin sister, who also has the exact same shunts placed in her head....

The Cumbusses contacted the Sovereign Patriot Group of Chico, California to help the family arrest the Sheriff Deputy who had custody of their son in the jail, and if need be, to arrest the Sheriff himself, Sheriff Mick Grey. Both the Jail and the Sheriff have suffered unique scrutiny lately as issues regarding irresponsibility and criminal actions being brought forward by the news media show an agency in complete disarray.

First, the Sheriff himself suffered an embarrassing lawsuit by an ex-lover who charged that Sheriff Grey irresponsibly gave her the herpes virus in having an affair with her when he was still married. This litigation is still pending by this woman, and is but part of the controversy surrounding the Butte County Jail.

Shortly thereafter, prisoners voiced charges against Jail Deputies, alleging that the Deputies were enlisting and instructing bully inmates to beat certain "unliked" prisoners....

Then, young 20-year-old, 110 pound Brady-Davis Cumbuss was found dead, shortly after being placed into the Jail's custody....

At the death, the NAACP along with Oroville Supervisor Vivian Myers and others, submitted court papers and proceeded to bury the young man's body without another autopsy. This was done over the protests of the Sovereign Patriot Group, who advised the father and each side of the family to have a second independent autopsy to confirm the pictures the family took of the body.

These graphic pictures show split lips, a cut on the arm, bumps on the head, slight swelling of the sides of the head, and bruises, the two most compelling ones being on the shoulder and the thigh. These pictures are in direct contravention of the Sheriff and the Sacramento Coroner's Office case, that the boy died of "natural causes...."

The Sovereign Patriot Group has had individuals of great courage come forward and tell their stories. From this information we attempted to air our show called "Sovereign America" on Thursday, October 19th at 8:30 PM. We responsibly called all the local media and our local representatives...to glean some support for the continued investigation to what could be perhaps one of the biggest stories ever to hit the Northern California area in some time.

However, two hours before the show was to air, a Trustee of Butte Community College "pulled" the show. This compelling show was NOT aired to the public, the media, and our local representatives who were waiting for this show to air and who would have been educated by the show....

This is blatant censorship. The Public Access Television should not be censored. What the Butte College Trustees did under pretense of concern for liable was to prohibit the public from a timely information on this important subject. Simply, Butte College TV, which is the carrier for Sovereign America, is but a medium. Sovereign America is aired with the standard disclaimers before the show releasing the broadcaster from any liability; their actions only prove that they were pulling this show only to censor it and to keep it from the public's view!

The bigger issue is: who inspired such censorship? If any outside authority can call a 'Good 'Ol Boy' network to censor timely information from the public's view—then this nation is in grave trouble. This should be a red flag to any freedom-loving American.

The Sovereign Patriot Group is fighting to bring forth justice. There appears to be a powerful and dark cloud hanging and prohibiting such actions. Like the Sheriff who defied his own law and refused to arrest his Deputy, Butte College is acting in bad faith and against its own rules and laws....

It is time that Patriots bind together and hold people accountable to THEIR OWN LAW. Especially government agents and officials. These are laws that they normally impose upon all of us, yet, when they themselves are charged to suffer that same fate—those same laws—they refute and shun such laws and disobey them at will.

We need your help and support. People have needlessly died. We are convinced to the core of our being, that if 20-year-old Brady-Davis Cumbuss had NOT entered that jail, he would be alive today. However, the greater tragedy of this is by the fact that it is readily apparent that our Public Servants have somehow become our certain Masters—and they choose to obey no law....

Source: patriots@kaiwan.com (accessed 29 October 1995).

The Field Manual of the Free Militia

The following excerpts from The Field Manual of the Free Militia *have circulated widely on the Internet and display the synthesis of Christian ideology with militias evident in numerous paramilitary groups:*

Biblical authority

Before we can rightly consider arming and organizing ourselves as a militia, we must consider whether or not doing so is the right thing to do. Later on we will see that we have the historical and constitutional right to form a militia. But ultimately, right and wrong is determined by God's Will, and God's Will is determined from the Bible. Why turn to the Bible to answer our questions about right and wrong? If you are a Bible believer, you must be committed to following its moral standards. If you do not believe the Bible, you should still know and weigh what it says and use it to justify your actions to the Bible believers....

The Bible is word for word the word of God. Therefore it is completely true or without any errors. This is what we mean by inerrancy. Think about it. If God knows everything (1 John 3:20) and cannot lie (Hebrews 6:18), and if the Bible's words are God's words, then there cannot be any mistakes in the Bible. Otherwise, God would either have to be wrong himself or lying to us....

This leads us to the final point which needs to be made about the Bible: the Bible alone is authoritative, meaning that it, and only it, must be completely believed and obeyed. Since all of the Bible is God's word we cannot pick and choose what we want to obey. Since it is all true, we cannot neglect a portion of it by raising doubts about its reliability. Since it contains all we need for our Christian walks we cannot appeal to something or someone besides the Bible as our final authority on some issue.

We must make sure that whatever we do in any department of life, including the use of force, conforms to the truth and moral principles of the Bible....

A call to arms!

From every legitimate angle, we are justified in keeping and bearing arms as well as forming or joining a militia independent of government control. The Bible tells us we are morally right. The American Revolution shows us we have the historical right. The Constitution protects our legal right. Moreover, our Constitutional liberties are systematically being eroded and denied. The fact that officials are infringing upon gun rights on every front is simply a manifestation of their inner tendency to empower themselves. Left unchecked, this tendency will lead to genuine tyranny. Remember, "power corrupts and absolute power corrupts absolutely...."

So arm yourself. Organize yourselves. And prepare to fight if you have to.

Source: patriots@kaiwan.com (accessed 13 November 1995).

The United Nations Flag in Gainesville, Florida

Many in the militia movement distrust the United Nations, considering it a major instrument in advancing a One World government. The North Central Florida Regional Militia expressed this view in its complaint, dated November 1995, about the city of Gainesville flying a UN flag:

The policy for flying of flags from the city flagpole adopted by the City Commission dated January 9, 1995, as well as the action taken by the City Commission in permitting the United Nations Association to fly the United Nations flag from the city flagpole, have had the effect of converting the city flagpole into an open forum for the expression of ideas and freedom of speech. Thus, such expression is now protected in the exact same manner as the traditional ways of expressing one's ideas are by the First Amendment to the United States Constitution. Accordingly, the North Central Florida Regional Militia requests to be granted access to and time on the city flagpole equal to that which has been given to the United Nations Association. . . .

The flag that the North Central Florida Regional Militia has adopted for its own use is the historic flag flown originally by the Gadsden Militia during the Revolutionary War. This flag can best be described as having a yellow background, upon which appears a coiled rattlesnake and the motto, "Don't tread on me."

Source: patriots@kaiwan.com (accessed 5 November 1995).

The New World Order Is a Vampire

A vampire lurks that can only be killed by driving a stake through its heart: The vampire is the New World Order. So claims the author of Operation Vampire Killer 2000, *a publication that seeks to unite police and law enforcement officials in blocking efforts to weaken state governments and push the entire nation under the rule of a leftist system:*

They, the Globalists, have stated that the date of termination of the American way of life is the year 2000. Therefore, it is fitting that our date to terminate, at the very least, their plan, is also the year 2000. LET IT BE WELL UNDERSTOOD, WE PROTECTORS OF THE AMERI- CAN PEOPLE HAVE NOT ASKED FOR THIS BATTLE. IT IS OUR NATION'S ENEMIES WHO HAVE BROUGHT THIS FIGHT TO THE DOOR OF EVERY GOOD AMERICAN. BE IT RESOLVED:

- Our prayer and promise is to do all within our power, as faithful countrymen, to overthrow this evil, treasonous plan in a completely non-violent, lawful manner.
- Our sworn duty is to protect the people of this nation and its constitutional, republican form of government from any enemy that would come against it.
- Our pledge is that WE WILL, BY EVERY MEANS GIVEN UNTO US, UPHOLD OUR OATHS AND FULFILL OUR SWORN DUTY TO OUR COUNTRYMEN.

PUTTING THE STAKE THROUGH DRACULA'S HEART
WHAT CAN WE DO, WHAT SHOULD WE DO? The Globalist's agenda is a diabolical program which, through patient gradualism, is slowly draining the moral, economic and political life blood from the United States and the hard working American people.

We in America, Officers and private citizens alike, are fortunate that at this moment in our history we can still LAWFULLY EXTERMINATE these parasitical Global Blood Suckers by placing numerous "STAKES" made of words, paper, pen, and hard work through their hardened hearts.

STATES BEING ABOLISHED

Study the constitution of your state. You may find that your state constitution no longer describes the boundaries of the state—effectively abolishing the state. At last check, the only states that still lay out their boundaries in their constitutions are Washington, Idaho, Montana, North and South Dakota, Wyoming, Iowa, Wisconsin, Indiana, Nevada, Utah, Colorado, Kansas, Arizona, New Mexico and Arkansas, Mississippi, Tennessee, Alabama and Florida.—*Spotlight* 1/18/88

When the state borders are no longer in the State Constitution, it is the signal that the State has lost its sovereignty (and its State Citizens). Now a CENTRAL GOVERNMENT HAS BEEN FORMED WHICH IS THE STEP INTO INTERNATIONAL COMMUNISM THROUGH THE UNITED NATIONS...WAKE UP AMERICA!

Vote Down Home Rule! THIS IS A DESIGNED AND PLANNED POLITICAL REVOLUTION. This is being done through the ballot box to destroy our State Constitutions and State Governments while we are kept busy fighting brush fires and fanning windmills on lesser matters of importance or of no significance. Obtain a copy of your present State Constitution and a copy of my proposed changes of your State Constitution. Keep watch for attempts to remove boundaries.

The prohibition in both the State and the United States Constitution are very clearly defined and impregnable. The only way that these changes can be made, of course, is to change the Constitutions. The perpetrators of Regional and World Government well know this. They well know that the STATE GOVERNMENTS WILL HAVE TO BE ABOLISHED BEFORE THEY CAN FORCE REGIONAL, METROPOLITAN AND WORLD GOVERNMENT IN THE UNITED STATES—This has already been done in 30 of the 40 states!

Source: American Citizens & Lawmen Association, *Operation Vampire Killer 2000* (Phoenix, Arizona, 1992), 5.

A Solution to the United Nations Problem

The Committee to Restore the Constitution, headquartered in Fort Collins, Colorado, supports paramilitary activity and warns about the movement toward a One World government. In 1995, the organization's director, Archibald E. Roberts, warned in a letter about the encroachment on American sovereignty by the United Nations:

The United Nations Charter is a constitution for world government designed to undermine our way of life, to take away our liberties and embroil our armed forces in 'no-win wars' all over the globe.

Objective: Use U.S. military to force all nations into line and deliver them up to world government administration.

The United Nations Charter has replaced the Constitution of the United States as the law of the land. (Review of the United Nations Charter. Doc #87, page 289, United States Senate, 7 January 1954)....

The people, source of all political power, are responsible for instructing state lawmakers to direct their agents in Washington to confine the functions of government to limitations defined in the Constitution of the United States....

Launch your tactical operation to challenge the men and the system who seek to rob you of your heritage....

Source: Archibald E. Roberts, "A Solution to the United Nations Problem," letter, n.d., 1995?.

Discrimination: an Unbecoming Trait of Patriots?

In Aide-de-Camp, *the official newsletter of the United States Militia Association, Samuel Sherwood inveighs against racism and anti-Semitism. To him, neither has a place in militias, and he especially takes to task* Spotlight, *the influential publication issued by the Liberty Lobby. Nevertheless, he believes that American sovereignty is under assault:*

Not all people are well read, well founded in the Constitution, or understand the meaning of the words being used in most of the causes in which they ally themselves. This being the case, it becomes easy for people to be led away down the path of deception, all the while thinking they are supporting the principles of truth and freedom, but are not. The scriptures in Luke 21:8, and Galatians 6:7 says, respectively:

And he said, Take heed that ye be not deceived: for many shall come in my name, saying, I am Christ and the time draweth near: go ye not therefore after them.

Be not deceived, God is not mocked: for whatsoever a man soweth, that shall he also reap....

One of the more notable examples of this deception comes from the *Spotlight* news magazine. Most readers are well meaning and sincere, but well meaning and sincere does not translate into constitutional soundness. The *Spotlight* is full of half truths, innuendoes, and partial facts, from which it is impossible for anyone to be able to come to a knowledge of the truth....

For someone to read that a Jew who works for a bank is advocating government protections and controls for the world banking system that gives it an advantage over other banks in the U.S. and destroys the sovereignty of banking operations both domestically and internationally, he may think that all Jews are bad and conspirators to destroy America. The problem is that the *Spotlight* did not report on the Irishman, Englishman, Japanese, Italian, and Saudi who all supported the same thing.

The problem comes when the person reading this trash reads over and over and over again that Jews are advocating a world bank, world monetary unit, world government, etc., etc., ad nauseam. These people never stop to ask themselves how these Jews are able to do this in opposition to the national interest of all of the nations involved. So, they react in the limited knowledge they have and hate Jews.

Source: "Discrimination, An Unbecoming Trait of 'Patriots'?" *Aide-de-Camp*, October 1995, 1.

The Protocols of the Meetings of the Learned Elders of Zion

In the early twentieth century, The Protocols of the Meetings of the Learned Elders of Zion *appeared in Europe. The publication—purported to be the minutes from a secret meeting of Jewish leaders, is now known to be a fake. The* Protocols *claims that Jews directed the French Revolution to weaken the Gentile (or Goyim) elite, cause turmoil, give the masses a false sense of authority, and move more quickly toward the day when people would turn to Jewish leadership for order and world control. The following excerpts display this account and the other strategies Jewish leaders allegedly devised. The* Protocols *appeals to conspiratorial theorists and to anti-Semitism, both present in segments of the militia movement, although not always in the combined state found in this document:*

We Shall End Liberty

Far back in ancient times we were the first to cry among the masses of the people the words "Liberty, Equality, Fraternity"—words many times repeated since those days by stupid poll-parrots who from all sides round flew down upon these baits and with them carried away the well-being of the world, true freedom of the individual, formerly so well guarded against the pressure of the mob. The would-be wise men of the Goyim, the intellectuals, could not make anything out of the uttered words in their abstractness; did not note the contradiction of their meaning and inter-relation; did not see that in nature there is no equality, cannot be freedom; that Nature herself has established inequality of minds of characters, and capacities, just as immutably as she has established subordination to her laws; never stopped to think that the mob is a blind thing, that upstarts selected from among it to bear rule are, in regard to the political, the same blind men as the mob itself, that the adept, though he be a fool, can yet rule, whereas the non-adept, even if he were a genius, understands nothing in the political—to all these things the Goyim paid no regard; yet all the time it was based upon these things that dynastic rule rested; the father passed on to the son a knowledge of the course of political affairs in such wise that none should know it but members of the dynasty and none could betray it to the governed. As time went on, the meaning of the dynastic transference of the true position of affairs in the political was lost, and this aided the success of our cause. In all corners of the earth the words "Liberty, Equality, Fraternity" brought to our ranks, thanks to our blind agents, whole legions who bore our banners with enthusiasm. And all the time, these words were canked-worms at work boring into the well-being of the Goyim, putting an end everywhere to peace, quiet, solidarity, and destroying all the foundations of the Goya States. As you will see later, this helped us to our triumph; it gave us the possibility, among other things, of getting in to our hands the master card—the destruction of the privileges, or in other words of the very existence of the aristocracy of the Goyim, that class which was the only defense peoples and countries had against us. On the ruins of the natural and genealogical aristocracy of the Goyim we have set up the aristocracy of our educated class headed by the aristocracy of money. The qualifications for this aristocracy we have established in wealth, which is dependent upon us, and in knowledge, for which our learned elders provide the motive force. Our triumph has been rendered easier by the fact that in our relations the men whom we wanted to have always worked upon the most sensitive chords of the human mind, upon the cash account, upon the cupidity, upon the instability, for material needs of man; and each one of these human weaknesses, taken alone, is sufficient to paralyze initiative, for it hands over the will of men to the disposition of him who has bought their activities. The abstraction of freedom has enabled us to persuade the mob in all countries that their government is nothing but the steward of the people who are the owners of the country, and that the steward may be replaced like a worn-out grave. It is this possibility of replacing the representatives of the people which has placed them at our disposal, and as it were, given us the power of appointment.

We Shall Destroy

By such measures we shall obtain the power of destroying little by little, step by step, all that at the outset when we enter on our rights, we are compelled to introduce into the constitutions of States to prepare for the transition to an imperceptible abolition of every kind of constitution, and then the time is come to turn every form of government into our despotism. The recognition of our despot may also come before the destruction of the constitution; the moment for this recognition will come when the people, utterly wearied by the irregularities and incompetence—a matter which we shall arrange for—of their rulers, will clamor: "Away with them and give us one king over all the earth who will mite us and annihilate the causes of discords—frontiers, nationalities, religions, state debts—who will give us peace and quiet, which we cannot find under our rules and representatives."

BUT YOU YOURSELVES PERFECTLY WELL KNOW THAT TO PRODUCE THE POSSIBILITY OF THE EXPRESSION OF SUCH

WISHES BY ALL THE NATIONS IT IS INDISPENSABLE TO TROU-
BLE IN ALL COUNTRIES THE PEOPLE'S RELATION WITH THEIR
GOVERNMENTS SO AS TO UTTERLY EXHAUST HUMANITY WITH
DISSENSION, HATRED, STRUGGLE, ENVY AND EVEN THE USE OF
TORTURE; BY STARVATION, BY THE INOCULATION OF DIS-
EASES, BY WANT, SO THAT THE GOYIM SEE NO OTHER ISSUE,
THAN TO TAKE REFUGE IN OUR COMPLETE SOVEREIGNTY IN
MONEY AND ALL ELSE. But if we give the nations of the world a
breathing space the moment we long for is hardly likely ever to arrive.

Poverty Our Weapon

All people are chained down to heavy toil by poverty more firmly
than ever they were chained by slavery and serfdom; from these, one
way and another, they might free themselves, these could be settled
with, but from want they will never get away. We have included in the
constitution such rights as to the masses appear fictitious and not actual
rights. All these so-called "People's Rights" can exist only in idea, an
idea which can never be realized in practical life. What is it to the proletariat labourer, bowed double over his heavy toil, crushed by his lot
in life, if talkers get the right to babble, if journalists get the right to
scribble, any nonsense side by side with good stuff, once the proletariat
has no other profit out of the constitution save only those pitiful
crumbs which we fling them from our table in return for their voting in
favour of what we dictate, in favour of the men we place in power, the
servants of our agent... Republican rights for a poor man are no more
than a bitter piece of irony, for the necessity he is under of toiling
almost all day gives him no present use of them, but on the other hand
robs him of all guarantee of regular and certain earnings by making
him dependent on strikes by his comrades or lockouts by his masters.

Protocol No. 6

We shall soon begin to establish huge monopolies, reservoirs of
colossal riches, upon which even large fortunes of the Goyim will
depend to such an extent that they will go the bottom together with the
credit of the States on the day after the political smals.

You gentlemen here present who are economists, just strike an esti-
mate of the significance of this combination. In every possible way we
must develop the significance of our Super-Government by representing it as the Protector and Benefactor of all those who voluntarily sub-
mit to us. The aristocracy of the Goyim as a political force, is dead—we
need not take it into account; but as landed proprietors they can still be
harmful to us from the fact that they are self-sufficing in the resources
upon which they live. It is essential therefore for us at whatever cost
to deprive them of their land. This object will be best attained by
increasing the burdens upon landed property in loading lands with
debt. These measures will check land holding and keep it in a state of
humble and unconditional submission. The aristocrats of the Goyim,
being hereditarily incapable of contenting themselves with little, will
rapidly burn up and fizzle out.

Destructive Education

Do not suppose for a moment that these statements are empty words: think carefully of the successes we arranged for Darwinism, Marxism, Nietzscheism. To us Jews, at any rate it should be, plain to see what a distinguishable importance these directives have had up on the minds of the Goyim. It is indispensable for us to take account of the thoughts, characters, tendencies of the nations in order to avoid making slips in the political and in the direction of administrative affairs. The triumph of our system of which the component parts of the machinery may be variously disposed according to the temperament of the peoples met on our way, will fail of success if the practical application of it be not based upon summing up of the lessons of the past in the light of the present. In the hands of the States of today there is a great force that creates the movement of thought in the people, and that is the press. The part played by the press is to keep pointing out requirements supposed to be indispensable, to give voice to the complaints of the people, to express and to create discontent. It is in the press that the triumph of freedom of speech finds its incarnation, but the Goyim States have not known how to make use of this force; and it has fallen into our hands. Through the press as we have gained the power to influence while remaining ourselves in the shade; thanks to the press we have got the gold in our hands, notwithstanding that we have had to gather it out of oceans of blood and tears. But it has paid us, though we have sacrificed many of our people. Each victim on our side is worth in the sight of God a thousand Goyim.

We Shall Destroy God

But even freedom might be harmless and have its place in the State economy without injury to the well-being of the peoples if rested upon the foundation of faith in God, upon the brotherhood of humanity, unconnected with the conception of equality, which is negatived by the very laws of creation, for they have established subordination. With such a faith as this a people might be governed by a wardship of parishes, and would walk contentedly and humbly under the guiding hand of its spiritual pastor submitting to the dispositions of God upon earth. This is the reason why it is indispensable for us to undermine all faith, to tear out of the minds of the Goyim the very principle of Godhead and the spirit, and to put in its place arithmetical calculators and material needs. In order to give the Goyim no time to think and take note, their minds must be diverted towards industry and trade. Thus, all the nations will be swallowed up in the pursuit of gain, and in the race for it will not take note of their common foe. But again in order that freedom may once for all disintegrate and ruin the communities of the Goyim, we must put industry on a speculative basis: the result of this will be that what is withdrawn from the land by industry will slip through the hands and pass into speculation, that is, to our classes. The intensified struggle for superiority and shocks delivered to economic life will create, nay, have already created, disenchanted cold and heartless communities. Such communities will foster a strong aversion towards the higher political and towards religion. Their only guide is gain, that is Gold, which they will erect into a veritable cult, for the sake of those material delights which it can give. Then will the hour strike when, not for the sake of attaining the good—not even to win wealth, but solely out of hatred towards the privileged, the lower-classes of the Goyim will follow our lead against our rivals for power, the intellectuals of the Goyim.

Source: Sergiei Aleksandrovich Nilus, *The Protocols of the Meetings of the Learned Elders of Zion*, trans. Victor E. Marsden. (Houston: Pyramid Book Shop, 1934), passim.

A Well-Regulated Militia

In a statement issued during the summer of 1995, the Michigan Militia insisted on both the need for a militia and on its legality:

A WELL REGULATED MILITIA? TODAY?

What is the Militia?

Section 311, Title 10 of the United States Code recognizes the unorganized militia of the United States as all able-bodied male citizens between 17 and 45 years of age who are not members of the National Guard or the Naval Militia. The law also includes provisions for militia participation by female, older and prospective citizens. The militia is LEGAL according to U.S. law. The militia is NOT a renegade organization as portrayed by the media and some politicians.

What is its purpose?

The purpose of the militia is the defense of the Republic and the State from all its enemies, whether they be foreign or domestic. We do this by maintaining a program of training and preparedness for emergency situations as well as by educating ourselves and others about potential dangers to our constitutionally protected way of life in these United States of America ....

What kind of training does the militia do?

Militia training includes a variety of areas that would increase our effectiveness in any time of National or State emergency. These include but are not necessarily limited to first aid, self defense, organization, transportation and navigation, communication, equipment maintenance and usage, as well as training in military field tactics. Training is typically held at times and places convenient to the participating unit and is held year-round to ensure a constant state of readiness. Most militia members find personal training to be a source of personal growth and esprit de corps. Militia training includes the mind as well as the body. Study of the Constitution and historical issues will be a significant part of your militia training. Militia members share knowledge in all these areas in order to provide for a strong defense of freedom.

What about racism or sexism in the militia?

There is none. The militia welcomes members of all races and creeds as well as of both genders. A member may hold any position that they are qualified to fill. Despite recent media attempts to portray us as otherwise, we are an organization that welcomes all who share our cause. YOU are invited to join our noble cause... the defense of liberty.

Is the militia a threat to a peaceful society?

The militia is more accurately called a guarantor of a peaceful society. The militia is strictly a DEFENSIVE organization. Our function is to preserve and defend the Constitution of the United States of America and the State of Michigan as well as the citizenry at large....

Source: http://www.grfin.org/%7Eheiny/cmrm.html (accessed 2 March 1996).

The Militia Mission

The 15th Brigade of the Central Michigan Regional Militia, part of the Michigan Militia, has laid out its mission and goals. It stresses educating people about the Constitution and protecting liberty:

Mission: To defend the Constitution of the State of Michigan and the Constitution of the United States of America. To uphold and defend the Bill of Rights, seen as unalienable, given by God to free men that they remain free. To insure that all citizens regardless of race, color, religion, sex, physical characteristics, or national origin shall have the right and opportunity to due process of law as established and guaranteed by the Great Documents which guide this Great Nation.

Goals: It shall be the goal of the Fifteenth Brigade of the Central Michigan Regional Militia to:

- Present itself to the citizens of this region as a well regulated, well-trained, well-equipped, and knowledgeable militia unit comprised of ordinary citizens rather than professional soldiers.
- Establish a cohesive command structure able to instruct and to task as need arises.
- Train its members in the many disciplines necessary to the function of the militia as a whole, and as members individually.
- Educate its members in areas of history, law, and principle from knowledge imparted from this country's historical record and from the Bible, which has been the greatest single guiding influence for all great nations desiring to be free.
- Inform its members of local, national, and global events imperiling the Constitution and impacting the direction of the country.
- Encourage its members to stand against tyranny, globalism, moral relativism, humanism, and the New World Order threatening to undermine our form of government and these United States of America.

- Uphold the pure Constitutional rule of law whereby all citizens have the right to trial by a jury of their peers in a court of law.

Source: http://www.grfin.org/%7Eheiny/cmrm.html (accessed 2 March 1996).

Militias and the Anti-Defamation League

Jews for the Preservation of Firearms Ownership recently issued a news release condemning the Anti-Defamation League for slurs against the militia movement:

June 30, 1995—"The Anti-Defamation League, headquartered at the United Nations Plaza, New York, has again attacked the patriotism of honest Americans with a misleading report. Beyond The Bombing: The Militia Menace Grows asserts that there is 'militia activity' in 40 states. The only documentation is a terse introductory statement that the material was compiled with the assistance of the ADL's 'regional offices,'" Aaron Zelman, Executive Director of JPFO said today.

Zelman pointed out that the ADL report contains little documentation such as newspaper articles. "The ADL's report is a tract. Its innuendo and assertions are designed to frighten Americans, rather than to inform and to educate." Zelman said. "JPFO challenges the ADL to reveal its source material, if it exists, so that independent researchers can verify the 'accuracy' of the ADL report. JPFO Special Reports have always contained detailed source citations. JPFO bases its reports on publicly available facts. The ADL should not publish allegations without also publishing source citations!" said Zelman....

Zelman went further: "We need to be very clear that the ADL defames all militia members as being racists, hate mongers, bigots, etc. This is wrong! The ADL even labels as an 'anti-Semite' Norm Resnick, an Orthodox Jew. They do so because he hosts a 'patriot' radio talk show in Colorado which encourages firearms ownership .... "

Source: News release, Jews for the Preservation of Firearms Ownership, 30 June 1995.

The Michigan Militia and Waco

In August 1995, the Michigan Militia offered its own questions and criticism concerning the events at Waco:

QUESTIONS ABOUT WACO

Were the small children and babies inside the 'compound' treated as hostages?

ANSWER: No.

Were they gassed?

ANSWER: Yes.

For how long were they gassed before they burned to death?

ANSWER: Six hours

Has the U.S. government signed an agreement not to use this gas on
foreign enemies?
ANSWER: Yes.
Does the manufacturer of this gas warn that it might cause fires?
ANSWER: Yes.
Does the manufacturer of this gas warn against its use in enclosed
areas?
ANSWER: Yes.
Did Attorney General Janet Reno authorize the use of this gas in an
enclosed wooden structure knowing inside were two pregnant women
and more than 20 children and babies?
ANSWER: Yes....

Source: http://www.grfin.org/%7Eheiny/cmrm.html (accessed
2 December 1995).

The National Rifle Association and Militias

*In November 1994, the National Rifle Association issued its official
position regarding militias, recognizing their right to exist but refus-
ing to sponsor their emergence:*

The Board of Directors of the National Rifle Association of America
has not adopted a formal policy regarding the formation of citizen militia groups, such as has occurred in numerous states. However, by its
Bylaws and policies the NRA strongly supports the Constitution of the
United States, and the Second Amendment to that document, which
guarantee the right of citizens to participate in militias for proper, lawful and constitutional purposes. Although the NRA has not been
involved in the formation of any citizen militia units, neither has the
NRA discouraged, nor would NRA contemplate discouraging, exercise
of any constitutional right.

It is the NRA's view, based on law (Article I, section 8 of the U.S.
Constitution; Title 10, U.S. Code, Section 311(a)), court precedents, and
legal and historical interpretation, that all able-bodied persons, explicitly those between the ages of 17 and 45, are members of the Federal
unorganized militia, except members of the organized state guards (for
example, State Defense Forces which exist in about two dozen states),
the National Guards of the various states (which also serve as a part of
the National Guard of the United States, a military reserve subject to
nationalization by the President of the United States), and certain government officials. An "organized citizen militia" must be created under
the constitution itself and/or the laws of a state.

Title 10, U.S.C., clearly affirms the existence of the citizen militia; it
is little changed since the original Militia Act of 1792 (except for the
addition in this century of recognition of the third type of militia, the
Federally supported National Guard, in addition to the enrolled and
un-enrolled militia).

Further, the individual right to own firearms is guaranteed by the Constitution, but the right to own firearms is not at all dependent upon the militia clause. The militia clause of the Second Amendment merely adds to the reason for the right, which is a common law right....

Source: Institute for Alternative Journalism, *Militias in America 1995* (San Francisco, 1995), 41.

The South Carolina Civilian Militia

The South Carolina Civilian Militia, organized by Ian Roebuck, joined the chorus of militia groups criticizing the events at Waco and a subsequent congressional inquiry into them. The South Carolina group called the hearings an injustice for which both Democrats and Republicans were to blame:

By the third day new material was showing up that showed obvious obstruction of justice being performed by the justice department (Butch Reno's Office of Injustice). One of the Davidians defense lawyers, whose client was acquitted on all counts and now lives in England, testified that the documents which show this obstruction clearly indicate that Justice ordered a halt to investigations into the shootings at WACO because the investigations were turning up evidence which would prove the innocence of the captured Davidians!....

These hearings are not being broadcast to the public, except by C-SPAN. The C-SPAN broadcast is usually not starting till after midnight and goes to about 5 in the morning....

THE IDEA IS TO FEED THE AMERICAN SLEEPING PUBLIC HALF-TRUTHS AND KEEP THEM IGNORANT AS TO THE TERRIBLE REAL INJUSTICES COMMITTED BY THE PRESENT ADMINISTRATION AND IN THE END BOTH PARTIES (DEMOCRAT COMMICRAT AND REPUBLICAN NAZICAN) WILL BE ABLE TO SAY THEY HELD HEARINGS, SO WHAT'S THE PROBLEM?

HERE IS THE PROBLEM: THERE ARE NOW ENOUGH AMERICANS AWAKE TO SEE THIS TACTIC FOR WHAT IT IS!

Source: http://pages.prodigy.com/SC/militia/militia.html (accessed 2 March 1996).

The South Carolina Civilian Militia and the Michael Hill Shooting

The South Carolina Civilian Militia criticized not only Waco, but also the shooting of a militia leader, Michael Hill, by police in a small Ohio town in June 1995. To this militia, the incident represented an attempt to silence the entire militia movement:

On June 28, 1995, autopsy results allege that Michael Hill was murdered in cold blood by Frazyburg, Ohio, police officer Matthew May.

This was first revealed by three eye witnesses and later confirmed by an independent autopsy. In Officer May's report, he stated that Michael Hill left his car with his gun in both hands pointing straight at Officer May.

Witnesses say Sgt. May stepped out of his car with weapon drawn and killed Chaplain Hill without provocation by firing four shots. Three shots hit the chaplain and killed him. Officer May claimed Chaplain Hill stepped out of the car holding a .45 semiautomatic in both hands, thus contradicting three witnesses. In addition news reports do not mention eye witnesses. Ken Adams [executive director of the National Confederation of Civilian Militias] is very concerned about conflicting reports on the incident. He stated, "I hope that shooting militia members by law enforcement officials is not becoming a sporting event...."

Adams...smells incompetence or a cover-up and a possible conspiracy in the shooting.... With an FBI investigation still pending, and with the failure of the Grand Jury to hear all witnesses, Mr. Adams commented, "This is an outrage!"

Soon after the killing of Michael Hill, Muskingum County's Sheriff Bernie Gibson, members from the county Prosecutor's office, Officer Mays, the Coroner, and allegedly other county officials possibly conspired to cover-up the murder of Michael Hill by Officer Mays. Within hours of the cold-blooded murder, and before Mr. Hill was laid to rest, Sheriff Gibson had already stated that he believed Officer Mays' account of the killing and flagrantly disregarded the testimony of three eye witnesses. After pressure from the NCCM and their legal counsel, Nancy Lord, the County Prosecutor reluctantly called witnesses before the Grand Jury, but intentionally and willfully disregarded testimony from others, including Mrs. Hill, even though they were told they would be called to testify.

The NCCM and this nation's militias will not sit silently by while our people are shot down.... We have not let up on WACO, Ruby Ridge, or the Vince Foster killing, and we will not let up on Michael Hill's murder....

The eyes of the nation and the nation's militias will be on Muskingum County until the truth concerning the murder of Michael Hill is properly investigated and the guilty are held accountable.

Source: http://pages.prodigy.com/SC/militia/militia.html (accessed 4 January 1996).

The New Jersey Militia and Motor Vehicle Law

Militias are often suspicious of government actions—in this case, in its newsletter for November 1995, the New Jersey Militia questions a recent state law that requires the inspection of automobiles:

The soon to be infamous N.J. Senate Bill #1700 which concerns "motor vehicle inspection and registration" states...that anyone who fails to "have a motor vehicle examined" ... or "fails or refuses to place the motor vehicle in proper condition," etc., etc .... faces a fine "of not more than $200.00 ... and/or imprisonment for not less than 30 days." (Second offense)

These penalties certainly exceed the "$20.00" specified in the Seventh Amendment. But, on page 19, line 14, S1700 states: "The hearing in any such proceeding shall be without a jury. "

Will Richard Kamin, Director of N.J.D.M.V., ... raise his voice in righteous indignation and denounce the legislators in Trenton who passed S1700, and Governor "Czarina" Whitman who signed it? The answer is, of course, no ....

On November 17th 1994, Mr. Kamin spoke to a private meeting on various issues at Linden, N.J. When someone at the meeting remarked that if S1700 was fully enforced there would be rioting in the streets, Mr. Kamin remarked: "That's why they took your guns away first."

Source: *New Jersey Militia Newsletter*, November 1995, 1.

A Militia Petitions Congress

On 22 July 1995, the Militia of the United States of America forwarded a petition to Congress with language unmistakably similar to that found in the 1776 Declaration of Independence. The opposition to any encroachment on the right to bear arms rings especially strong:

DECLARATION OF GRIEVANCE

"But when a long train of abuses and usurpation, pursuing invariably the same object evinces a design to reduce them under absolute despotism, it is their right, their duty, to throw off such government, and to provide new guard for their future security." (Quoted from the Declaration of Independence.)

Therefore, We the people do declare that as of this day, July 22, 1995, Congress shall make no further law or regulation abridging, infringing, or encroaching upon the Second Amendment to the United States Constitution. This includes but is not limited to so-called "counter-terrorism," "anti-terrorism," or "anti-militia" legislation, Executive Orders, Presidential Directives, and Treaties which are outside the scope of the federal powers enumerated in the United States Constitution.

Any unjust attack upon any part of the militia will be considered an attack upon the militia as a whole and upon their Constitutional basis to provide for the defense of their families, states and nation against all enemies, foreign and domestic.

We oppose any world government organization that would infringe upon our sovereignty as Americans or that would supersede the United States Constitution.

Any action taken against the American people by United Nations forces, including the quartering of United Nations troops or stationing of United Nations equipment on American soil by treaty, legislation or Executive Order, will be opposed by the militia.

Any act declaring martial law or a state of emergency which would deprive the American people of life, liberty or property, without due process of law, shall be considered an act in contravention to the United States Constitution.

Any violation of the Posse Comitatus Act will be considered an act of aggression against the American people.

Any alteration of the United States Constitution not in accordance with Article V will not be tolerated.

The Founding Fathers, in the original Declaration of Independence, put forth the principle that when government which derives its powers from the consent of the governed, no longer protects the unalienable rights of the governed, then a people scorned, ignored, and plundered by unconstitutional acts are compelled to exercise their RIGHT and DUTY to take up arms in response to acts of war against the American people.

We appeal to our Just God, Who rules over the Destiny of Nations, in this righteous cause. BLESSED IS THE NATION WHOSE GOD IS THE LORD (Psalm 33:12).

Source: patriots@kaiwan.com (accessed 28 August 1995).

Complaints About Unconstitutional Legislation

On the Internet in November 1995, militias praised remarks made by Charles R. Duke, a state senator from District 9 in Colorado. Duke warned about recent congressional legislation that allowed unconstitutional searches:

Anyone who believes things are "okay" in our government today is, at the very least, very badly misinformed. While we, the public, are entertained by O.J. Simpson and Colin Powell, the enemies of our Constitution are busy stealing our rights.

There is some editorial attention, after the fact, being paid to the wiretaps granted to the FBI last year (before Oklahoma City) by the Digital Telephony Act of 1994. This is not a pending bill. It is already law and authorizes millions of wiretaps against innocent and law-abiding citizens without a warrant or probable cause of any kind.

Students of our Constitution already know we have a Fourth Amendment to protect us from these Gestapo-like tactics. That Amendment states we have a right to be secure in our persons, houses, papers, and effects, against unreasonable searches and seizures. The Amendment also states that right: " . . . shall not be violated, and no Warrants shall issue, but upon probable cause, supported by Oath or affirmation, and particularly describing the places to be searched, and the persons or things to be seized." This Amendment was added to our Constitution because, in 1761, prior to the War for Independence, King

George was issuing Writs of Assistance to his tax collectors to allow warrant-less searches of ships, warehouses, and homes. This practice was so despised by those who believed in the sovereign rights of the individual, it earned a place of honor as being one of the enumerated prohibitions, the collection of which became our Bill of Rights, against the intrusion of government....

Source: patriots@kaiwan.com (accessed 20 November 1995).

Militias React to Troops in Bosnia

After President Bill Clinton decided to send American troops into Bosnia, some militia groups renewed their complaints about executive orders issued by the president. These diminished the rights of the people, they said, and, as in the case of Clinton's action, often entangled the United States in unnecessary engagements overseas:

None [of the executive orders that are now in effect] could have been created without the Emergency War Powers Act in 1933 against the people of our own country. Every president has had and most have used this dictatorship power and the congress has never opposed them. When a president sends our troops to foreign lands on a whim and declares it "in our best interest," congress could deny funding to stop him but in the end they never do. Today Clinton is using his dictatorship to send our troops to Bosnia, knowing that this country is bankrupt, the public is against it, congress is opposed and he doesn't care. Why? Because it is the interest of the Fortune 500 and all global investors to keep countries under control for corporate profit and free trade. It makes no difference that this country is the largest debtor nation in the world now because the Federal Reserve Bank will print the phony money at no cost and charge interest to American citizens and increase our debt. Note that one of the executive orders will give our assets to foreign lands to pay our debt. Americans will only become involved when England and its Bank of London, who is one of the owners of the Federal Reserve banking cartel, will want American land (including your homes and everything you own), which is the collateral in the deals made by our government since 1933....

Source: patriots@kaiwan.com (accessed 24 November 1995).

Alabama Militias Warn the FBI

Late in 1994, several Alabama militias joined together to issue an open letter to the FBI. Convinced that the federal government planned to crush them, the militias warned they would not be treated as another Ruby Ridge or Waco:

Gentlemen,

It has come to Our attention that a major operation against the legal citizen militias of northern Alabama is being contemplated by your Birmingham offices. We have been told that there have recently been significant shifts in resources and manpower away from legitimate criminal investigations and toward this "Z.B.O." (ATF parlance for "Zee Beeg One" or a major assault like Waco). This is of great concern to us as the Birmingham ATF office is currently being run by James Cavanaugh, an (as yet) un-indicted Federal criminal who was on the planning and command team responsible for the botched Waco raid that led to mass murder. While Mr. Cavanaugh will soon be very busy testifying to Congress and others about his involvement at Waco, we believe he intends a strike at us to try to retrieve his stained reputation within his own agency. As for the FBI, we believe that the traditional disdain the agency has shown for the unconstitutional cowboys of the ATF has been overridden by strict orders from Director Louis Freeh to cooperate. Is the FBI seriously contemplating sending their fabulously ill-named "Hostage Rescue Team" to Alabama to "rescue" some "hostages" down here?

If so, let's have some "rules of engagement" to forestall any tragedy. First, as you know if you read our literature, we are legal formations in every regard. We do not advocate force, violence, or the overthrow of the government. Our groups do not traffic in firearms or illegal items. If you wish to know what we plan, call us up and ask us. Second, if you think you have reasonable cause to execute a search warrant, come and knock on our doors in broad daylight, ACCOMPANIED BY NEWS MEDIA WITH CAMERAS ROLLING. (And do bring them with you instead of calling them after your thuggery is done, like the ATF did recently at the Trader's Gun Shop raid in Birmingham.) Unlike Mr. Cavanaugh and his BATF thugs we have nothing to hide....

WE WILL NOT PLAY THAT GAME BY YOUR ILLEGAL RULES. As law-abiding American citizens, we have all the Constitutional protections we need, plus one: the long recognized legitimate right of individual and collective self-defense when confronted by an illegal attack, whether it comes from street criminals or an out-of-control Federal agency....

To the leaders of the ATF and FBI here and in Washington we say this: Reconsider what you appear to be about to do. If we are attacked in the Waco style without warning, without the opportunity to respond in a peaceful way to any charges you may think you can stick on us, then good, law-abiding people will be killed on both sides without any reason. Also, and more importantly from your perspective, you will lack any political fig leaf to hide behind. You are already gearing up to try to explain the unexplainable and unforgivable actions at Waco, Ruby Ridge and elsewhere. The Republican Congress, to your chagrin, has your bureaucratic fruit in its hands, and your careers and the future survival of your agencies hang in the balance. The fallout from any Waco-style fiasco here will finish you for good and all, but it will be slim comfort to those who will lie in the newly-made graves in Alabama. For God's sake, and your own, back off this stupid plan and any others you might have around the country. Transfer Cavanaugh out of Alabama back to Washington....

By authority of the following:

The Sons of Liberty, Southern Command

The Gadsden Minutemen

The Crispus Attucks Detachment, Birmingham

The Mobile Regulators

The Committee of Seventy Six, Huntsville

The Sand Mountain Militia Company

Company A, 1st Alabama Volunteers

The Shelby County Citizen's Militia Co.'s A & B

The Dogtown Ranger Platoon

Source: "An Open Letter to the ATF and FBI," December 1994.

Citizens for the Reinstatement of a Constitutional Government

In 1995, the group Citizens for the Reinstatement of a Constitutional Government, based in Charlotte, North Carolina, outlined its goals and the expected means to achieve them. The document stresses the Second Amendment and Christianity:

Goals:

1. To make the Holy Bible and the United States Constitution the law of the land.
2. To return to "We The People" the unalienable rights to life, liberty, and property.

To accomplish these goals we will:

1. Remove treasonous politicians and corrupt judges from positions of authority, by whatever legal means possible, and return authority to the people.
2. Preserve our Second Amendment right to keep and bear firearms in order to secure for ourselves and our progeny a free state.
3. Support Christian education and home schooling.
4. Expose fraud perpetrated by the IRS, the lending institutions and the state against the sovereign citizen.
5. Return America to the Constitutionally mandated tax laws.
6. Abolish the Federal Reserve and return our country to the gold and silver standard, thereby removing the huge national debt.
7. Remove the United States from membership in the United Nations, in order to secure for all time, under God, our national sovereignty.

Source: http://www.infi.net/extra/militias/m-index.htm (accessed 2 March 1996).

A Conspiracy to Alter the Constitution

A warning went out in August 1995 about attempts by a select group to initiate a substantial alteration of the Constitution. The author of this work, Trisha Katson, saw a conspiracy underway. The right-wing Constitution Party distributed her essay, portions of which follow:

Danger: The internationalists' plans to change the US Constitution are alive and well!

Promoters of the so-called Conference of the States (COS) stung by their stunning defeat this year at the hands of the patriots nationwide , are back. The same forces which had hoped to make fundamental, structural, long-term changes in America's constitutional form of government are now planning what they're calling a "federalism summit" in Cincinnati on October 22–24. The meeting will be a prelude for a convention in Philadelphia in 1996.

A delegation of six legislators—equally divided between the Democrat and Republican leaders—from each state that passes resolutions of participation are expected to attend ....

The summit will hear testimony from "experts" and "scholars" on ways to downgrade our constitutional concept of separation of powers....

One scheduled speaker is University of Virginia professor A. E. "Dick" Howard. Howard is a member of the summit's Scholars Subcommittee advising the summit's Steering Committee. Howard is an advocate of changing America's form of government to a parliamentary system with the legislative and executive branches combined ....

Beware all ... constitutionist groups, and patriots of any calling. The insurrectionists are going to keep it up until they wear us down, or so at least that is what they think. Never, never give up. Protect and defend your state constitutions because they are the foundation documents that created government which in turn created the federal Constitution.

Source: patriots@kaiwan.com (accessed 30 August 1995).

A National Database Threatens Individual Liberty

"Big Brother" seemed ever more real as Congress debated a bill to provide for a national identification system. This anonymous essay considers the threat posed by such legislation. The government would be able to gather information on personal aspects of a person's life using sophisticated tracking techniques:

Imagine an America in which every citizen is required to carry a biometrically-encoded identification card as a precondition for conducting business. Imagine having your retina scanned every time you need to prove your identification. Imagine carrying a card containing your entire medical, academic, social, and financial history. Now, imagine that bureaucrats, police officers, and social workers have access under certain circumstances to the information on your card. Finally, imagine an America in which it is illegal to seek any employment without approval from the United States government.

This future may be more real than many Americans would like to think if Congressional lawmakers are allowed to proceed with their most recent attempt at monitoring the private lives of American citizens.

Enter S. 269, the latest attempt by Congress to mandate a computer-driven, biometrically-verifiable national identification system. If enacted into law, S. 269 would require the most comprehensive registration and tracking system of American citizens by the federal government in history. Some experts have speculated that once the system envisioned by S. 269 is in place, the scope of the identity card could be expanded to include information of a highly personal nature, such as credit and spending history and medical, educational, and social records....

Why would Congress and the Clinton Administration consider such a plan? Some Americans believe that America is in the midst of an illegal immigration crisis. Politicians want to show their constituents that they are taking strong action against illegal immigration. These politicians argue that the best way to control illegal immigration is to give the government the right to approve all employee hiring in America. By using advanced technology to register, track and store information on every citizen, they argue, it will be easy to spot illegal immigrants.

Senator Dianne Feinstein, an original drafter of the proposal, recently explained in a Capitol Hill magazine that it is her intention to see Congress immediately implement a national identity system where every American is required to carry a card with a "magnetic strip on which the bearer's unique voice, retina pattern, or fingerprint is digitally encoded...."

Source: patriots@kaiwan.com (accessed 10 October 1995).

Militias: Monitoring the Movement

An Analysis of Militias in America

In April 1995, the Center for Democratic Renewal, based in Atlanta, Georgia, issued a summation of what it considered the main characteristics of militias:

Summary

1. Militias have a dual strategy: to organize paramilitary groups while denying that they do so.
2. They deliberately mislead the media and the public.
3. They appear to violate laws against paramilitary groups in at least 24 states.

4. They are connected and organized even when they say they aren't.

5. Their agenda is racist and anti-Semitic even when they say it isn't.

6. They are linked to mainstream politicians who legitimize their cause.

7. They are prone to violence and not only organized for defensive purposes. They pose a serious threat to our society.

8. They use a "Leaderless Resistance" model in which a small cell of people commit the violence while other members often don't know about the cell or the violence.

9. They will probably commit more violence. Oklahoma City may be just the beginning. Janet Reno's personal security should be sharply increased.

10. Their recorded telephone lines (hatelines) and literature promised to make April 19 a "Day of Remembrance."

11. We do not need new laws to stop paramilitary organizing but better enforcement of existing ones. There are laws in 24 states banning paramilitary groups like militias.

Source: Center for Democratic Renewal, "An Analysis of Militia in America," 25 April 1995, 1.

The U.S. Senate Investigates

Given the concerns that the Oklahoma City bombing might be linked to the intensifying militia movement, the Subcommittee on Terrorism, Technology, and Government Information of the Senate Committee on the Judiciary decided to launch an investigation. At a hearing held on 15 June 1995 in Washington, D.C., the committee members heard testimony from militia members and those monitoring them, such as state district attorneys. The following information appears here: the original news release from Chairman Arlen Specter announcing the hearing (labeled evidence A), testimony from public officials involved in monitoring the militias (labeled evidence B), and testimony from leaders in the militia movement (labeled evidence C).

Source for the following: U.S. Senate, Judiciary Subcommittee on Terrorism, Technology, and Government Information, 104th Congress, 1st session, 15 June 1995. Obtained from the office of Senator Richard Shelby (Republican, Alabama).

Evidence A

SENATOR SPECTER HOLDS HEARING ON MILITIA GROUPS

Washington, D.C., June 15—To investigate the citizen militia movement in America, the Judiciary Subcommittee on Terrorism, Technology and Government Information will hold a hearing today, chaired by U.S. Senator Arlen Specter (R-PA).

"In the wake of April's tragic bombing in Oklahoma City, the militia movement has received increased public attention," Senator Specter said. "My concern is not about the simple existence of these groups, but about the connection between these groups and acts of violence against the government and law enforcement officials."

The focus of today's hearing is to examine the magnitude of these organizations, the nature of their activities, the reasons for their existence, and the extent to which they pose a threat to American citizens. This is the fourth in a series of hearings held by Senator Specter to examine terrorism.

"The right of free association is protected. However, when those words or associations are combined with acts or threats of imminent violence, the protections of the Constitution are lost. The rights of the American people to be safe and the government to perform its duties must take precedence. There is a clear distinction between political dissent and discourse and violence based on a political belief," the Pennsylvania Senator said.

In its most recent report, the private watchdog group Klanwatch stated that at least 224 militia groups operate in the United States, and 45 have ties to neo-Nazi and other white supremacist organizations.

"The Constitution provides expressly for the freedom of speech and association through the First Amendment and the right to bear arms through the Second Amendment. However, inherent in the Constitution's protection of 'ordered liberty' is the right of government to restrict the exercise of those freedoms if they are found to pose a 'clear and present danger' to the public," Senator Specter said.

Evidence B

The following statement was presented by Arlen Specter (R, Pa.), the Chairman of the Subcommittee on Terrorism, Technology, and Government Information:

Today's hearing has been called to examine the militia movement in the United States. I am glad, seemingly at long last, to be able to convene this hearing. Immediately following the tragic bombing in Oklahoma City, I stated publicly that I would convene a series of hearings in this Subcommittee on, among other topics, the nature and extent of the terrorist threat in this country, the counter-terrorism legislation, which has since been passed by the Senate, the militia movement, and the role of the federal government in the Waco, Texas, and Ruby Ridge, Idaho incidents.

To date, we have held hearings on the first two subjects, as well as an additional hearing on bomb-making manuals available over the Internet. Today's hearing was originally scheduled for May 25, but because of continuous votes on the Budget Resolution, which would have precluded an effective hearing, it was postponed and rescheduled for today. It is my hope that in the near future we will conduct hearings on Waco and Ruby Ridge.

In the wake of April's tragic bombing in Oklahoma City, the militia movement has received increased public attention. The objective of this hearing is to examine the magnitude of these organizations, the nature of their activities, the reasons for their existence and the extent to which they pose a threat to this country.

In its most recent report, the private watchdog group Klanwatch stated that at least 224 militias operate in this country, and that 45 have ties to neo-Nazi and other white supremacist organizations. According to information gathered by watchdog organizations, from which the Subcommittee has received large amounts of information and with whom we have been in extensive contact, militias are active in 39 states and are rumored to be present in all 50 states. These militias flourish despite the fact that 17 states prohibit the formation of militias, 17 others, including Pennsylvania, prohibit paramilitary training, and 7 additional states prohibit both anti-militia and anti-paramilitary training. Obviously, some militias have been formed in states where their very existence is illegal.

It is not, however, the simple existence of these groups that gives rise to concern; rather, it is the connection between these groups and acts of violence against the government and law enforcement officials. Certain militia members are on public record as advocating the "trial" and hanging of public officials for "treason" and have condoned the terrible bombing in Oklahoma City.

Words alone, no matter how odious or ludicrous, are protected by the First Amendment. The right to associate with whomever one chooses is similarly protected. However, when those words or associations are combined with acts or threats of imminent violence, the protections of the Constitution are lost, and the rights of the American people to be safe and the government to perform its duties must take precedent. There is a clear distinction between political dissent or discourse and violence based on a political belief.

Americans became all too aware of the volatile nature of the beliefs of some who associate themselves with the militia movement soon after the bombing in Oklahoma City. Media portrayals of militia groups and their relationship with federal, state, and local law enforcement, however, have consisted primarily of conjecture and sound bites.

It is apparent that not all who associate themselves with militias are violent, or racist, or hate the government. These people express legitimate concerns for the abridgment of certain rights by the government, and the lack of accountability for government decisions and actions. There are militia groups in my home state of Pennsylvania. The May 17, 1995, edition of the *Washington Post* included an extensive piece on the effect of the militia movement on the small town of

Meadville, Pennsylvania. From the article it was obvious that not all those who belonged to the militia or sympathized with their positions advocated violence. Yet, many were clearly concerned about the infringement of the government on their rights.

The Constitution provides expressly for the freedom of speech and association through the First Amendment and the right to bear arms through the Second Amendment. The Constitution, however, is not a "suicide pact." Inherent in the Constitution's protection of "ordered liberty" is the right of government to restrict the exercise of those freedoms if they are conducted in such a manner as to pose a "clear and present danger" to the public.

The other party to this issue is law enforcement, whether state, local or federal. Our law enforcement officials must be able to carry out their duties without the threat of violent acts against them by any American. Disagreement with law enforcement officials' legitimate and legal performance of their duties is never justification for violent acts or resistance by any American. The Constitution provides safeguards that prevent the abuse of Americans by law enforcement. Congress also has an oversight role, especially the Judiciary Committee, to oversee federal law enforcement. These safeguards against the abuse of police power must be balanced against both public safety interests and the rights of the accused or targeted group.

The duty of Congress to oversee federal law enforcement agencies must not be taken lightly. Unfortunately, there is some argument that Congress' failure to conduct hearings inquiring into the facts of Waco, Texas, and the Randy Weaver case in Ruby Ridge, Idaho, was perhaps a contributing cause of the tragic situation in Oklahoma City. For this reason, I believe it is important for the Judiciary Committee to hold oversight hearings on the Waco and Ruby Ridge incidents as soon as possible. No matter what happened at Waco there can be no possible justification for the bombing of the Federal Building in Oklahoma City.

I do not believe there is any justification whatsoever for the slaughter of innocent men, women, and children as occurred on April 19. The bomb not only blew away a building, but devastated the lives of millions of Americans. I cannot understand how anyone, aware of the devastation caused by that act, can say he "understands" what led someone to commit such a deed, as Norman Olson of the Michigan Militia, one of our witnesses today, stated on the "60 Minutes" television program the Sunday after the bombing.

Federal, state and local law enforcement and the militia movement are equally represented with witnesses at this hearing. It is my hope that we will have a full discussion, and come away with a better understanding of all sides. We will also hear from members of both Houses of Congress who take decidedly different views of the militia movement. This is the type of full, open discourse encouraged and facilitated by the Constitution, and it is the foundation of our democracy.

We have a large number of witnesses to shed light on the militia movement. We are honored to have on our first panel two distinguished Senators, Max Baucus of Montana and Carl Levin of Michigan. Our second panel consists of law enforcement officials who are knowledgeable about the militia movement: Assistant Director Bob Bryant of the FBI; Deputy Associate Director Jim Brown of the Bureau of Alcohol, Tobacco and Firearms; Colonel Fred Mills, Superintendent of the Missouri State Highway Patrol; Richard Romley, the county prosecutor from Maricopa County, Arizona; and John Bohlman, the county prosecutor of Musselshell County, Montana. Our third panel today consists of several militia founders and members: Ken Adams from Michigan; Norman Olson, also from Michigan; James Johnson from Ohio; and two witnesses from Montana, John Trochmann and Robert Fletcher, who are joined by their legal counsel, John DeCamp, of Omaha, Nebraska. We welcome all of our witnesses and look forward to their testimony.

The following statement was presented by James L. Brown, deputy associate director for criminal enforcement within the Bureau of Alcohol, Tobacco, and Firearms:

Mr. Chairman and members of the Subcommittee, I appreciate this opportunity to discuss with you what ATF has learned about some of the militia groups in the United States.

Since the tragic bombing of the Alfred P. Murrah Building in Oklahoma City on April 19, much of the American public has learned for the first time through the media about the militia movement.

ATF has a long history of working to prevent violence associated with firearms and explosives violations. ATF's unique jurisdiction over the federal firearms laws allows us to focus on armed career criminals and drug traffickers, and international firearms traffickers. Our expertise in explosives led to the discovery of a key piece of evidence in the World Trade Center bombing, ultimately bringing the perpetrators to justice.

Paramilitary terrorist activity within the United States is not a new phenomenon. Its origins in the second half of this century date back to 1960, with the establishment of the Minuteman organization. The organization founded and coordinated by Robert DePugh, was reportedly intended to resist the spread of communism in the United States by the use of guerrilla tactics. ATF conducted over 60 investigations nationwide of members of the Minutemen from the late 1960s to the early 1980s.

From 1976 to the mid-1980s, ATF conducted 43 investigations of members and associates of the Posse Comitatus, a group opposed to "government intrusion." On February 13, 1983, a member of the Posse Comitatus in Medina, North Dakota, succeeded in bringing the group to national notoriety. On that date, [Gordon] Kahl and others engaged in an armed confrontation with federal and local law enforcement officers, resulting in the death of two U.S. marshals and the wounding of three other federal, county, and local enforcement officers. Before he was finally apprehended, Kahl shot and killed the sheriff of Lawrence County, Arkansas. The ideology of the Posse Comitatus is very similar to that of today's militias.

At this point, I'd like to give you some examples of the types of allegations that have been found in some of the militia propaganda in this country. These are not necessarily representative of the views of all militia members, however. Certainly there are members of militia groups who are upstanding, law-abiding citizens.

As a result of criminal investigations conducted by ATF, along with information received from other law enforcement agencies, open source documents, and publications distributed by militias, ATF estimates militias exist in approximately 40 states.

A May 11, 1995, Gannett News Service article quoting the Center for Democratic Renewal, a private Atlanta group that monitors militias, reports that there are up to 100,000 militia members in at least 30 states.

Accurate estimates reflecting the total number of militias, the number and specific states involved, and the total militia membership nationwide are not available.

As you are aware, the incident in Oklahoma City has generated much speculation in the media about militia groups and anti-government views. While we do not investigate groups based on their beliefs, we do pursue investigations on individual suspects based on evidence of violations of the law. Through these investigations we have gained some insight into militias.

During the past decade, several national and global events provided the environment for the formation of militias. Militias include members with a spectrum of views. They range from ideas which are extreme, violent and paranoid, to active opposition to the firearms laws. Some militias believe that they are the "people's response" to a wide range of issues that include the supposed takeover of the United States by the United Nations. Most are primarily concerned about firearms laws.

In April 1994, a militia promoter called for an armed march on Washington, D.C., to arrest members of congress unless they complied with a list of demands including the repeal of gun control legislation. Although the march was later canceled, this proposed march fostered the concept of militias nationwide.

One theory promoted by some of today's militia members is that the democratic United States will be replaced by the New World Order. A national militia speaker furthers the notion that the Illuminati (a group of national and international government and military officials) will round up all non-Christian and Christian patriots and confiscate their guns, and haul them off in black helicopters to concentration camps. A 1994 news article quotes this spokesperson as saying that urban street gangs would be part of the "home invasion of the

patriots." Also included in this invasion force would be foreign mercenaries, including Nepalese gurkhas and royal Hong Kong police. The
operation would supposedly be controlled by the Federal Emergency
Management Agency, a multi-jurisdictional task force comprised of
the "Fincen Police," ATF, and the FBI, and other federal enforcement
agencies.

Militias apparently forming independently across the United
States, are able to share many of the same philosophies and agendas,
due to an efficient networking system. This system utilizes militia-ori-
ented publications, computer bulletin board services, commercial radio
stations, videos, public forums, and short-wave radio to spread their
rhetoric.

Federal authorities are likened to Nazis and are called baby killers
by some militia advocates. Hateful descriptions of the president and
the attorney general of the United States, found in some militia-related
letters and literature are so vile that they cannot be repeated here. The
most recent propaganda circulating among some militia supporters is
that the president ordered the Oklahoma City bombing.

Federal and local enforcement personnel have been threatened,
harassed, assaulted, and shot. A white supremacist with militia lean-
ings shot and wounded a Missouri state trooper in September1994. In
November 1994 an adherent of a militia philosophy shot Nashville
metro police officers when they stopped him on suspicion of drunken
driving.

ATF has successfully investigated and charged several members of
the present-day militia movement with violations of federal firearms
and explosives laws. I want to emphasize that we do not investigate
these people based on their beliefs; we pursue investigations on individual suspects based on violations or intended violations of the law.
I would like to highlight a couple of those investigations:

American Patriots. On March 24, 1994, the Las Vegas Metro Police
responded to a report of shots being fired on a Las Vegas street. The
officers then encountered two armed suspects with a Mak 90 semi-
automatic rifle and numerous hand grenades. ATF's assistance was
requested, and a federal search warrant was executed at the suspects'
residences, yielding numerous hand grenades, pipe bombs, and other
explosives, along with drugs, illegal firearms, and thousands of rounds
of ammunition. Upon questioning, the suspects claimed membership
with the American patriots and affiliation with the ARM (presumably
Aryan Resistance Movement). The suspects stated that war had been
declared against the police. They were hostile toward the ATF agents
and made several references to Waco. Both have been convicted of
possession of unregistered machine-guns.

American Citizen Alliance and the Liberty Group. While purchas-
ing 50 ammunition magazines from a firearms dealer in Maitland,
Florida, a suspect made references to militia activity while in the presence of a police detective. He spoke about a plan in place to kill federal

judges, members of Congress, and special agents. He also advised that he had 60 Ruger rifles. An inquiry into the suspect's background revealed his status as a convicted felon, and he was arrested by ATF on October 15, 1994. At the time of his arrest, he had a Ruger rifle with a silencer. The suspect has five associates, also members of the American Citizen Alliance, who are defendants in federal cases as the result of their role in placing unlawful liens against the properties of federal district court judges. The original suspect pled guilty to possession of an unregistered machine-gun and was sentenced on April 19, 1995.

ATF has joined with Department of Justice agencies (FBI and DEA) and other treasury agencies in the fight against violent crime. ATF has been at the forefront of that battle due to our unique position of being vested with the enforcement of the federal firearms and explosives laws and the regulation of those industries.

ATF's expertise in explosives enforcement has been well tested throughout the last 25 years. ATF personnel, through years of experience and advanced training, have developed unparalleled proficiency in post-blast analysis and the logistics involved with investigating post-blast crime scenes of any size. This experience is recognized and highly regarded by investigators within the enforcement community.

To strengthen its investigative capacity, ATF is researching the effects of large-scale vehicle bombs. Through this enforcement will derive much-needed information relative to the explosives signature, blast effect, debris distance, and residue retrieval. The analysis of such characteristics and the development of computer modeling of such explosions will have a significant impact on the development of investigative leads in connection with large and complex bombings such as the World Trade Center and Oklahoma City.

In conclusion, the men and women of ATF investigate and apprehend some of the most violent criminals in America on a daily basis. During our extensive planning for the execution of search and arrest warrants, we anticipate—and expect—violators to be armed with firearms or to have in their possession destructive devices. In fact, the possession or use of a firearm or bomb is the primary element of proof for many of the statutes we enforce. Unfortunately, and sadly, the responsibility of apprehending the nation's most violent criminals has taken its toll on our agency, resulting in the deaths of 183 special agents in the line of duty.

Mr. Chairman, I would like to take this opportunity to thank you for allowing me to speak here today on behalf of ATF. We commend your leadership and efforts to pursue initiatives that will make the American society safer and more secure. I would also like to assure you that ATF will continue to actively investigate all crimes, such as those that I have mentioned, that involve violations of the federal firearms, explosives, and arson laws. ATF is committed to assisting state and local law enforcement in its continuing fight against crime and violence. Thank you for your time. I would be happy to answer any questions.

The following statement was presented by Richard M. Romley, an attorney in Maricopa County in Phoenix, Arizona:

Mr. Chairman and members of the subcommittee, thank you very much for giving me the opportunity to appear before you today, and to discuss with you the growing concern about militia movements in the United States; and more specifically, in my home state of Arizona.

As Maricopa county attorney I am the chief prosecutor in a county whose population is approximately two and one-half million people. It encompasses twenty-three cities and towns, including the city of Phoenix. I am responsible for more than two hundred and fifty prosecuting attorneys whose primary role is to investigate and prosecute the more than forty thousand felony offenses reported to my office each year.

The horror of Oklahoma City has unfortunately thrust Arizona onto the front pages of our nation's newspapers. As most of us know, the accused bomber—Timothy Mcveigh—lived in Arizona. We also know that numerous associates of Mr. Mcveigh also reside in Arizona and it has been reported that they have connections with various militia organizations.

Arizona, like other states, is experiencing a proliferation of militias. Thirteen groups have recently been identified. Some leaders of these groups spew messages of hate and conspiracy, messages rooted in anti-Semitism and racism, messages which create images of "black helicopters" and international military troops hiding in caves waiting for a signal to usurp our democracy. However, these messages are so outrageous that they often fall on deaf ears, even among their own members. Therefore, we must be careful not to label all members of militias as supporters of the ranting of these extremists. Our focus must be on the fanatic fringe of the militia movement who maliciously seek to sow the seeds of violent discontent.

It is this fanatical fringe claiming to be patriotic Americans who attack by intimidation and violence the very core of our democracy. In my jurisdiction we have had direct experience with some of these extremists. My office has prosecuted numerous individuals whose fanaticism was based on racial or religious prejudice and a desire to violently destroy confidence in our democratically elected government. Let me tell you about one case. It involved a member of a white-supremacist group called the "Arizona White Battalion" who was also associated with a group called "the freemen," a tax protesting, anti-government organization. This person conspired to place bombs at more than thirty-seven locations. His targets included synagogues, day care centers and government buildings. His plan was to detonate the bombs during peak occupation of these buildings. Fortunately, he was apprehended before he could carry out his plan, and is now serving a long prison sentence. As horrible as his intentions were, they become even more troublesome when we consider that this potential mad bomber was only sixteen years old when he first laid down his plan of destruction. Sixteen years old when the seeds of hate had already taken root.

So-called "patriots" refuse to acknowledge that in a representative democracy you do not challenge laws by insurrection, you bring your grievances to the ballot box or to the courts. In their quest for notoriety, power and financial gain these fanatical individuals shroud their insurrection in patriotism. It is difficult to explain their underlying motives. They have declared war on the very system that guarantees them the freedoms they demand. It is as if, in the absence of a real threat or enemy, they have turned inward against their own government.

In the face of such attacks it may be tempting to react quickly and harshly. This is where I urge caution. We must not be stampeded into quick, but ill-conceived action because of the horror of immediate events. We must engage in calm and thoughtful deliberation before we choose our course of action. It must be consistent with our constitutionally guaranteed freedoms, for we as Americans, have the right to question and criticize our government.

If there is one common denominator among the extremists in these groups, it is that they all strive for the opportunity of martyrdom. We must be careful not to give them that opportunity. If our decisions are made in haste, we help create false martyrs around whom they could rally the disaffected and misguided. We must ensure that government does not self-fulfill the prophecy of those who seek to destroy.

However, we in law enforcement must be vigilant. When these extremists encourage change through violent means rather than just talk, we need to step up and say enough is enough. If an individual steps over the line of lawlessness, we must act swiftly. As a prosecutor I have no patience with those who break the law or who encourage others to do so. As one who is on the front line in the battle against crime and extremism, I applaud the senate's passage of the anti-terrorism legislation. You have given law enforcement tools with which to combat this menace.

Specifically, I support the increased penalties, the additional investigatory tools, the authorization to hire law enforcement officers, and the commitment to finance a new anti-terrorism center to facilitate the sharing of information among law enforcement agencies.

I also strongly support habeas corpus reform. As a prosecutor I feel the frustration of delayed justice. For too long habeas corpus has been used by the convicted as a tactical device of obstruction rather than as a substantive review of appropriate legal issues. Your passage of this reform is long overdue. This legislation will help ensure that our citizens need not live in fear that horrors such as the World Trade Center bombing or the federal courthouse bombing in Oklahoma will occur in their communities. Protecting our right to be free of crime and terrorism is not a partisan issue. I again applaud the senate for its bipartisan support of these anti-terrorism measures. I would encourage the House of Representatives and the president to adopt this same bipartisan approach and send a clear message to those who would undermine the rule of law that we will protect ourselves and our democracy against their fanaticism.

Thank you again for giving me this opportunity. I would be happy to answer any questions that the committee may wish to ask.

The following statement was presented by John Bohlman, county attorney in Musselshell County, Montana:

In my day to day work activities since becoming county attorney on January 1, 1995, I have little contact with any members of the Militia of Montana or members of any other militia group. Even prior to my taking office as county attorney, I was aware that the militia activity in Montana was primarily taking place in the western part of Montana. As Noxon, Montana, is over 500 miles northwest of my hometown of Roundup, Montana, I was not very attentive to Militia of Montana activities. I was much more concerned with the eastern Montana "Freemen" who were very active in Musselshell and Garfield Counties. I believe that one of the reasons that the "Freemen" made their most violent threats and took their most aggressive actions in Garfield County is the fact that Garfield County has a total population of less than 1,500 people and that the total law enforcement presence consists of a sheriff and his undersheriff. Fugitives from state and federal warrants are currently making their base of operation a log home in Musselshell County where the total population is about 4,400 people and the Sheriff's Department consists of five officers.

In spite of the absence of a militia organization in Musselshell County, I have had direct dealings with the Militia of Montana and other militia and "patriot" group members since March 3, 1995. During the week beginning February 27, 1995, the Musselshell County Sheriff's Department was on alert that an organization known as the "Freemen," and/or members of similar organizations, were planning to kidnap a judge and/or county prosecutor in eastern Montana. As the information was related to me by the Sheriff of Musselshell County, the federal agency supplying the warning stated that it was believed that Garfield County Attorney Nick Mumion, the District Court Judge that served Garfield County, and Musselshell County's District Judge Roy C. Rodeghiero were considered the most likely targets, and that the victim was to be put on trial before the organization members, convicted, executed by hanging, and that the whole event was to be videotaped. Based on that information, the Musselshell County Sheriff placed reserve deputies in the Musselshell County Courthouse to increase security for Judge Rodeghiero. The Judge was also accompanied to work in the mornings and home in the evenings by Sheriff's deputies.

On the afternoon of March 3, 1995, two men were arrested for violation of the state's concealed weapon law, a misdemeanor, after they had been stopped by a deputy for driving a pickup with no license plates. (Earlier, one of the two men had been in the county courthouse and had spent time on each floor, including being just outside the judge's office.) That stop led to the deputy finding that the driver also had no driver's license. When the two men exited the pickup, the deputy learned that both men were carrying concealed weapons without permits, and both men were placed under arrest. Shortly after the arrest, the Sheriff's deputies learned that the two men had in their possession a large amount of weapons and ammunition which included bullets that would pierce class II body armor commonly worn by law enforcement officers, approximately 30 plastic "flex-cuffs" and a role of duct tape, approximately $26,000 in cash and approximately $60,000 in gold and silver coins, a video camera and film and a 35 mm. Minolta camera with additional lenses, and sophisticated radio communication equipment. At the time of this discovery, the deputies concluded that they had disrupted the attempt to kidnap and kill a judge about which we had been warned by a federal agency. A few days after the arrest, a hand drawn map carried in the pocket of one of the men, Frank Ellena, was identified as a map of the town of Jordan, Montana. The map clearly marked for identification the home of the Sheriff and the home of the county prosecutor, Nick Mumion, who had successfully convicted a member of the Freeman group who was sentenced to ten (10) years in prison.

At approximately 6 o'clock p.m. on March 3, 1995, and only about 90 minutes after the first two men were jailed, two vehicles containing six men entered the parking area of the Musselshell County Sheriff's Department and parked facing the door in what appeared to the deputies to be an effort to control entrance to the Sheriff's Department. The first deputy to see the vehicles believed that when the vehicles entered the parking area, at least one occupant in each vehicle was speaking into a remote, hand held radio transmitter/receiver. (When the first two men were stopped, they too were talking into a remote, hand held radio transmitter/receiver.) Two men remained in one car, and three men entered the jail and made what the deputies described as a demand that the evidence recently taken be turned over to them. The jail lacks security due to its age and design, so the evidence, guns, etc., was in clear view of the three men. As the demand or request was being made, one of the deputies saw a gun concealed on one of the men when that man's jacket opened. The two deputies immediately placed the three individuals under arrest. It was believed by the deputies that these three men and the two men in the car outside were coconspirators of the first two men arrested.

After securing the three individuals arrested inside the jail, the two deputies went outside to the white car which contained two men. According to the deputies, one of the two men was speaking into a hand-held radio transmitter/receiver as the deputies approached and both men locked the doors of the two-door car. The officers had their weapons drawn and demanded that the two men exit the car. The two men refused and one continued to talk into a radio. One deputy saw a gun tucked into the front of the passenger's pants and the driver began unzipping his jacket as if reaching for a gun. The driver's side window was broken by one deputy and the passenger then opened his door. Both men were placed under arrest and a check of both men showed that both men were carrying handguns and that the driver did have a handgun in a shoulder holster under his jacket.

I learned later that night that the passenger in the two-door car was John Trochmann, a founder of the Militia of Montana. I did not know anything about him until I read the newspaper the following day and then read an Esquire magazine interview with John Trochmann. Within an hour after the arrest of John Trochmann, telephone calls began coming into the jail from all over Montana, and from other states as well. In the week that followed, the jail received hundreds of telephone calls from all over the United States demanding that the arrested individuals be released and making threats against the Sheriff and his deputies. My office telephone was ringing continuously and my secretary and I received approximately 40 threats on our lives and threats that included my secretary's family. One caller identified himself as being with the Militia of Montana and made threatening comments about my secretary's adopted Korean daughter. Because of the racial comments made by some of the callers, my secretary drove to another state during the night to hide her daughter. One of the deputies sent his family out-of-town after he received a call that neither of the two arresting deputies could find a hole deep enough to hide in. Some callers stated that armed men from militia organizations in various states would come to Roundup to see that justice was done to those of us responsible for the arrest of the "fine patriot John Trochmann." Many callers stated that they knew my phones were "bugged" by the FBI and that these 7 men had been arrested on false charges as part of an FBI scheme to get John Trochmann into custody. Interestingly, Randy Trochmann, a cofounder of MOM, gave press releases disavowing any link between John Trochmann and MOM and the "Freemen" organization. He stated that the "Freemen" were extremist and that John Trochmann was in Musselshell County to attempt to negotiate a settlement of the tensions between the "Freemen" and local law enforcement. However, facts sharply contradict those press releases. In the January 24, 1995, issue of *Taking Aim*, MOM's newsletter, John Trochmann wrote an extensive article explaining how to set up replacement governments at the county level and how to create the so-called assets that are the basis of money crimes being actively committed by at least two of the "Freemen" operating out of Musselshell County. Mr. Trochmann even thanked three "Freemen" leaders for teaching these techniques and he encouraged readers to go and study with the "Freemen" so that the techniques could be implemented. The article went so far as to state that MOM would help interested individuals make arrangements to spend the necessary time with the "Freemen."

In concluding my written statement about the militias, I want to state that on a personal level I am opposed to such organizations because I believe they are attempting to impose their political will by force and the threat of force. It is impossible to lump them into a single classification at this time because the different groups have some common ground, but they also have very distinct variations. My opinion is that they are predominately racist and that they are composed of members who do not fundamentally agree with equality of citizens and the principle of one-person, one-vote. However, as a prosecutor for the State of Montana, my only public concern is that laws not be broken and that when the laws are broken, those criminals responsible are apprehended and dealt with fairly by our criminal legal system. I am concerned that militias will spawn lawbreakers who will be immune from prosecution due to actual violent resistance by the lawbreakers' militia associates or due to the threat of violence readily projected by MOM and the North America Militia. I believe my fear has been realized already in the person of John Trochmann. Mr. Trochmann and an associate recently committed what I consider to have been misdemeanor assaults on Shaun McLaughlin and his camera man, both TV news reporters from Oklahoma City, while the two reporters were on a public road. I believe that no charges resulted from that event. When Mr. Trochmann was in the Musselshell County Jail he claimed to have a concealed weapon permit. However, the permit had no expiration date when state law requires a 4 year expiration on such permits, "none" fills the space where the person is to identify a social security number, and the permit was not recorded as required with the Montana Department of Justice. However, the state attorney general's office declined prosecution. At MOM meetings and in public statements, Mr. Trochmann has made it clear that he and the Militia of Montana are protecting Gordon Sellner from arrest. Gordon Sellner is charged with shooting a deputy sheriff. The use of force, deception, or intimidation to purposely prevent or obstruct anyone from performing an act that might aid in the apprehension of Mr. Sellner is a crime in Montana. Similarly, Calvin Greenup was able to avoid arrest for crimes he committed in Rivalli County, Montana, for quite some time because of his violent threats and leadership position with the North America Militia.

FREEMAN

For the past four years, the activities of Rodney Skurdal have become bolder and bolder and more threatening in regards to violence toward public servants. Mr. Skurdal is a Montana leader of a group which Montanans refer to as "Freemen." The name comes from their use of the term "freeman character" when identifying themselves. The group particularly targets county government officials and judges as traitors who are to be executed. The group members reveal racism in their own writings, and their version of law combines the Magna Carta, the Bible, old English common-law, and a 19th century state constitution. They also apply different aspects of the United States Constitution to varying classes of citizenship as identified by the group. In Garfield County, Montana, bounties were posted by the

"Freemen" for various public officials and those officials were to be executed by hanging. Around the state of Montana, there are a variety of felony warrants for the arrest of Rodney Skurdal and LeRoy Schweitzer stemming from their Freemen related criminal acts. However, they continue to operate out of a log home in Musselshell County that the IRS "seized" for failure to pay taxes, but from which Rodney Skurdal has never been evicted. There is also a federal warrant for the arrest of LeRoy Schweitzer.

The "Freemen" are promoting and selling bogus money orders which they claim must be accepted as payment of debts. Rodney Skurdal recently issued a $20,000,000 bogus money order which was deposited in a bank by the mayor of the town of Cascade, Montana. "Certified Bank Checks" signed by LeRoy Schweitzer on check blanks printed by Skurdal and Schweitzer and written on a closed account for which they never had signature authorization, are being sent to militiamen, "Freemen", and other anti-government activists around the country. The "Freemen" publish in a local newspaper what they consider to be proper notice to claimed debtors, including the United States Government and agencies of the government, and then make their judgment based on those published notices. They also publish notice of the creation of their courts. I have attached as Exhibit 4a a copy of a page of our local newspaper dated June 7, 1995, in which various notices are given and in which a group in Michigan published notice of their creation of their "One Supreme Court in Common Law venue." Recently, the "Freemen" documents declare that their courts have been recognized by the 10th Circuit Court of Appeals. However, I have read the opinion which they cite, and I don't see any of the claims made by the "Freemen" as being stated in that opinion.

I recently charged six (6) "Freemen" for felony crimes committed in Musselshell County, Montana. Those charges stem from a written demand they made on a Justice of the Peace that he appear in their court located at the address of Rodney Skurdal's log home, and that the Justice of the Peace produce evidence and prove the pending misdemeanor cases against two "Freemen" for carrying concealed weapons. I have attached copies of two of the documents which led to the charges as Exhibit 5. I have also attached a copy of the new Montana law under which I charged the six "Freemen" as Exhibit 6. To this date, only one of the men has been arrested and he is presently released from jail on $7,500 bail.

I don't believe that the promotion and creation of parallel courts by the "Freemen" can be comprehended by my written explanation. Therefore, I am attaching as Exhibit 7 the most recent documents received by myself and others in Musselshell County. To assist the reader, I have underlined the parts I consider most revealing. The one million dollar check referred to in the documents was not actually among the documents received by our county clerk and recorder. The most astounding thing about these documents is that they appear to have been also sent to the 9th Circuit Court of Appeals for those justices to sign one of the documents above the signatures of our local self-appointed "Freemen" justices.

Finally, because the documents attached as Exhibit 7 claim that Frank Ellena was a prisoner of war and that his arrest was an act of war, I have attached as Exhibit 8 some pages of transcripts from Mr. Ellena's appearance in district court for arraignment and bail reduction. Although Mr. Ellena was very cooperative and stated that the terms and conditions of his bail reduction were agreeable to him, he now claims that he was justifiably lying in order to escape our "evil trap."

The community in which I live is under an unusual strain. Many people are strongly objectionable to the actions of the "Freemen" and they strongly object that many residents who are on public assistance or otherwise take advantage of public services are so vocal with their opposition to taxes, county officials, and government in general. However, there is also a fear that should one speak out against these individuals, that one's property or person will be harmed. The liens filed by the "Freemen" may seem like a joke unless you are the person attempting to sell your property and you learn you can't buy title insurance because a Freeman has a million dollar lien filed against the property. The community is further aggravated because the most militant individuals are able to break laws without punishment. It is particularly frustrating to see some people continue to not pay taxes for many years with what appears to be impunity because those people threaten violence. If this trend continues, more and more people will believe that the Freemen interpretation of law is correct; and even if they don't believe that they will at least see the obvious: that guns are cheaper than taxes!

The following statement was made by Senator Max Baucus (Democrat, Montana), the ranking minority member of the Subcommittee on Terrorism, Technology, and Government Information:

Mr. Chairman, thank you for calling this hearing and inviting me to testify.

Since the Oklahoma City bombing, we have learned a great deal about the so-called militia movement in this country. I do not claim any special expertise on the national phenomenon. But I have watched it develop in my own state, and I am very pleased to relay what I know to the Subcommittee.

In essence, I would like to address three questions. First, what are the Montana militia groups like, and who leads them? Second, what problems, if any, have they caused in Montana? And third, what solutions to these problems exist?

First, however, I would say this. I understand anger with government. Often people are right to be angry at government. But those who express their anger through hate rhetoric and violence are few. The vast, vast majority of Montanans reject hate, obey the law and cherish our peaceful, democratic values. That is true for conservatives, liberals,

Democrats, Republicans, property owners, environmentalists, gun controllers, NRA members, everybody. Militia groups are the exception; and they are a small exception.

MILITIA AND FREEMEN

Now let me begin by describing the groups and their leaders.

The groups have a fairly small following. Law enforcement officers who have studied the militia and freemen closely believe there are about 25–30 hard-core leaders, while about 500 people have casually attended militia meetings at one time or another.

The movement as a whole is made up of three loosely connected groups. One is the so-called "Militia of Montana," based in the northwestern town of Noxon, and led by Mr. John Trochmann and Mr. Bob Fletcher. A second is the "North American Volunteer Militia," several hundred miles to the south in Darby. And the third is the so-called "freemen," active in large, thinly-populated Eastern Montana counties like Musselshell and Garfield.

The Militia of Montana is the largest and best known. The Darby group and the freemen are much smaller. However, the three have very evident links. The Militia of Montana newsletter, *Taking Aim*, ran an article this past year praising the freemen philosophy and offering to bring militia members to meet them for training. Mr. Trochmann himself showed up heavily armed in the Musselshell County seat of Roundup after two freemen leaders were arrested last March. The leaders [of the militia and freemen movements] tend to share two fundamental beliefs. One is their fear of government. This ranges all the way from "world government" and international conspiracies to common obligations of citizenship. An example is Musselshell County Freemen leader Rodney Skurdal—now ducking a warrant for tax evasion— who offered the following "proof' of government tyranny in a document he filed at the County Courthouse last year:

"A Social Security card/number, marriage licenses, drivers licenses, insurance, vehicle registration, welfare from the corporations, electrical inspections, permits to build your private home, income taxes, property taxes..."

The second is a deep strain of racism and anti-Semitism. Mr. Skurdal, who says marriage licenses are tyranny also believes people who are not white are "beasts;" only whites go to heaven; and Jews are children of Satan.

The Militia of Montana is a bit more cautious. Its public literature uses anti-Semitic code words like "shadow government" and "banking elites," rather than open attacks. When challenged, Militia leaders issue unconvincing quasi-denials of the type offered by Director Bob Fletcher:

"If the bulk of the banking elite are Jewish, is that anti-Semitic? The people who are doing this are the international banking elite, and if they are all Jews, so be it, but that's not the case. I don't care if they're Arabs or monkeys."

JOHN TROCHMANN AS EXAMPLE

Later today you will hear from Mr. John Trochmann, the founder of the "Militia of Montana." He is an interesting example of the movement's leadership.

Mr. Trochmann is a native of Minnesota. He moved to the small town of Noxon, Montana—population 350—in 1987. Here he can take advantage of his long association with the neo-Nazi "Aryan Nations," based about an hour's drive away in Hayden Lake, Idaho. Mr. Trochmann has denied this association. But Aryan Nations "President" Richard Butler stated in his letter on April 5th, and reaffirmed to the *Missoulian*, that Trochmann visited the compound many times and helped write the group's "code of conduct."

During his first years in Noxon, Mr. Trochmann promoted the views of the Aryan Nations and the freemen. A document he filed in the Sanders County Courthouse in January 26, 1992, is an example. In it, he claims citizenship in the "Republic of the State of Montana," and uses the Dred Scott decision to show that only "the white race" has Constitutional rights. He also explicitly repudiates the USA, saying:

"I am not now, nor have I ever been, a citizen of the United States, or a resident of its subordinate territories...I am not, nor have I ever been a member of the armed forces of the State of Montana or the United States...I have no Social Security account or taxpayer/employer account numbers, driver's license, or any other nexus with any City, County, State or Federal governments."

He found a more marketable agenda when he founded the "Militia of Montana" in February, 1994. He no longer talks about denying his country; instead he adopts a "patriot" agenda. He plays down his racial views—although he occasionally slips, as he did a few weeks ago when a constituent heard him railing against the "Jews Media." But most of the time he claims to be an ordinary American worried about an overly powerful federal government.

Mr. Trochmann's direction of the Militia, though, is just as alarming as his previous efforts. Militia mail order catalogs are full of videos and booklets which train people to use "improvised munitions," "booby traps," "sniper training," "espionage and sabotage," and so on.

In a country as big as ours, some disturbed people in our country are sure to use it. Last November, Mr. Trochmann told a journalist that the government might be planning a large and destructive event that would take place on April 19, 1995.

This was, of course, the date of the terrible Oklahoma City bombing. There may be no connection—but it is quite certain that people are reading what he puts out, many of them are disturbed, and some of them may well act on it.

THE ECONOMIC PRICE

The next question is what the "militia" movement has meant to Montana. Unfortunately, it has meant a lot.

Since the Oklahoma City bombing, Montana militia and freemen leaders have been all over the media. They have appeared on ABC, NBC, CNN, C-SPAN and CBS; in *USA Today*, the *New York Times* and the *Washington Post*; on Japanese TV, Australian radio, the BBC, German newspapers and probably more. They are doing a very good job of giving our quiet, beautiful state the image of a nest of violent kooks and radicals.

They hurt the Montana economy. In Ravalli County, where police and judges get regular threats from local militia leaders, the Stevensville Chamber of Commerce had to cancel its annual Balloon Festival this year. Tourism is in danger—I have already gotten letters from outsiders saying they intend to boycott Montana because of the militia presence. And economic development professionals say it is already getting harder to attract business.

THREATS TO LAW ENFORCEMENT AND ORDINARY CITIZENS

But the economic price is less than the price we pay in loss of our sense of public safety and security.

Since the militias formed, terrorist acts and anti-Semitic incidents have become noticeably more frequent. We have had two women's clinics bombed and burned. We have had a Jewish cemetery desecrated in Butte; an anti-Semitic daubing on a school wall in Big Timber; and a Jewish child taunted in Helena.

A constituent from Ravalli County wrote me in early April, referring to North American Volunteer Militia members:

"You see Freemen with guns in the post office, grocery store and gas stations. If it gets to any one of them that a person doesn't like the 'Freemen,' they will call or confront a person face to face. They tell people that 'we are all going to die like the Jews.'"

Threats against law enforcement have become routine in some areas. Garfield County, Attorney Nick Mumion recalls threats the "Freemen" made against him last year.

"They told me they weren't going to bother building a gallows. They were just going to let me swing from the bridge."

And Marshal Larry Rose in Darby had this experience when he pulled over a car with 1992 license plates last April 5th:

"They had weapons and they were shaking them at us and yelling that they were going to kill us. We backed off a little bit and then left because we could see that it could turn into a blood bath."

NO COMPROMISE ON RIGHTS

Now let us look at the solution to these problems. I believe it comes in three parts—

First, we must enforce the law. Paramilitary training is illegal in Montana. Tax evasion and threats against law enforcement are illegal everywhere, as far as I know. And Montana law enforcement knows very well who is violating these laws—whether it is the fellow in Darby threatening to shoot down helicopters, or the man in Musselshell with a four-year-old warrant out on him for tax evasion.

At least in Montana, we do not need new wire-tapping authority to deal with these crimes. We need not compromise our basic rights to free speech, to bear arms, to free association and to privacy in any way. We need to arrest the criminals. In some cases, they are so well-armed and so unstable that a small rural police department needs help in dealing with them. Perhaps some extra manpower or a new squad car. But that's about it.

ADDRESS FUNDAMENTAL CONCERNS

Second, we must address the concerns and frustration that lead some ordinary people—people who are not criminals or neo-Nazis—to consider joining militia groups.

When President Clinton visited Montana last week, he spoke out strongly against the militias. But he also took the time to ask one of our ranchers, Tom Breltbach, why an ordinary person might listen to the conspiracy theories offered by people like the militia and freemen leaders. Tom said it is pretty simple:

"As [people] feel more pressured economically, they feel more desperate, and become willing to resort to desperate measures."

There is a lot of truth to that. Most casual militia members are not Nazis or criminals. But they are angry. Angry about slow income growth, economic pressure on working families, and some of Washington's decisions on bread-and-butter issues.

I'll give you an example. Back in February, some loggers in the Flathead Valley in northwestern Montana called me up. They said that OSHA, the Occupational Safety and Health Administration, had ordered them to buy steel-toed, chainsaw-resistant boots to protect their feet. They had two weeks grace, and after that it was no boots, no work.

Well, steel-toed boots may sound good in Washington. But in Montana they can make the job more dangerous, not less. On a cold day they make your feet go numb. When your feet go numb out on a steep hill, you can slip and fall. And that's no joke when you're holding a live chainsaw.

Because these loggers acted so fast, I was able to get to the Secretary of Labor and stop the regulations. But the fact is, nobody at a desk in Washington should be telling people in the Flathead what kind of shoes to wear. And to threatening someone's job over it is an outrage. You can expect people to be mad about it.

COMMUNITY MUST SPEAK OUT

And third, the community must speak out. We must set clear standards of what is right and what is wrong.

Most casual militia members are angry. They are angry about slow income growth, economic pressure on working families, and some of the federal government's decisions on bread-and-butter issues like forest management, regulation and the like. Those are legitimate complaints and we should try to fix them.

But there is a right way and a wrong way to deal with anger. Unlike the Flathead Valley loggers, militia members choose an unacceptable way to deal with that frustration. Intimidating loggers, your neighbors, and spreading hate rhetoric are not going to solve anybody's problems.

More important, to do any of that is wrong. And we should not hesitate to say they are wrong. Hate rhetoric, anti-Semitism, and calls for violence are wrong . They have no place in our community. And as the community asserts that basic American value, the hate groups will be defeated.

I know, because I have seen it happen before.

THE BILLINGS MENORAH MOVEMENT

In November 1993, a group of "Skinheads" came to a Jewish house in Billings, and threw a bottle through the glass door. A few days later they put a brick through the window of another Jewish house, with a five-year-old boy in the room. Then they smashed the windows of Catholic High School, which had a "Happy Hanukah" sign for its marquee.

Events like these can isolate their victims. They can silence people of good will and open broader campaigns of hate and violence. But that did not happen. Instead, people all over Billings rallied with their Jewish neighbors.

As our Billings Police Chief at the time, Wayne Inman, said, "Hate crimes and hate groups are a community responsibility." And the Billings community met that responsibility.

The *Billings Gazette* printed, as a full-page advertisement, thousands of paper menorahs. People all over town clipped them out of the paper and pasted them in their windows as a sign of solidarity. Billings held the largest Martin Luther King Day march ever in our state. And the Skinheads left town. I believe the same will happen with the "militia" and "freemen" too.

CONCLUSION

Mr. Chairman, one final word. I first thought it was sad and ironic that these groups, with their anti-Semitic agenda, had emerged as we prepared to mark the fiftieth anniversary of the victory over Nazi Germany. But my opinion has changed.

The militia leaders get a lot of attention. But far more important are the thousands of Montanans who have stood up in this past year for the values that make America special. They may not be getting the headlines. But they are the real story.

People in law enforcement. Sheriffs and prosecutors like John Bohlman, Chuck Maxwell, Nick Mumion, George Corn and Bob Slomski. Police and judges in small mill towns, like Larry Rose, Marty Bethel and Jeff Langton. Men and women who put themselves on the line to preserve the democratic process. To maintain the rule of law. To guarantee the safety of their friends and neighbors.

Community groups. People like Ken Toole and Christine Kaufman in the Montana Human Rights Network, Cheye Ann Butler in the Northwest Montana Human Rights Alliance and Tim McWilliams in the Sanders County Coalition for Human Dignity, who are willing to stand up, tell the truth, and expose these groups for what they are.

And ordinary citizens all over Montana. Parents telling their children hate is wrong. Teachers giving their time to make sure their students know the truth. People coming together to protect Larry Rose's house in Darby, pasting menorahs in their windows in Billings, writing letters to local papers and telling hate groups to stay out of town.

Mr. Chairman, as we recalled the end of the war in Europe last Memorial Day, I heard people saying the heroism of World War II is gone. But I guarantee you, it is here today—if we take the time to look....

Robert M. Bryant, assistant director of the National Security Division of the FBI, told of the circumstance under which the FBI investigated militia groups in the past and the circumstance under which future investigations will proceed:

Good morning, Mr. Chairman and members of the subcommittee. I appreciate your invitation to appear before the subcommittee today as you discuss the militia movement in the United States. This offers me, on behalf of the FBI, the opportunity to clarify misunderstandings about the nature of the FBI's investigative jurisdiction as it may relate to militias or militia members.

Let me assure you that the FBI is doing everything within its mandate to prevent acts of terrorism from occurring. If an incident does occur, the FBI will mount whatever lawful effort it takes to solve the crime and apprehend the individual terrorists or terrorist group. The swift and effective investigation of terrorist acts, culminating in arrests, convictions, and incarcerations, sends a powerful message to terrorists and helps deter future acts of terrorism.

The FBI does investigate specific individual groups where there is a reasonable indication of criminal activity, but because these are pending investigations I cannot discuss them. These investigations are governed by the attorney general guidelines regarding general crimes, racketeering enterprises, and domestic security/terrorism investigations.

FBI domestic counter-terrorism investigations under the guidelines are limited to occasions when there is a reasonable indication that two or more persons are engaged in an enterprise for the purpose of furthering political or social goals wholly or in part through activities that involve force or violence and a violation of the criminal laws of the United States. A consideration the guidelines prescribe in determining whether an investigation is warranted is the danger to privacy and free expression posed by an investigation.

In addition, we may investigate individuals under the general crimes portion of the guidelines. Full investigations under these provisions may be initiated when "facts or circumstances reasonably indicate that a federal crime has been, is being, or will be committed." For investigations of groups under the domestic security provisions and of individuals under the general crimes provisions, there must be an objective, factual basis regarding criminal activity. More limited inquiries may be conducted when information is received which, although short of a reasonable indication of criminal activities, responsible handling requires some further scrutiny beyond the prompt and extremely limited checking out of initial leads.

One recent example of the type of investigation we do conduct led to the arrests and convictions of two men from Minnesota: Duane Baker and Leroy Wheeler, who claimed to be members of a tax protest group called the Patriots Council. Baker and Wheeler manufactured a quantity of ricin, a highly toxic derivative of the castor bean. They planned to use the ricin to kill a police officer who had served eviction papers on one of the group's members. Following their arrests on August 4, 1994, they were convicted of violations of the biological weapons anti-terrorist act of 1989.

A second example involved individuals linked to a militia group who learned that Russian-made tanks were located at a local military base. Apparently fearing that these tanks were the prelude to a Russian-led invasion of the U.S. by the United Nations, some individuals took it upon themselves to plan to destroy these tanks. In fact, the tanks were captured by the U.S. Army from the Iraqis during desert storm and are being used for training our own soldiers, as well as for research and development to improve U.S. tanks and combat tactics. These misguided individuals were foiled before any damage could be done.

Finally, in the mid-1980s, some groups, which could now be viewed as paramilitary in nature, engaged in a wide range of criminal activity, including bank robberies, counterfeiting, seditious conspiracy homicide, bombings threats to federal authorities including judges, and *illegal* possession and use of weapons and explosives. These are the types of activities that will receive the full investigative attention of the FBI. Organizations that are peaceful and do not plan to violate the laws of the United States are of no investigative interest to the FBI.

As a result of a 1982 presidential directive, the Department of Justice delegated lead agency responsibility for combating terrorism within the United States to the FBI. In this role, when a terrorist incident has occurred, the FBI functions as the on-scene crisis manager for the U.S. government and is responsible for the direction and coordination of all law enforcement efforts to resolve the situation. Additionally, the FBI is responsible for the collection of intelligence to identify and prevent terrorist acts before they occur, but only within the parameters of the attorney general guidelines.

Combating terrorism is a difficult and complex endeavor. Through many years of experience in many different aspects of our responsibilities, the FBI has learned that cooperation with other members of the law enforcement community and the support of the American public are essential for the FBI to be effective in countering terrorism.

Evidence C

Norm Olson, until shortly before this testimony was head of the Michigan Militia, presented the following statement in reaction to critics of the militia movement:

Thank you for the opportunity to testify today. The following statement will attempt to answer the question of the legitimacy and the need of the citizen militia.

Not only does the Constitution specifically allow the formation of a Federal army, it also recognizes the inherent right of the people to form militias. Further, it recognizes that the citizen and his personal armaments are the foundation of the militia. The arming of the militia is not left to the state but to the citizen. However, should the state choose to arm its citizen militia, it is free to do so (bearing in mind that the Constitution is not a document limiting the citizen, but rather limiting the power of government). But should the state fail to arm its citizen militia, the right of the people to keep and bear arms becomes the source of the guarantee that the state will not be found defenseless in the presence of a threat to its security. It makes no sense whatsoever to look to the Constitution of the United States or that of any state for *permission* to form a citizen militia since, logically, the power to permit is also the power to deny. If brought to its logical conclusion in this case, government may deny the citizen the right to form a militia. It this were to happen, the state would assert itself as the principle of the contract making the people the agents. Liberty then would depend on the state's grant of liberty. Such a concept is foreign to American thought.

While the Second Amendment to the U.S. Constitution acknowledges the existence of state militias and recognizes their necessity for the security of a free state; and while it also recognizes that the right of the people to keep and bear arms shall not be infringed, *the Second Amendment is not the source of the right to form a militia nor to keep and bear arms*. Those rights existed in the states prior to the formation of the federal union. In fact, the right to form militias and to keep and bear arms existed from antiquity. The enumeration of those rights in the Constitution only underscores their natural occurrence and importance.

According to the Tenth Amendment, ultimate power over the militia is not delegated to the Federal government by the Constitution nor to the states, but resides with the people. Consequently, the power of the militia remains in the hands of the people. Again, the fundamental function of the militia in society remains with the people. Therefore, the Second Amendment recognizes that the militia's existence and the security of the state rests ultimately in the people who volunteer their persons to constitute the militia and their arms to supply its firepower.

The primary defense of the state rests with the citizen militia bearing its own arms. *Fundamentally, it is not the state that defends the people, but the people who defend the state.*

The second line of defense of the state consists in the statutory organization known as the National Guard. Whereas the National Guard is solely the creation of statutory law, the militia derives its existence from the inherent inalienable rights which existed before the Constitution and whose importance are such that they merited specific recognition in that document. While the National Guard came into existence as a result of legislative activity, the militia existed before there was a nation or a constitutional form of government. The militias consisting of people owning and bearing personal weapons is the very authority out of which the United States Constitution grew. This point must be emphasized. Neither the citizen's militia nor the citizen's private arsenal can be an appropriate subject for federal regulation. *It was the armed militia of the American colonies whose own efforts ultimately led to the establishment of the United States of America!*

While some say that the right to keep and bear arms is granted to Americans by the Constitution, just the opposite is true. The federal government itself is the citizen. We the people, are the parent of the child we call government. You, Senators, are part of the child that We The People gave life to. The increasing amount of Federal encroachment into our lives indicates the need for parental corrective action. In short, the Federal government needs a good spanking to make it behave.

One other important point needs to be made. Since the Constitution is the limiting document upon the government, the government cannot become greater than the granting power, that is the servant cannot become greater than his master. Therefore, should the Chief Executive or other branch of government or all branches together act to suspend the Constitution under a rule of martial law, all power granted to government would be canceled and defer back to the granting power, the people. *Martial law shall not be possible in this country as long as the people recognize the Bill of Rights as inalienable.*

Since the power of self-defense and the defense of the state is ultimately vested in the people, there is no possible way that a Governor or the Chief Executive of the United States, or any legislative body can "outlaw" the citizen militia for to do so would rob inherent power from the people. If that were to happen, our entire form of government would cease.

Historically, we have found that the Governor's militia, that is the National Guard, is intended to reduce the need for the citizen militia. Simply, if the National Guard did its job in securing the state, the citizen militia would not emerge. That it has emerged so dramatically seems to indicate that the people do not feel secure. Simply stated, the growing threat of centralizing federal government is frightening

America, hence the emergence of the citizen militia. When government is given back to the people at the lowest level, the citizen militia will return to its natural place, resident within the body of the people. Civil war and revolution can be avoided by re-investing governing power to the people.

To summarize: Citizen militias are historic lawful entities predating constitutions. Such militias are "grandfathered" into the very system of government they created. The Constitution grants no right to form militias, but merely recognizes the existing natural right of all people to defend and protect themselves. The governments created out of well armed and free people are to be constantly obedient to the people. Any attempt to take the means of freedom from the people is an act of rebellion against the people.

In order to resist a rebellious and disobedient government, the citizen militia must not be connected in any way with that government lest the body politic lose its fearful countenance as the only sure threat to a government bent on converting free people into slaves.

John Trochmann, one of the founders of the Militia of Montana (MOM), and Bob Fletcher, at that time the chief spokesman for the organization, presented their statement stressing the necessity of a militia in the face of intrusive federal power. They tie their complaint to the view that taxes, the United Nations, and a banking elite were cause for the erosion of individual liberty and the expansion of tyranny in America:

GREETINGS FROM MONTANA:

It is saddening that this opportunity to address the Senate has arisen out of the Oklahoma tragedy. We *wholeheartedly* denounce this deplorable act of violence. We have had and will continue to assist in any manner to apprehend all persons that may have planned and/or carried out that dastardly deed at what ever level they may hide.

At the present time we view the militia movement as a giant neighborhood watch. The movement is made up of a cross section of Americans from all walks of life, with one singular mandate which is public and overt: the return to the Constitution of the United States, as your oath implies.

The Declaration of Independence gives excellent insight as to why people feel the need to group together and participate in militia/patriot organizations. This document speaks for itself once again as it did over 200 years ago when flagrant injustices continued "out of control" by oppressive public servants. We request that this document be entered into the permanent record as a partial support document to our statements.

The following are just a few examples as to why Americans are becoming more and more involved in militia/patriot organizations.

The high office of the presidency has been turned into a position of dictatorial oppression through the abusive use of executive orders and directives thus leaving Congress stripped of its authority. When the President overrules Congress by executive order, representative government fails.

When government defines human beings as a biological resource under the United Nations Ecosystem Management Program, maintaining that state and local laws are barriers to the goals of federal government, when the average citizen must work for half of each year just to pay their taxes, while billions of our tax dollars are forcibly sent to bail out the banking elite, while our fellow Americans are homeless, starving and without jobs, Congress wonders why their constituents get upset.

When government allows our military to be ordered and controlled by foreigners, under presidential order, allowing foreign armies to train on our soil, allowing our military to label "caring" patriots as the enemy, then turns their tanks loose on U.S. citizens to murder and destroy or directs a sniper to shoot a mother in the face while holding her infant in her arms, you bet your constituents get upset.

When government refuses to hold hearings on government sanctioned abuses, and white washes those hearings that are held, when government tampers with or destroys evidence needed to solve a crime and now considers the very idea of infringing upon the people's rights of freedom of speech, assembly and the right to redress after having destroyed the second and the fourth article, how can senators and representatives even question the loyalties of concerned Americans without first cleaning their own house.

"The law perverted and the police powers of the state perverted along with it!! The law not only turns from its proper purpose, but made to follow a totally contrary purpose. The law becomes the weapon of every kind of greed. Instead of checking crime, the law itself becomes guilty of the evils it is supposed to pursue." Frenchman, Frederick Bastiat 1884.

We the people have had about all we can stand of the twisted, slanted, bias media in America who take their signals from a few private, covert interest groups bent on destroying what's left of the American way. We respectfully request that you rely upon your own investigations, steering clear of the media and their rumor-gossip mills of dis-information.

Although most everyone in the movement has assembled around the First Amendment "Freedom of speech and the right to peaceably assemble" we have not forgotten what our founding fathers have stated about the second, former president James Madison—"A well regulated militia, composed of the body of the people, trained to arms, is the best and most natural defense of a free country"; former vice president Eldridge Gerry—"I ask what is the purpose of the militia? To off set the need of large standing armies—the bane of liberty."

Why would he call the armed forces the bane of liberty? Why is the Pentagon waging an active campaign to win over the populace? Why does military FM 41-10 (Civil Affairs Manual: The Steps Necessary For The Over Throw Of A Nation) seem to be so applicable to America today?

May God be with America as He watches over the shoulders of you who write her laws. A nation can survive its fools and even the ambitious, but it can not survive treason from within. America has nothing to fear from patriots maintaining "vigilance." She should, however, fear those that would "outlaw" vigilance.

What to Do When the Militia Comes to Town

In 1995, Kenneth Stern and Ken Toole wrote critically about the militia movement in a report issued by the American Jewish Committee. Their words expressed a fear that militias posed a serious threat to American democracy:

Ken Toole:

There is a tendency to view extremist activity as a law-enforcement issue. But the law addresses the symptoms and ignores the cure. Law-enforcement agencies confront the illegal acts committed by extremist groups and their members. Throughout history law-enforcement action has sometimes unintentionally increased public support for these groups by creating martyrs. The law does not, and should not, deal with the ideology that drives these groups.

The lesson that emerges from history is that these groups are hindered more by the attitudes of the community than they are by laws. Fear and silence allow hate groups to flourish. People coming together, organizing and speaking out—saying "Not in my town!"—make the extremists' tasks that much more difficult.

Kenneth Stern:

At least forty states have militia groups. Between 10,000 and 40,000 Americans belong to these private armies. Imagine what it must be like having one in your community. Militia members are politically active, threatening public officials, talking about the need to "war" with their enemies. How comfortable would you be signing a letter to the editor, showing up at a community meeting, running for office?

Source: Ken Toole, *What to Do When the Militia Comes to Town*, New York: American Jewish Committee, 1995, v, 29–30.

Paramilitary Training Sites

In April 1996, the Southern Poverty Law Center reported that active paramilitary training sites existed in several states. The group listed the locations of the most prominent ones in use during 1994 and 1995 as follows:

Alabama
Etowah County, used by the Gadsden Minutemen
Coosa County, used by the Central Alabama Militia

Arizona
Kingman, used by the Arizona Patriots

Florida
Key Largo, used by the 1st Regiment Florida State Militia

Georgia
Hall County, group name unknown

Kentucky
Boone County, used by the Defenders of Liberty

Louisiana
Lafayette, used by the Militia of Louisiana

Michigan
Wolverine, used by the Michigan Regional Militia

Minnesota
Pope County, group name unknown

Missouri
Kansas City, used by the Missouri 51st Militia

New Hampshire
Plainfield, used by the Constitution Defense Militia

New Mexico
Raton, used by the New Mexico Militia

New York
Chemung County, used by the Citizens Militia

Ohio
Pike County, used by the Ohio Patriots
Clermont County, used by the Ohio Patriots
Cleveland, used by the Ohio Unorganized Militia

Oregon
Jefferson County, used by the Central Oregon Regional Militia

Rhode Island
Providence, used by the Rhode Island Militia

South Dakota
Gregory, used by the Tri-States Militia

Texas
Texas-Oklahoma border area, used by the North Texas
Constitutional Militia

Utah
Near Zion National Park, used by the Army of Israel

Washington
Snohomish County, used by the Washington State Militia

Wisconsin
Waupaca County, used by the Militia of Wisconsin
Vernon County, used by the Militia of Wisconsin

Paramilitary training sites were known to be functioning also in northern Idaho and in New Jersey.

Source: *False Patriots: The Threat of Antigovernment Extremists.* Southern Poverty Law Center, 1996, 21.

Directory of Organizations

T his chapter includes lists of three types of organizations: militias, militia support groups (dedicated to assisting militias in their formation and growth), and groups that monitor militias and militia support groups. In the case of militias, it should be noted that only a selective list is included here, one emphasizing higher-profile organizations in terms of offering information and being receptive to correspondence. Militias come and go, and some maintain a clandestine existence or prefer exposure only through the Internet (see Bibliography for Internet sites). Except for the most prominent among them, it is often difficult to determine a precise contact point, and descriptions have been provided only for those militias which have obtained some longevity and a national profile. Thus militia addresses given below, including telephone and fax numbers (provided when the information was available), should be checked for recent changes. A search on the Internet is advised.

Militias and Militia Support Groups

American Justice Federation (AJF)
3850 South Emerson Avenue
Indianapolis, IN 46203
(317) 780-5200
Fax: (317) 780-5209

Under Linda Thompson's tutelage, this organization encourages the formation of militias to protect constitutional rights. The AJF believes that a government conspiracy exists aimed at oppressing the American people. This message is communicated via numerous videotapes, some books, and its news computer network, all available by special order.

Publications: The AJF publishes *USA News.*

Committee to Restore the Constitution
P.O. Box 986
Fort Collins, CO 80522
(970) 484-2575

This organization believes that local control and individual rights have been undermined by the federal government. It subscribes to conspiracy theories, including the belief that revolutionary internationalists want to destroy the Constitution and replace the republic with a corporate state. The group is supportive of militias as protective of liberty.

Publications: This organization issues *The Bulletin of the Committee to Restore the Constitution* monthly and promotes a book, *The Republic: Decline and Future Promise*, written by its director, Archibald Roberts.

Congress of Florida Militias
3745 Racker Highway
Winter Haven, FL 33889
(813) 293-3197

Continental Militia
1st Missouri Volunteers
P.O. Box 31233
Des Peres, MO 63131

Jews for the Preservation of Firearms Ownership (JPFO)
2872 South Wentworth Avenue
Milwaukee, WI 53207

(414) 769-0760
Fax: (414) 483-8435

This group is not a militia organization; rather, it was organized to fight gun control legislation, which it considers a threat to liberty. Despite its nonmilitia status, JPFO has supported militia organizations as legal formations. It issues newsletters, special reports, and numerous books condemning gun control.

Publications: JPFO publishes *The Firearms Sentinel*, available with membership.

Michigan Militia
304 South Maple Island Road
Muskeogon, MI 49442
(616) 788-4754
Fax: (616) 788-5001
http://www.grfn.org/%7Eheiny/cmrm.html

The Michigan Militia, also known as the North Michigan Regional Militia, grew considerably in 1995 and encompasses local militias in several areas of the state, including the active Kent County Fifteenth Brigade. General Lynn Jon Van Huizen, a gun shop owner, is the current commander of the Michigan Militia Corps.

Publications: This militia publishes the *Weekly Update*, available either in hard copy or through e-mail.

Military Studies Group
1131-0 Tolland Turnpike
Suite 124
Manchester, CT 06040
(203) 645-1736

Militia of Montana (MOM)
P.O. Box 1486
Noxon, MT 59853
(406) 847-2735
Fax: (406) 847-2246

MOM is the most prolific of the militias in terms of producing and distributing written material, tape recordings, and videotapes. The organization publishes a training manual, and a voluminous catalog stocked with books, articles, and videotapes to order.

Publications: MOM issues *Taking Aim*, a bimonthly newsletter.

New Jersey Militia
P.O. Box 10176
Trenton, NJ 08650
(609) 695-2733

This group, founded in December 1994, publishes a monthly newsletter and welcomes subscribers. It adheres to several conspiracy theories and advises that correspondents place parentheses around the zip code above to signify their protest against federal bureaucratic devices that infringe on individual liberty.

Publications: The New Jersey Militia Newsletter is published on a monthly basis.

New Mexico Militia
P.O. Box 153
Mountainair, NM 87036
(505) 847-2831
Fax: (505) 897-8789

Ohio Unorganized Militia
P.O. Box 4404
Columbus, OH 43204-4404
(614) 444-5840
Fax: (614) 444-5865

This militia dedicates itself to defending the integrity of the Constitution and insists it will emphasize educational functions, such as historical research, publications, and lectures.

Pennsylvania Militia
9th Regiment Company
P.O. Box 1396
Morrisville, PA 19067

Rhode Island Militia Unit 215
780 Victory Highway (Route 102)
West Greenwich, RI 02817

San Diego Militia
P.O.Box 12361
La Jolla, CA 92039
(619) 272-1789
e-mail: militia@tomlinson.com

South Carolina Civilian Militia
P.O. Box 805
Greenville, SC 29602

Fax: (864) 268-6442

http://pages.prodigy.com/SC/militia/militia.html

The South Carolina Civilian Militia recently complained about the unfair, secretive nature of congressional hearings on Waco. It claims, too, that militiaman Michael Hill was murdered in cold blood by a police officer in Frazyburg, Ohio, in the summer of 1995.

United States Militia Association (USMA)
17 South Cleveland Avenue
Blackfoot, ID 83221
(208) 785-1032

The USMA advocates forming militias within the guidelines provided by law. Although it rejects racism, anti-Semitism, and most conspiratorial theories, it holds that there has been an assault on individual liberty by the federal government through incorrect or misguided policies.

Publications: Aide-de-Camp, the official USMA newsletter, is published monthly.

West Virginia Militia
Box 10
Wileyville, WV 26186
(304) 889-2786

Yavapai County Militia
15568 South Black Mountain Road
Mayer, AZ 86333
(602) 407-8236

Organizations That Monitor Militias

American Jewish Committee (AJC)
165 East 56th Street
New York, NY 10022-2746
(212) 751-4000
Fax: (212) 751-4019

As part of its overall mission to ensure the security of Jews everywhere, this organization traces the ties militias have to anti-Semitic and racist groups. The fax number above is that of Ken Stern who wrote *A Force Upon the Plain*, a book critical of militias. Stern is a lawyer and prominent analyst of the militia movement for the American Jewish Committee. The AJC maintains an extensive archives on some militias and far-right and hate groups.

Publications: The *AJC Journal* is published every six to eight weeks and is available with membership in the organization.

Anti-Defamation League (ADL) of B'nai B'rith
823 UN Plaza
New York, NY 10017
(212) 490-2525
Fax: (212) 867-0779

The ADL has issued reports on the Skinheads, Ku Klux Klan, Identity Christianity, the Liberty Lobby, and other racist and anti-Semitic groups. In 1994 and again in 1995 it released detailed reports on the militia movement. The organization's book *Extremism on the Right*, published in 1988, provides information on right-wing leaders.

Publication: ADL On the Frontline is a monthly newsletter provided to members.

Bay Area Coalition for Our Reproductive Rights (BACORR)
750 La Playa #730
San Francisco, CA 94121
(415) 437-4032
Fax (415) 431-2523
e-mail tburghardt@igc.apc.org

Primarily involved in upholding women's right to choice and in protecting abortion clinics, BACORR has also investigated the ties between anti-abortionists and militias.

Publications: Publishes a quarterly journal of anti-racist activism entitled *Turning the Tide.*

Center for Democratic Renewal
P.O. Box 50469
Atlanta, GA 30302
(404) 221-0025
Fax: (404) 221-0045

This is one of the largest regional groups that monitors racist activities and right-wing extremism. For a modest contribution, this organization will research militia group activities.

Publications: The CDR prints a complete list of publications and issues a bimonthly newsletter titled *Monitor.*

Coalition for Human Dignity (CHD)
P.O. Box 40344
Portland, OR 97240
(503) 281-5823
Fax: (503) 281-8673

The CHD monitors efforts by radical right groups in the Pacific Northwest, including militias.

Publications: The CHD publishes *Dignity Report,* a monthly journal.

Institute for Alternative Journalism
77 Federal Street
San Francisco, CA 94107
(415) 284-1420
Fax: (415) 284-1414

This group promotes diversity in news reporting. It recently issued a report, *Militias in America, 1995* that includes news articles from around the nation concerning the growth of the militia movement.

Institute for Research and Education on Human Rights
P.O. Box 411552
Kansas City, MO 64141
(404) 373-5169

Daniel Levitas, this group's expert witness, has testified extensively on the activities of right-wing extremists, including the Ku Klux Klan, Aryan Nations, and the Skinheads.

Montana Human Rights Network
P.O. Box 9184
Helena, MT 59604
(406) 442-5506

This is a nonprofit organization that monitors far right groups in Montana, including militias.

Publications: The group issues *Human Rights Network News,* a monthly newsletter.

Northwest Coalition Against Malicious Harassment
P.O. Box 16776
Seattle, WA 98116
(206) 233-9136
Fax: (206) 233-0611

This organization monitors extremism in the Pacific Northwest with special attention to hate groups and their activities.

Publications: The Northwest Deacon, a newsletter, is issued every three months.

People Against Racist Terror (PART)
P.O. Box 1055
Culver City, CA 90232
(310) 288-5003

PART has issued numerous reports on racism, anti-Semitism, and white supremacy, including an analysis of Bo Gritz.

Publications: PART publishes a newsletter entitled, *Turning the Tide.*

Political Research Associates (PRA)
678 Massachusetts Avenue
Suite 702
Cambridge, MA 02139
(617) 661-9313
Fax: (617) 661-0059

The PRA compiles and distributes extensive information on right-wing movements, including militias, and has numerous reports available for a fee. Chip Berlet, a political analyst with the PRA, is considered to be an expert in the field of right-wing political activity and has done extensive research into the militia movement.

Publications: The Public Eye, issued monthly, publishes investigations of the far right.

Southern Poverty Law Center
P.O. Box 548
Montgomery, AL 36101-0548
(334) 264-0286
Fax: (334) 264-8891

Through its Klanwatch project, this organization monitors militia groups affiliated with white supremacists.

Publications: The SPLC publishes a monthly newsletter, the *Klanwatch Intelligence Report*, that includes a militia update column.

Western States Center
522 SW 5th Avenue, #1390
Portland, OR 97204
(503) 228-8866
Fax: (503) 228-1965

This group reports on links between the anti-environmentalist Wise Use movement and militias. Some of the projects of the Western States Center are cosponsored by the American Federation of Labor-Congress of Industrial Organizations.

Publications: The *Western States Center News* is published three times per year.

Selected Print Resources

6

T his chapter of print resources includes the following: annotated listings of books, articles, and reports. These publications are relevant to militias and the militia movement.

Books

The focus in this section is on books that are readily available from library sources. This section includes works on colonial and Revolutionary America to enable the reader to draw connections between the contemporary period and the past, an aspect often overlooked in writings about militias. Throughout, emphasis is on those books that discuss militias or issues important to them (e.g., the incidents at Ruby Ridge, Idaho, and Waco, Texas). Although there are some references to more peripheral organizations (e.g., the Ku Klux Klan) and leaders (e.g., David Duke), they are included only as a starting point for interested readers and thus the listing for them is not as extensive as for works dealing directly with militias. The militias listed in chapter 5 of this book can be contacted as sources for a large number of books regarding conspiracy theories.

Most of the listings below include ISBN or LCCN numbers. In a few instances, the numbers are unavailable, usually because the particular book has been published by an individual or by a small private press.

Aho, James A. *The Politics of Righteousness: Idaho Christian Patriotism*. Seattle: University of Washington Press, 1990. 323p. ISBN 0295969970.

This sociological study traces the origin of Christian rights groups in Idaho and details the complex ideological differences and similarities among constitutionalists and racialists. It includes an appendix with primary documents.

Anderson, Fred. *A People's Army: Massachusetts Soldiers and Society in the Seven Years' War*. Chapel Hill: University of North Carolina Press, 1984. 274p. ISBN 0807816116.

Analyzes the role of the Massachusetts militia in colonial warfare.

Banning, Lance. *The Jeffersonian Persuasion: Evolution of a Party Ideology*. Ithaca, NY: Cornell University Press, 1978. ISBN 0801411513.

Although not directly about militias, this book provides insight into the Republican ideology dominant in the late 1700s and early 1800s that placed a premium on citizen militias to help maintain liberty. Banning traces the status of these ideas in a changing political climate.

Barkun, Michael. *Religion and the Racist Right: The Origins of the Christian Identity Movement*. Chapel Hill: University of North Carolina Press, 1994. 290p. ISBN 0807821454.

Surveys the connection between the Christian Identity movement in the United States and the earlier British-Israelist movement in Europe. Much of the discussion deals with ideology, particularly the virulent anti-Semitism found in the Order, Aryan Nations, and Posse Comitatus.

Bell, Daniel, ed. *The Radical Right*. 1964. Reprint, Stratford, NH: Ayer, 1977. 468p. ISBN 78167309.

Includes essays that evaluate the emergence of right-wing politics in America, largely during the 1950s and early 1960s. The analyses, although somewhat dated, include several observations pertinent to contemporary society.

Bennett, David H. *The Party of Fear: From Nativist Movements to the New Right in American History*. Chapel Hill: University of North Carolina Press, 1988. 509p. ISBN 0807817724.

Presents the argument that the New Right, which emerged in the 1980s, is different from previous far right movements in that it does not stress nativism; on the other hand, it is similar in its reliance on fear.

Bennett, Walter Hartwell, ed. *Letters from the Federal Farmer to a Republican*. Tuscaloosa: University of Alabama Press, 1978. 145p. ISBN 0817351132.

Contains the letters of Richard Henry Lee published in the 1780s as an argument against ratifying the Constitution. Lee considers an armed citizenry important to protecting liberty and worries that the federal government will create an all-powerful standing army.

Birnbaum, Louis. *Red Dawn at Lexington*. Boston: Houghton Mifflin, 1986. 402p. ISBN 0395388147.

An overview of the events in Massachusetts Bay leading up to the Revolutionary War, with a chapter covering the showdown at Lexington and Concord between the Minutemen and regular militias on one side, and the British on the other.

Boorstin, Daniel. *The Americans: The Colonial Experience*. New York: Vintage Books, 1958. 434p. LCCN 58-9884.

A general history of colonial America. Chapter 54 assesses the militias in the colonies as departing from English practices and developing in reaction to particular American needs. The myth of a constantly prepared citizenry hampered the development of a professional army and helps account for the American propensity, at least in its early years, to disarm after emergencies.

Brown, Richard Maxwell. *Strain of Violence: Historical Studies of American Violence and Vigilantism*. New York: Oxford University Press, 1975. 397p. ISBN 0195019431.

Analyzes the tradition of violence in American society by discussing its colonial origins, its expression through nineteenth-century vigilantism, and its role in white-black relations. It provides important historical context for understanding the contemporary tendency toward violence, including the formation of militias.

Broyles, J. Allen. *The John Birch Society: Anatomy of a Protest*. Boston: Beacon Press, 1964. 169p. LCCN 64-13536.

A sociological and ideological analysis of the John Birch Society, based mainly on interviews. It contains biographical information about the John Birch Society's founder, Robert Welch.

Buel, Richard, Jr. *Dear Liberty: Connecticut's Mobilization for the Revolutionary War*. Middleton, CT: Wesleyan University Press, 1980. 425p. ISBN 0819550477.

Presents an analysis of Connecticut's use of its militia to mobilize for the Revolution.

Chalmers, David M. *Hooded Americanism: The History of the Ku Klux Klan*. Durham, NC: Duke University Press, 1981. 477p. ISBN 0822307308.

Presents a detailed historical survey from the formation of the early Ku Klux Klan in 1867 to the modern Klan of the 1970s. It includes an extensive bibliography, valuable to additional reading and research on the topic.

Coates, James. *Armed and Dangerous: The Rise of the Survivalist Right*. New York: Hill and Wang, 1987. 294p. ISBN 0809027429.

Surveys the ideology of right-wing extremism and discusses the Order, Identity Christians, the Posse Comitatus, and their predecessors, especially the Minutemen.

Cohn, Norman. *Warrant for Genocide: The Myth of the Jewish World Conspiracy and the Protocols of the Elders of Zion*. New York: Harper and Row, 1969. 303p.

Refutes the validity of the conspiratorial plot laid out in the *Protocols of the Meetings of the Learned Elders of Zion* and traces the popularity of the myth over time, including its appeal in Nazi Germany.

Cooke, Jacob E. *The Federalist*. Hanover, NH: Wesleyan University Press, 1964. 672p. ISBN 0819530166.

The most authoritative compilation of *The Federalist* written in the 1780s by Alexander Hamilton, James Madison, and John Jay. It contains extensive explanatory notes and includes Federalist No. 29, which deals with militias.

Cooper, Jerry. *The Militia and the National Guard in America Since Colonial Times: A Research Guide*. Westport, CT: Greenwood Press, 1993. 185p. ISBN 0313277214.

Includes an extensive bibliography along with historiographical essays pertaining to citizen militias and the National Guard, especially militias in the seventeenth through early nineteenth centuries.

Cooper, Milton William. *Behold a Pale Horse*. Sedona, AZ: Light Technology Publishing, 1991. 500p. ISBN 0929385225.

A far rightist details the many conspiracy theories held as truth among segments of the militia movement. Information is included on the New World Order, the Federal Emergency Management Agency, treasonous activities in high places, UFO sightings and investigations, and links between U.S. Army intelligence and a Satanic church. The book contains a reprint of the *Protocols of the Meetings of the Learned Elders of Zion*.

Corcoran, James. *Bitter Harvest: Gordon Kahl and the Posse Comitatus, Murder in the Heartland*. New York: Viking, 1990. 274p. ISBN 0670815616.

Details Gordon Kahl's troubles with the federal government, including the shoot-outs in North Dakota and Arkansas. It presents excellent background concerning the Posse Comitatus and paramilitary activities.

Cottrol, Robert J., ed. *Gun Control and the Constitution: Sources and Explorations on the Second Amendment*. New York: Garland Publishing, 1993. 320p. ISBN 0815312717.

An excellent starting point for delving into early American views toward guns, this book contains several essays exploring the English common law tradition respecting firearms and the relationship among citizenship, republicanism, and the right to bear arms.

Cress, Lawrence D. *Citizens in Arms: The Army and the Militia in American Society to the War of 1812*. Chapel Hill: University of North Carolina Press, 1982. 238p. ISBN 080781508x.

Analyzes the influence of English Opposition and moderate Whig thought on the status of the early American militia and regular army and concludes that by 1820 the latter was accepted as an integral part of a properly functioning government.

Davidson, Bill R. *To Keep and Bear Arms*. Boulder, CO: Sycamore Land Books, 1979. 258p. ISBN 0873641450.

The author strongly opposes most efforts at gun control and advocates the formation of a citizen militia as essential to defend America from external aggression. The militia, he advises, should be well trained and under the authority of the state governor.

Davis, David Brion. *The Fear of Conspiracy: Images of Un-American Subversion from the Revolution to the Present*. Ithaca, NY: Cornell University Press, 1971. 369p. ISBN 080140598x.

A collection of evidence, both primary and secondary, displaying the conspiratorial mentality evident in America during socially tense periods, such as the American Revolution, the conflict over slavery, the influx of new immigrants, and the threat of communism.

Dees, Morris, and James Corcoran. *Gathering Storm: America's Militia Threat*. New York: Harper Collins, 1996. 254p. ISBN 006017403x.

Morris Dees is head of the Southern Poverty Law Center, an organization sharply critical of the militia movement. The authors tie the militias to anti-Semitism and racism, and thus focus on Christian Identity, *The Turner Diaries*, and neo-Nazis, as well as the incidents at Ruby Ridge, Idaho, and Waco, Texas.

DePugh, Robert B. *Blueprint for Victory*. Norborne, MO: Robert B. DePugh, 1966. 110p.

In the 1960s, most of what Robert DePugh had to say in this book was considered extreme. In the 1990s, large parts of it have entered the conservative mainstream, and his ideas continue as a strong influence on the militia movement.

Diamond, Sara. *Spiritual Warfare: The Politics of the Christian Right*. Montreal: Black Rose Books, 1990. 292p. ISBN 092168659.

Although not directly about militias, this book contains an informative chapter about charismatic Christians and the Christian Identity movement that helps in understanding the fervency found within the extreme right wing.

Epstein, Benjamin R., and Arnold Forster. *The Radical Right: Report on the John Birch Society and Its Allies*. New York: Vintage Books, 1967. 239p. LCCN 68-2744.

In addition to the John Birch Society, this book discusses right-wing ideology, the devices used in spreading extremist propaganda, and the status of several leaders and organizations in the mid-1960s, including the Liberty Lobby and the Christian Crusade.

Finch, Philip. *God, Guts, and Guns*. New York: Seaview/Putnam, 1983. 240p. ISBN 0399310126.

Presents America's radical right in the 1950s through the early 1980s in a lively, insightful manner by using interviews as a major source. It clarifies several attempts at forming militias.

Fischer, David Hackett. *Paul Revere's Ride*. New York: Oxford University Press, 1994. 445p. ISBN 0195088476.

Studies the actions of the American revolutionaries, including the militias, from the position that individual decisions, while shaped by larger cultural factors, determine the unfolding of events. It contains an excellent historiographical essay tracing the myths surrounding Paul Revere's ride.

Galvin, John R. *The Minute Men: The First Fight—Myths and Realities of the American Revolution*. Washington, DC: Pergamon-Brassey's International Defense Publishers, 1989. 274p. ISBN 008036733x.

Emphasizes the continuity between the early colonial period, when colonists organized militias—including quick-response units—and the formation of the minutemen who battled the British at Concord. The long-standing minutemen tradition meant that these men were well prepared for the fight.

George, John, and Laird Wilcox. *Nazis, Communists, Klansmen, and Others on the Fringe*. Buffalo, New York: Prometheus Books, 1992. 523p. ISBN 0879756802.

A survey of political extremism of both the left and right, this book includes chapters on the Minutemen, the Black Panthers, Gerald L. K. Smith, and Lyndon LaRouche. An extensive bibliography is divided into a "left bibliography" and a "right bibliography," providing a wealth of resources in understanding extremist mentalities.

Gibson, James William. *Warrior Dreams: Paramilitary Culture in Post-Vietnam America*. New York: Hill and Wang, 1994. 357p. ISBN 0809096668.

Gibson asserts that in the 1980s, American culture was infused with warrior dreams in reaction to losing the war in Vietnam, economic difficulties, an influx of immigrants, and legal and economic gains by women. Warrior dreams extolled paramilitary activity by men to protect American liberty. These dreams restored masculinity. They appeared in magazines such as *Soldier of Fortune* and in the Rambo movies. Warrior dreams appeared, too, in the rise of paramilitary groups, including racist ones such as the Posse Comitatus.

Gross, Richard A. *The Minutemen and Their World*. New York: Hill and Wang, 1976. 242p. ISBN 0809069334.

Reflects the methodology known as new social history. Gross analyzes the rise of the minutemen in Concord amid changing economic and social conditions that produced tensions and instability in the traditional community setting.

Hamm, Mark S. *American Skinheads: The Criminology and Control of Hate Crime*. Westport, CT: Praeger, 1993. 243p. ISBN 0275943550.

A sociological and historical analysis of the Skinheads, this book concludes that the single most important factor in young people joining this extreme right group was the organizational activities of Tom Metzger.

Higginbotham, Don. *The War for American Independence: Military Attitudes, Policies, and Practices, 1763–1789*. New York: Macmillan, 1971. 509p. LCCN 74-132454.

An overview of the Revolutionary War, this book includes the role of the militia.

Hofstadter, Richard. *The Paranoid Style in American Politics and Other Essays*. Chicago: University of Chicago Press, 1965. 314p. ISBN 0226348172.

Any study of contemporary radicalism in American society, particularly that of the right-wing, should begin with Hofstadter. Although this book was written 30 years ago, its definition of the paranoid style remains accurate, and its conclusions about radicalism in the 1950s and 1960s in many ways are applicable to the 1990s; indeed, some statements are fascinatingly prescient.

Jackson, Kenneth T. *The Ku Klux Klan in the City, 1915–1930*. New York: Oxford University Press, 1967. 326p. LCCN 67-28129.

Concludes that the second Ku Klux Klan movement immediately after World War I and into the 1920s drew its most dynamic support from the cities. The KKK had an enormous impact on society and was not an aberration but, instead, typically American.

Jones, J. Harry, Jr. *The Minutemen*. Garden City, NY: Doubleday, 1968. 426p. LCCN 68-17786.

An extensive, detailed study of the militant right-wing Minutemen, founded in 1961 by Robert DePugh. Jones reveals the ideology and psychological motivation behind the group.

Keith, James. *Black Helicopters Over America: Strikeforce for the New World Order*. Lilburn, GA: Illuminet Press, 1994. 154p. ISBN 1881532054.

Keith provides an account of the many sightings in the United States of black helicopters, an instrument, the author believes, of the New World Order. The book discusses, too, the creation of detention centers and a national police force, all intended to crush American liberty. This is an interesting insight into the conspiracy mentality—its beliefs and fears.

King, Dennis. *Lyndon LaRouche and the New American Fascism*. New York: Doubleday, 1989. 415p. ISBN 0385238800.

Analyzes Lyndon LaRouche's transformation from leftist to rightist and the substantial political influence he developed in the 1980s, especially with the Reagan administration. LaRouche included in his activities militia training and at one point envisioned a coup that would bring him to power.

Kohn, Richard H. *Eagle and Sword: The Federalists and the Creation of the Military Establishment in America, 1783–1802*. New York: Free Press, 1975. 443p. ISBN 0029175518.

Details the Federalist effort to establish a professional regular army to supplant the militias.

Langguth, A. J. *Patriots: The Men Who Started the American Revolution*. New York: Simon and Schuster, 1988. 637p. ISBN 0-671-52375-9.

Includes sketches of famous leaders from the American Revolution and of events where the colonists acted en masse against the British. Also included is a lively account of the militias at Lexington and Concord in 1775 and important surveys of major battles in the Revolutionary War.

Leppard, David. *Fire and Blood: The True Story of David Koresh and the Waco Siege*. London: Fourth Estate, 1993. 182p. ISBN 1857021665.

Provides a lurid account of Koresh's life from his teenage years—when he immersed himself in the Bible and learned to play the guitar—to the cataclysmic end at Waco, Texas. The author, a British journalist, focuses on the Branch Davidian shootout with federal agents and the ensuing 51-day siege. He considers the Branch Davidians an evil cult; even so, the federal government, he believes, was misguided in its response.

Lewis, James R., ed. *From the Ashes: Making Sense of Waco*. Lanham, MD: Rowman and Littlefield Publishers, 1994. 269p. ISBN 0847679144.

Contains 46 brief essays concerning the Branch Davidians and the siege at Waco, Texas. The authors reject the view that David Koresh engaged in child abuse or that the Davidians committed suicide. The federal government, they believe, persecuted Koresh's group.

Lipset, Seymour Martin, and Earl Raab. *The Politics of Unreason: Right-Wing Extremism in America, 1790–1970*. New York: Harper & Row, 1970. 547p. LCCN 67-22529.

Includes extensive statistical analyses drawn from surveys concerning social and economic influences on behavior. For the post-World War II period, the authors focus on McCarthyism, the John Birch Society, and George Wallace.

Macdonald, Andrew. *The Turner Diaries*. Hillsboro, WV: National Vanguard Books, 1978. 211p. ISBN 0937944025.

The novel written by William Pierce under the pen name Andrew Macdonald. Anti-Semitic and racist, the story spins conspiracy theories and may have influenced the person or persons involved in the 1995 bombing at Oklahoma City, Oklahoma. One passage of the book presents a bombing scene similar to that which occurred at the Alfred P. Murrah Federal Building in that city.

Maclean, Nancy. *Behind the Mask of Chivalry: The Making of the Second Ku Klux Klan*. New York: Oxford University Press, 1994. 292p. ISBN 0195072340.

A historical analysis of the Klan during the 1920s that uses a case study of the organization in Athens, Georgia, to focus on cultural and ideological influences and the expression of reactionary populism. The book also includes an extensive bibliography.

Mahon, John K. *The American Militia: Decade of Decision, 1789–1800*. Gainesville: University of Florida Press, 1960. 69p. LCCN 60-63132.

The author concludes that state militias were highly effective in the early republic.

Martin, James Kirby, and Lender, Mark Edward. *A Respectable Army: The Military Origins of the Republic, 1763–1789*. Arlington Heights, IL: Harlan Davidson, 1982. 240p. ISBN 0882958127.

The focus here is on the Continental Army and the role of Whig militia ideology in hampering the war effort against the British.

Mintz, Frank P. *The Liberty Lobby and the American Right: Race, Conspiracy, and Culture*. Westport, CT: Greenwood Press, 1985. 251p. ISBN 031324393x.

Emphasizes the ideological roots of right-wing extremism and provides a historical account of the Liberty Lobby into the 1980s.

Moore, Jack B. *Skinheads Shaved for Battle: A Cultural History of American Skinheads*. Bowling Green, OH: Bowling Green State University Popular Press, 1993. 200p. ISBN 0879725826.

Focuses on the Skinhead movement in the United States and provides background concerning the movement in England. It includes substantial discussion about the relationship of Skinheads to music.

Nilus, Sergiei Aleksandrovich. *The Protocols of the Meetings of the Learned Elders of Zion*. Translated by Victor E. Marsden. Houston: Pyramid Book Shop, 1934. 71p. LCCN 34-18166.

One of the most important documents among extremists, especially right-wingers. It purports to be an official Zionist document detailing plans formulated in 1918 to establish a One World government.

Porteous, Skipp. Foreword to *The Field Manual of the Free Militia*. Great Barrington, MA: Riverwalk Press, 1996. 108p.

The Field Manual is presented by Skipp Porteous, who is affiliated with the Institute for First Amendment Studies, a group that opposes militias. They offer *The Field Manual* to show the racist and anti-Semitic extremists in the militias. Porteous considers paramilitary groups "unnecessary" and "dangerous." The *Field Manual*, issued originally by the Wisconsin Free Militia, has circulated since 1994 and expresses a Christian Identity ideology.

Ridgeway, James. *Blood in the Face: The Ku Klux Klan, Aryan Nations, Nazi Skinheads, and the Rise of a New White Culture*. New York: Thunder's Mouth Press, 1990. 203p. ISBN 156025002x.

Surveys far right groups, mainly paramilitary, and traces their common belief in a worldwide conspiracy, largely by Jews, to crush liberty and end white civilization. It includes primary documents and photographs.

Rose, Douglas D., ed. *The Emergence of David Duke and the Politics of Race*. Chapel Hill: University of North Carolina Press, 1992. 269p. ISBN 0807820431.

Essays by academics and journalists analyzing David Duke's support, his attachment to racism and anti-Semitism, and his use of the media are included in this book. Each selection contains an extensive bibliography.

Rosswurm, Stephen. *Arms, Country, and Class: The Philadelphia Militia and the "Lower Sort" During the American Revolution, 1775–1783*. New Brunswick: Rutgers University Press, 1987. 373p. ISBN 0813512484.

Historians continue to debate the extent to which the American Revolution was an internal conflict pitting class against class. This work asserts that class conflict existed in Philadelphia and that the militia pushed for radical political restructuring.

Royster, Charles. *A Revolutionary People at War: The Continental Army and American Character, 1775–1783*. Chapel Hill: University of North Carolina Press, 1979. 452p. ISBN 0807813850.

Concludes that the militia was ineffective in the American Revolution, but faith in it as an expression of community virtue remained strong.

Selesky, Harold E. *War and Society in Colonial Connecticut*. New Haven: Yale University Press, 1990. 278p. ISBN 0300045522.

Finds that the Connecticut militia system was different from that in other colonies and from England.

Shea, William L. *The Virginia Militia in the Seventeenth Century*. Baton Rouge: Louisiana State University Press, 1983. 154p. ISBN 0807111066.

Asserts that the colonial Virginia militia changed considerably from the early to late seventeenth century and in the later period resembled the system existing in England.

Sherwood, M. Samuel. *Establishing an Independent Militia in the United States*. Blackfoot, ID: Founders Press Publishing, 1995. 61p.

Explains the intent of the founding fathers regarding the formation of militias and clarifies the policy positions of the United States Militia Association, which the author founded. It differentiates the USMA from white supremacist and anti-Semitic groups and inveighs against forming militias without the approval of county governments.

Shy, John. *A People Numerous and Armed: Reflections on the Military Struggle for American Independence*. Ann Arbor: University of Michigan Press, 1990. 356p. ISBN 0472094319.

Contains essays that place the military aspects of the American Revolution within the context of broad social, political, and economic changes. Shy believes a dynamic rather than static situation existed, one in which the militias differed from colony to colony and changed over time. He sees the militia as effectively meeting the demands placed on it in the Revolutionary War.

Simkin, Jay, and Aaron Zelman. *Gun Control: Gateway to Tyranny*. Milwaukee, WI: Jews for the Preservation of Firearms Ownership, 1993. 139p. ISBN 0964230410.

Presents evidence that gun control legislation enacted by Congress has been based on provisions of gun control legislation used in Nazi Germany.

Simkin, Jay, Aaron Zelman, and Alan M. Rice. *Lethal Laws: Gun Control is the Key to Genocide*. Milwaukee, WI: Jews for the Preservation of Firearms Ownership, 1994. 347p. ISBN 0964230402.

Argues that inhibiting gun ownership by law-abiding adults takes away an important defense against genocide. Hence, gun control must be ended.

Smoot, Dan. *The Invisible Government*. Boston: Western Islands, 1962. 240p. ISBN 0882791257.

The views of a Bircher amid the cold war concerning a conspiracy to make America part of a one-world socialist system are presented.

Stern, Kenneth S. *A Force Upon the Plain: The Militia Movement and the Politics of Hate*. New York: Simon and Schuster, 1996. 303p. ISBN 0684819163.

A well-researched analysis of the militia movement focusing on Ruby Ridge, Idaho, and Waco, Texas, as stimulants of its growth. Stern, a lawyer and writer and considered to be an expert on hate and hate groups, sees racism and anti-Semitism as central to the militias. Although he concludes that militia membership does not exceed some 40,000, he sees these organizations reflective of intolerance, which lately has been rampant in American society. The book includes an extensive bibliography that will lead the reader to articles in small-town newspapers.

Tugwell, Rexford G. *The Emerging Constitution*. New York: Harper's Magazine Press, 1974. 642p. ISBN 0061282251.

The result of research at the Center for the Study of Democratic Institutions. The author emphasizes the need for changing the U.S. Constitution, preferably with amendments. Provided here, though, is the full text of what an entirely new constitution might look like, one intended to eliminate or reduce current political problems. The document is entitled the Newstates Constitution and due to its provisions has raised enormous opposition within the militia movement.

Walter, Jess. *Every Knee Shall Bow: The Truth and Tragedy of Ruby Ridge and the Randy Weaver Family*. New York: Regan Books, 1995. 375p. ISBN 006039174x.

A detailed and gripping account of the Weaver family and the shoot-out at Ruby Ridge, Idaho, that stirred the formation of militias. The author portrays a divided America and addresses the questions of racism and excessive government power.

Weisman, Charles A. *America: Free, White, and Christian*. Burnsville: MN: Charles A. Weisman, 1989. 172p.

The author argues that the origins of America are rooted in colonial Christianity. The nation's founders never intended religious or racial pluralism, for they knew no nation could survive long with it.

Whisker, James B. *The Militia*. Lewiston, NY: The Edwin Mellen Press, 1992. 210p. ISBN 0773495533.

Summarizes the place of militias in different political settings, including American republican government and overseas authoritarian regimes. The author discusses Machiavelli and other philosophical sources that support a citizen soldiery.

Yockey, Francis Parker. *Imperium*. Newport Beach, CA: Noontide Press, 1962. 626p. ISBN 0911038523.

A popular book in extremist circles, *Imperium* portrays Jews as a threat to civilization and calls Hitler a hero.

Zatarain, Michael. *David Duke: Evolution of a Klansman*. Gretna, LA: Pelican, 1990. 304p. ISBN 0882898175.

The author assesses David Duke through personal interviews with him and his supporters, as well as through print resources.

Principal Articles

The mainstream press continues to publish articles in ever-expanding quantities about the militia movement and developments related to it. The following list includes the more insightful newspaper and newsmagazine articles on militias that appeared immediately after the bombing at Oklahoma City, Oklahoma, and an extensive coverage of articles from other magazines. In addition to these, the list covers articles from historical journals and books concerning developments in early America to allow the reader to draw connections with the past.

Barkun, Michael. "Militias, Christian Identity, and the Radical Right." *Christian Century*, 2–9 August 1995, 738–740.

Traces the links between militias and religious ideology and concludes that a danger exists: The militias may eventually embrace racism and anti-Semitism on a large scale.

Berlet, Chip, and Matthew N. Lyons. "Militia Nation." *The Progressive*, June 1995, 22–25.

The authors find that militias represent populist discontent and in many instances have legitimate grievances.

Blumenthal, Sydney. "Her Own Private Idaho." *New Yorker*, 10 July 1995, 27–33.

Connects the election of Congresswoman Helen Chenoweth (Republican, Idaho) to economic tensions, far-right appeals, and support from militia groups.

"Bob Fletcher Rising in Militia of Montana." *Human Rights Network News*, March 1995, 2.

This article, in a publication of the Montana Human Rights Network, reports the rise of Bob Fletcher in the hierarchy of the Militia of Montana. An astute businessman and polished speaker, Fletcher does not have the direct links to the white supremacist movement for which Militia of Montana leader John Trochmann is noted.

Boucher, Ronald L. "The Colonial Militia as a Social Institution: Salem, Massachusetts, 1764–1775," *Military Affairs* 37 (December 1973), 125–129.

Analyzes the changes in the militia in Massachusetts after the French and Indian War.

Breen, Timothy. "English Origins and New World Development: The Case of the Covenanted Militia in Seventeenth Century Massachusetts," *Past and Present* 57 (1972), 74–96.

Asserts that the militia in Massachusetts reflected Puritan ideals with an emphasis on local control.

Brookheiser, Richard. "Patriots, Rebels, and Founding Fathers." *New York Times*, 16 June 1995, A15.

The founding fathers, especially George Washington, saw militias as dangerous. As in the case of Shays' Rebellion and the Whiskey Rebellion, militias could take the law into their own hands and threaten government stability.

Carp, E. Wayne. "The Problem of National Defense in the Early American Republic." In Jack P. Greene, ed., *The American Revolution: Its Character and Limits*. New York: New York University Press, 1987, 14–50.

This is both an interpretation of Whig thought concerning militias and standing armies and a historiographical overview of how historians have covered the ideological debate that occurred among Americans in the late 1700s and early 1800s.

Chandler, Noah. "Militias: Armed and Paranoid." *The Monitor*, Spring 1995, 6–7.

This writer for the Center for Democratic Renewal concludes that white supremacists and anti-Semites are using the militia movement to expand their following and influence in ways often unrecognized by militia members.

Cockburn, Alexander. "Neither Left nor Right." *The Nation*, 17–24 July 1995, 80–81.

A leftist commentator argues against maintaining the old political distinctions between left and right. He sees much validity to complaints about a national government that frequently bypasses democratic processes.

"Conspiracies, Helicopters, and Militias Prove a Dangerous Mix." *Human Rights Network*, March 1995, 2.

Describes the conspiracy theories held by some militia members in Montana.

"Contemporary Militia Movement More Than Thirty Years in the Making." *Klanwatch Intelligence Report*, June 1995, 12–13.

Traces the white supremacist wing of the militia movement back into the 1960s, when William Potter Gale founded the California Rangers.

Cooper, Marc. "Montana's Mother of All Militias." *The Nation*, 22 May 1995, 714–722.

Details the conspiracy theories held by the Trochmanns, who lead the Militia of Montana.

Cress, Lawrence Delbert. "Radical Whiggery and the Role of the Military: Ideological Roots of the American Revolutionary Militia." *Journal of the History of Ideas* 40 (January–March 1979), 43–60.

Traces Whig ideas in America that asserted the need for a republican militia to offset governmental power.

———. "A Question of Sovereignty: The Militia in Anglo-American Constitutional Debate, 1641–1827." In John W. Elsberg, ed., *The U.S. Army Bicentennial Series, Papers on the Constitution*. Washington, DC: U.S. Army Center of Military History, 1990, 123–149.

Concludes that state sovereignty over the militia in the early republic reflected the prominence of state authority over the federal government.

Doskoch, Peter. "The Mind of the Militias." *Psychology Today*, July/August 1995, 12–14, 70.

Defines the mindset of a typical contemporary militia member, emphasizing how the prevailing ideology demonizes the government and engages in paranoia.

"Enemies of the State." *Time*, 8 May 1995, 58–69.

Summarizes the locations of prominent local militias and lists their important leaders; it clarifies the rise of the militia movement and the differences among several groups of right-wing extremists.

"The Far Right Is Upon Us." *The Progressive*, June 1985, 8–10.

Criticizes both the militia movement and legislation proposed by President Bill Clinton to combat terrorism.

Farley, Christopher John. "The West is Wild Again." *Time*, 20 March 1995, 46.

Concludes that an anti-government insurgency in the West, stirred by federal land control measures, has appeared in its most extreme form in the militia movement.

Ferguson, Clyde R. "Carolina and Georgia Patriot and Loyalist Militias in Action, 1778–1783." In Jeffrey J. Crow and Larry E. Tise, eds., *The Southern Experience in the American Revolution*. Chapel Hill: University of North Carolina Press, 1978, 174–199.

Surveys the role of Patriot and Loyalist militias in the Revolution and sees them as crucial in determining the British response.

Flanders, Laura. "Far-Right Militias and Anti-Abortion Violence: Will the Media See the Connection?" *Extra!*, July/August 1995, 11–12.

Concludes that there exists more than a weak connection between the violence at abortion clinics and the militia movement. Many militias list their desire to close the clinics as a primary goal, and in some instances militia members and those who bomb the clinics are one and the same.

Glastris, Paul. "Patriot Games." *The Washington Monthly*. June 1995, 23–26.

Describes the often convoluted interpretations given to laws and the Constitution by militia groups.

Haggard, Carl D., and Nancy Haggard. "A Well-Regulated and Legal Militia." *Soldier of Fortune*, May 1995, 46–47, 86.

Clarifies the difference between organized and unorganized militias. It asserts that militias are legal, and in fact, any regulations against them are illegal. Moreover, the article maintains that militias are crucial in protecting liberty.

Halbrook, Stephen P. "The Right of the People or The Power of the Sates: Bearing Arms, Arming Militias, and the Second Amendment." *Valparaiso University Law Review*, 26 (1991), 131–207.

Presents an extensively documented argument that the Second Amendment refers to the people's right, apart from the state governments, to maintain a militia; the Bill of Rights was specifically considered to be protective of the general public; and the Constitution already has in its main body provisions for national and state supervision of militias.

Herbert, Bob. "Militia Madness." *New York Times*, 7 June 1995, A19.

Claims militias have run amok as evident in actions by members of the Minnesota Patriots Council and the Blue Ridge Hunt Club in Virginia.

Higgenbotham, Don. "The American Militia: A Traditional Institution with Revolutionary Responsibilities." In Don Higginbotham, ed., *Reconsiderations on the Revolutionary War: Selected Essays*. Westport, CT: Greenwood Press, 1983, 83–103.

Concludes that the colonial militia proved effective in the Revolution.

———. "The Debate over National Military Institutions: An Issue Slowly Resolved, 1775–1815." In William M. Fowler, Jr., and Wallace Cayle, eds., *The American Revolution: Changing Perspectives*. Boston: Northeastern University Press, 1979, 149–168.

Discusses the importance of radical Whig thought in Revolutionary America with its emphasis on a militia as a counterbalance to a standing army that might oppress the people.

―――. "The Military Institutions of Colonial America: The Rhetoric and the Reality." In Don Higgenbotham, *War and Society in Revolutionary America: The Wider Dimensions of Conflict*. Columbia, South Carolina: University of South Carolina Press, 1988, 19–42.

Concludes that as the Revolution neared, the colonial militias resembled more the system extant in England than one unique to America.

"Idaho Militia Leader Says Violence, Civil War Possible." *Idaho Falls Post-Register*, 12 March 1995, B6.

Reports the controversial comments of Sam Sherwood, head of the United States Militia Association, who allegedly threatened state legislators with violence. (The article by Mark Tanner in *Reason* [described later] offers a different version of Sherwood's remarks.)

Johnson, Dirk. "Paramilitary Groups Refocus On Local Government." *New York Times*, 12 November 1995, A10.

Describes efforts by militias in Michigan to take over township meetings and begin their own extralegal proceedings. The militias reject all restrictions on property use and claim that the township governments are in league with a conspiracy to establish a One World government.

Junas, Daniel. "Angry White Guys with Guns: The Rise of the Militias." *Covertaction Quarterly*, Spring 1995, 20–25.

Explains the rise of the militias through the activities of Bo Gritz and John Trochmann and the influences of the incidents at Ruby Ridge, Idaho, and Waco, Texas.

Kelly, Michael. "The Road to Paranoia." *New Yorker*, 19 June 1995, 60–75.

Discusses "fusion paranoia"—the convergence of far left and far right conspiratorial theories and how they have influenced both the militia movement and mainstream politics in the 1990s.

Ladd, Susan, and Stan Swofford. "Discontent Feeds Movement, Observers Say." *Greensboro News and Record*, 25–27 June 1995. Accessed at http://www.infi.net/extra/militias/m-index.htm.

The authors of this article see debate over social norms, economic hardship, and a weak political party structure as leading to the militia movement.

————. "Electronic Outlet: Computers Link Patriots." *Greensboro News and Record*, 25–27 June 1995. Accessed at http://www.infi.net/extra/militias/m-index.htm.

Describes the efforts of far-right patriot groups to exchange information through computer bulletin boards. It includes an interview with the leader of one such board in North Carolina.

————. "Fearing for Our Country." *Greensboro News and Record*, 25–27 June 1995. Accessed at http://www.infi.net/extra/militias/m-index.htm.

Traces the rise of patriot militia groups in North Carolina. The authors conclude that the militia movement is in many ways diffuse but with important links to white supremacy.

————. "On the Brink of Doom." *Greensboro News Leader*, 25–27 June 1995. Accessed at http://www.infi.net/extra/militias/m-index.htm.

Presents the views of Nord Davis, Jr., author of *Desert Shield and the New World Order* and proponent of Identity Christianity.

Leach, Douglas. "The Military System of Plymouth Colony." *New England Quarterly* 50 (September 1950), 342–364.

The author concludes that the Plymouth Colony militia became less effective as the seventeenth century drew to a close.

Levitas, Daniel. "Militia Forum." *The Nation*, 10 July 1995, 42.

Criticizes the Senate hearings led by Arlen Specter for failing to seriously expose militia extremism and, instead, providing a soapbox for militia leaders.

Maier, Pauline. "Popular Uprisings and Civil Authority in Eighteenth Century America." *William and Mary Quarterly*, 3rd series, 27 (January 1970), 3–35.

Provides an analysis of mob action in colonial America and its relationship to the later institutionalization of the militia under the Constitution.

Maxwell, Joe, and Andres Tapia. "Guns and Bibles: Militia Extremists Blend God and Country into a Potent Mixture." *Christianity Today*, 19 June 1995, 34–37, 45.

The authors see a complex mix of religious fervor within the militia movement, with some militias adhering to racism, but a good many infused with genuine evangelicalism.

"Militarism in America." *The Defense Monitor* 15 (#3, 1986), 1.

Concludes that the American public has become more militaristic in attitude because of a society that glorifies the military.

"Militia Update." *Klanwatch Intelligence Report*, March 1995, 8.

Presents recent reports on militia activities involving racism in Michigan, Montana, Florida, and Georgia.

"Militias: Armed and Furious." *Arizona Republic*, 23 April 1995. Accessed at http://paul.spu.edu/~sinnfein/arizona.htm/.

Traces the rise of militias in Arizona.

Naureckas, Jim. "The Oklahoma City Bombing: The Jihad that Wasn't." *Extra!*, July/August 1995, 6–10.

Presents an analysis of how the mainstream press originally portrayed the Oklahoma City bombing as the work of Middle Eastern terrorists. It shows the connection between the bombing and the polarized atmosphere created by right-wing militias.

"Neo-Nazi's Terrorist Novel: Likely Blueprint for Oklahoma Bombers." *Klanwatch Intelligence Report*, June 1995, 4.

Details the striking similarities between the bombing at Oklahoma City and the bombing attacks presented in the racist novel, *The Turner Diaries*.

Norden, Eric. "The Paramilitary Right." *Playboy*, June 1969, 104, 242+.

A detailed account of the formation of the 1960s Minutemen and their activities, including their involvement in terrorist assaults. It reveals a peculiar similarity between far-right and far-left ideas.

Parfrey, Adam, and Jim Redden. "Patriot Games." *Village Voice*, 11 October 1994, 26–31.

The authors cover the views and activities of controversial militia advocate Linda Thompson, who founded and leads the American Justice Federation. Thompson subscribes to many conspiracy theories, and through the AJF supports the growth of militias.

Pitcavage, Mark. "'Burthened in Defence of Our Rights': Opposition to Military Service in Ohio During the War of 1812." *Ohio History* (Summer/Fall 1995), 142–162.

This article contains references to the status of militias in the War of 1812.

———. "Ropes of Sand: Frontier Militias, 1810–1812." *Journal of the Early Republic*, 13 (Winter 1993), 481–500.

This prominent historian of America's early militias discusses their role in the War of 1812.

"The Plot." *Newsweek*, 8 May 1995, 29–34.

An account of the 1995 Oklahoma City bombing and its connection to militias, the article also includes references to Michael Koernke and militia strategy.

Pratt, Larry. "Firearms: The People's Liberty Teeth." *Guns and Ammo*, March 1995, 26–27.

The article argues that an effective militia is protection against tyranny, and this is why the Second Amendment must not be violated.

Pugh, Robert C. "The Revolutionary Militia in the Southern Campaign, 1780–1781." *William and Mary Quarterly*, 3rd series, 14 (April 1957), 154–175.

Concludes that the militia was crucial to the Patriot victory during the American Revolution, especially in the South.

"Racist Extremists Exploit Nationwide Militia Movement." *Klanwatch Intelligence Report*, December 1994, 1–4.

Traces the connections between some militia groups and white supremacists.

"Racist Leaders in the Militia Movement." *Klanwatch Intelligence Report*, December 1994, 5–7.

Provides brief sketches of what the Southern Poverty Law Center sees as white supremacists involved in the militia movement—including John Trochmann, James Wickstrom, Louis Beam, Pete Peters, Martin "Red" Beckman, Ray Southwell, Robert Pummer, and Wayne Gonyaw.

Radabaugh, Jack S. "The Militia of Colonial Massachusetts." *Military Affairs* 18 (Spring 1954), 1–18.

The author asserts a direct link existed between the Puritan militia system and the form of militias in England.

Ridgeway, James, and Leonard Zeskind. "Revolution U.S.A." *Village Voice*, 2 May 1995, 34–37.

Describes the various influences on the formation of militias, including Ruby Ridge, Idaho, and Waco, Texas, and clarifies the concept of "leaderless resistance."

Ross, Loretta J. "Military Nation: Saying It With A Gun." *The Progressive*, June 1995, 26–27.

The author describes the militia movement after the bombing at Oklahoma City, Oklahoma, as bolder and posing a serious threat to society.

Sennott, Charles M. "NRA Becomes Militias' Beacon." *Boston Globe*, 13 August 1995, 14–15.

As part of a series on the National Rifle Association, this article explains that group's intimate connections to the militia movement.

Shapiro, Joseph P. "An Epidemic of Fear and Loathing." *U.S. News and World Report*, 8 May 1995, 37–44.

Analyzes the militia movement as an expression of right-wing extremism. It discusses Ruby Ridge, Waco, shortwave radio broadcasts, and politicians who use incendiary language.

Shea, William L. "The First American Militia." *Military Affairs* 46 (Feb. 1982), 15–18.

Examines how the Virginia militia resembled that in England and, by the late 1600s, was led by a wealthy planter class.

Shy, John. "American Society in the War for Independence." In Don Higginbotham, ed., *Reconsiderations on the Revolutionary War: Selected Essays*. Westport, CT: Greenwood Press, 1978, 72–82.

This article sees the colonial militia as weakened by social factors but still playing an important role in the early republic.

———. "Hearts and Minds in the American Revolution: The Case of 'Long Bill' Scott and Peterborough, New Hampshire." In John Shy. *A People Numerous and Armed: Reflections on the Military Struggle for American Independence*. Ann Arbor, MI: University of Michigan Press, 1990, 163–179.

Examines how the militia in Peterborough kept the Loyalists at bay and buttressed local government.

————. "The Military Conflict Considered as a Revolutionary War." In John Shy. *A People Numerous and Armed: Reflections on the Military Struggle for American Independence*. Ann Arbor, MI: University of Michigan Press, 1990, 193–224.

Concludes that the militia helped win popular support for the Revolution.

Tanner, Mack. "Extreme Prejudice: How the Media Misrepresent the Militia Movement." *Reason*, July 1995, 42–47.

The author argues that the media has used sensationalist and provocative tactics to portray the entire militia movement as extremist, anti-Semitic, and racist. The article examines how, in fact, most militias reject such extremism and emphasize armed preparedness for defensive purposes so as to prevent government tyranny.

Tillson, Albert H., Jr. "The Militia and Popular Political Culture in the Upper Valley of Virginia, 1740–1775." *Virginia Magazine of History and Biography* 94 (July 1986), 285–306.

Concludes that the militia rank and file often resisted leadership from the wealthy officers.

Vest, Jason. "Militia Nation: Leader of the Fringe." *The Progressive*, June 1995, 28–29.

Describes the activities of Linda Thompson, leader of the American Justice Federation, especially her effective use of the Internet to promote militias.

Voll, Daniel. "At Home with M.O.M." *Esquire*, July 1995, 46–49+.

Describes the Militia of Montana and includes interviews with its leaders.

————. "The Right to Bear Sorrow." *Esquire*, March 1995, 75–82.

Through interviews, Voll traces middle America's attachment to guns and describes the militia movement in Pensacola, Florida, and Noxon, Montana.

Weisberg, Jacob. "Playing with Fire." *New York*, 8 May 1995, 28–35.

Evaluates the relationship between right-wing politics and political violence such as the Oklahoma City bombing, and concludes that an atmosphere of intolerance must be considered an important influence.

Wheeler, E. Milton. "Development and Organization of the North Carolina Militia." *North Carolina Historical Review* 41 (July 1964), 307–323.

Surveys the laws that governed the North Carolina militia from the late 1600s to the Revolutionary period.

Wilentz, Sean. "Bombs Bursting in Air, Still." *New York Times Magazine*, 25 June 1995, 40–41.

Places the Oklahoma City bombing and the militia movement in the context of American history, from the era of the Whiskey Rebellion in the 1790s into the twentieth century.

Williams, Leonard. "Ideological Parallels Between the New Left and the New Right." *Social Science Journal* 24 (1987), 317–327.

Concludes that both the New Left and New Right criticize the bureaucratization of society and the domination of political power by an entrenched elite. This criticism is a reaction to the problems produced by an advanced industrial society.

Wills, Gary. "The New Revolutionaries." *New York Review of Books*, 10 August 1995, 50–52.

A political commentator discusses the similarities between conspiracy ideas gripping many militias and widespread concerns on the part of Americans about a federal government that has become too powerful. He concludes that the new extremism is not paranoia but a coherent protest.

Zeskind, Leonard. "The Smell of Yesteryear: Militias and White Supremacy." *The Dignity Report*, Winter 1995, 20–23.

This article appears in the quarterly publication issued by the Coalition for Human Dignity and stresses the anti-Semitic and white supremacist nature of the militia movement.

Reports

Both militias and the groups that study them have issued numerous reports over the past few years. These are frequently updated and their size and scope often change. The reader is encouraged to study the list of organizations in chapter 5 of this book and contact groups directly for recent revisions.

American Citizens and Lawmen Association. *Operation Vampire Killer 2000*. Phoenix, AZ: American Citizens and Lawmen Association, 1992.

Purports to show proof of treasonous activities by prominent Americans to make the United States part of a socialist One World government. It urges police, National Guardsmen, and military officers to defend the people against this threat.

Anti-Defamation League. *Armed and Dangerous: Militias Take Aim at the Federal Government*. New York: Anti-Defamation League, 1994.

A survey of militia organizations in 13 states, including their leaders, size, and ideas.

————. *Beyond the Bombing: The Militia Menace Grows*. New York: Anti-Defamation League, 1995.

Updates the 1994 *Armed and Dangerous* report and concludes that the militia movement continues to expand. Militia activity is surveyed in 40 states.

————. *Extremism on the Right*. New York: Anti-Defamation League, 1988.

A synopsis of the activities of right-wing extremist organizations in the 1980s, including those engaged in paramilitary training and activities. Also included are biographical sketches of extremist leaders.

————. *Paranoia as Patriotism: Far-Right Influences on the Militia Movement*. New York: Anti-Defamation League, 1995.

Discusses the importance of the confrontation between Randy Weaver and federal agents at Ruby Ridge, Idaho, and the showdown at the Branch Davidian compound in Waco, Texas, to the rise of the militia movement. It also clarifies the central role of far-right extremist ideas that predate these incidents.

Berlet, Chip. *Armed Militias, Right Wing Populism, and Scapegoating*. Cambridge, MA: Political Research Associates, 1995.

Links the militia movement to conspiratorial, anti-government, racist, and anti-Semitic ideas.

Burghardt, Tom. *Leaderless Resistance and the Oklahoma City Bombing*. San Francisco: Bay Area Coalition for Reproductive Rights, 1995.

Raises the possibility that the Oklahoma City bombing was related to the strategy of leaderless resistance popular within the Christian Patriot militia.

————. *God, Guns, and Terror*. San Francisco: Bay Area Coalition for Reproductive Rights, 1994.

Traces the connection between Christian rightist anti-abortion groups and militias.

Burghart, Devin, and Robert Crawford. *Guns and Gavels: Common Law Courts, Militias and White Supremacy*. Portland, OR: Coalition for Human Dignity, 1996.

The authors provide profiles of leaders in the militia movement and present a survey of far-right and militia activities in the Northwest and several states outside the region. Much of the material is pertinent to the Freemen, a group that gained notoriety in 1996 for a confrontation with federal agents at a ranch near Jordan, Montana.

Crawford, Robert, S. L. Gardner, Jonathan Mozzochi, and R. L. Taylor. *The Northwest Imperative: Documenting A Decade of Hate*. Portland, OR: Coalition for Human Dignity, 1994.

Discusses the ideologies and activities of right-wing extremist groups in the Pacific Northwest.

Hazen, Don, Larry Smith, and Christine Triano, eds. *Militias in America, 1995*. San Francisco: Institute for Alternative Journalism, 1995.

A collection of newspaper articles about the militia movement shortly before and immediately after the bombing at Oklahoma City. A resource section with valuable information about organizations that monitor militias is included.

Klanwatch/Militia Task Force of the Southern Poverty Law Center. *False Patriots: The Threat of Antigovernment Extremists*. Montgomery, AL: Southern Poverty Law Center, 1996.

A detailed report focusing on the racist and anti-Semitic aspects of the militia movement. The report includes a map showing the distribution of militias across the United States, and it contains brief biographies of extremist leaders and a list of militias and patriot support groups active from 1994 to 1996.

Klanwatch Project of the Southern Poverty Law Center. *Hate, Violence, and White Supremacy: A Decade Review, 1980–1990*. Montgomery, AL: Southern Poverty Law Center, 1989.

Traces the rise of hate groups and paramilitary activity in the 1980s.

Montana Advisory Committee to the U.S. Commission on Civil Rights. *White Supremacist Activity in Montana*. Helena, MT: Montana Advisory Committee to the U.S. Commission on Civil Rights, 1994.

Not strictly a work about militias, this report describes the growth of white supremacist groups in Montana, some of whom engage in paramilitary activities.

Montana Human Rights Network. *Racist to the Roots: John Trochmann and the Militia of Montana, A Special Report*. Helena, MT: Montana Human Rights Network, 1995.

Traces the roots of the Militia of Montana in John Trochmann's United Citizens for Justice that organized in 1993. States that the group's leaders had extensive ties to white supremacy, with Trochmann himself an Identity Christian.

————. *A Season of Discontent: Militias, Constitutionalists and the Far Right in Montana*. Helena, MT: Montana Human Rights Network, 1994.

Analyzes connections between the militia movement in Montana and far-right extremist groups. It includes an appendix with articles reproduced from militia publications.

Ross, Loretta. *An Analysis of Militias in America*. Atlanta, GA: Center for Democratic Renewal, 1995.

Presents a brief overview of militia and paramilitary ties to white supremacy.

Stern, Kenneth S. *Militias: A Growing Danger*. New York: American Jewish Committee, 1995.

This analysis of the contemporary militia movement calls it a threat to national order, in general, and to government officials, specifically.

Toole, Ken. *What to Do When the Militia Comes to Town*. New York: American Jewish Committee, 1995.

Defines militia groups, summarizes their common characteristics, and advises what action should be taken when they threaten a community.

U.S. Senate. Judiciary Subcommittee on Terrorism, Technology, and Government Information. Statement of James L. Brown, Deputy Associate Director for Criminal Enforcement, Department of the Treasury, Bureau of Alcohol, Tobacco, and Firearms. 104th Congress, 1st session, 15 June 1995.

Explains efforts by the Bureau of Alcohol, Tobacco, and Firearms to investigate militia groups that have violated federal laws.

————. Statement of John Bohlman, Musselshell County (Montana) Attorney. 104th Congress, 1st session, 15 June 1995.

Presents an account of militia activities underway in and around the town of Roundup, Montana, that have led to an atmosphere of fear.

————. Statement of John Trochmann and Bob Fletcher of the Militia of Montana. 104th Congress, 1st session, 15 June 1995.

The militia movement is defended and claims are made that tyranny is taking over the United States.

————. Statement of Leroy Crenshaw. 104th Congress, 1st session, 15 June 1995.

The militia movement is defended by a Massachusetts African-American who believes the federal government is oppressive.

————. Statement of Missouri State Highway Patrol. 104th Congress, 1st session, 15 June 1995.

Includes a map of Missouri showing counties in which militias are active.

————. Statement of Norman Olson. 104th Congress, 1st session, 15 June 1995.

A leader in the Michigan militia movement condemns government tyranny and explains the people's "right" to form a militia.

――― . Statement of Richard M. Romley, Maricopa County (Arizona) Attorney. 104th Congress, 1st session, 15 June 1995.

A report on the growth of militias in Arizona.

――― . Statement of Robert M. Bryant, Assistant Director, National Security Division of the Federal Bureau of Investigation. 104th Congress, 1st session, 15 June 1995.

Clarifies the situations under which the FBI will investigate armed groups.

――― . Statement of Senator Arlen Specter, Chairman. 104th Congress, 1st session, 15 June 1995.

The scope of Specter's subcommittee investigation is clarified.

――― . Statement of Senator Max Baucus. 104th Congress, 1st session, 15 June 1995.

The status of militias in the senator's home state of Montana are discussed.

U.S. Senate. Senate Committee on the Judiciary. Testimony of Leroy Crenshaw. 104th Congress, 1st session, 25 May 1995.

Grievances against the federal government are outlined and assertions made that the Bill of Rights has been substantially violated.

Selected Nonprint Resources 7

This chapter includes lists of information found in three places: 1) commercial video and broadcast services and public radio, 2) militia shortwave radio, and 3) the Internet and World Wide Web.

Video and Broadcast Sources

Transcripts of the following television and radio programs are available for a fee from:

Journal Graphics, Incorporated
1535 Grant Street
Denver, CO 80203
Phone: 1-800-TALK-SHO

ABC News, *Nightline*, 22 May 1995.

The Militia of Montana is covered. Interviews with local residents in Noxon, the small town where MOM is located, are included along with reports on the reaction of some in the community who oppose the militia and consider its actions too extreme.

ABC News, *20/20*, 21 April 1995.

The show contains interviews with two prominent men from opposite sides of the political spectrum: Norm Olson, founder and leader of the Michigan Militia, and Morris Dees, head of the Southern Poverty Law Center in Montgomery, Alabama. Olson stresses the necessity to fight for liberty, while Dees focuses on white supremacist aspects of the militia movement.

ABC News, *World News Tonight*, 29 April 1995.

This brief report covers the forced resignation of Norman Olson and Ray Southwell from their leadership positions in the Michigan Militia and recent efforts by the Militia of Montana.

CNN, *Florida Militia Movement Recruits New Members*, 5 May 1995.

The expanding militia movement in Florida is covered; militia members express alarm over infringement of the Second Amendment and evidence of government oppression.

CNN, *The Michigan Militia*, 24 October 1994.

This includes reports on Norm Olson and Ray Southwell and their founding of the Michigan Militia.

CNN Special, *Oklahoma City*, 1 May 1995.

This includes coverage of the Militia of Montana and its involvement in Ravalli County. Militia supporters there refused to obtain driver's licenses and car tags.

National Public Radio (NPR), *Morning Edition*, 12 May 1995.

This is an interview with Bob Fletcher, former spokesman for the Militia of Montana. He accuses signers of the Greater Atlantic Trade Treaty (GATT) of engaging in an unconstitutional and immoral action.

Militia Shortwave Radio Broadcasts

The shortwave radio stations listed below broadcast nationwide and carry programs reflective of right-wing and militia ideas.

WHRI, Noblesville, Indiana, 7315 kilohertz.

This station's programs included *Truth for the Time*, an anti-government show presented by Pete Peters.

WINB, Philadelphia, Pennsylvania, 11950 kilohertz.
This station carries Christian Identity programs.

WRNO, New Orleans, Louisiana, 7355 kilohertz.
Several militant far-right programs are presented, including one with William Pierce, author of *The Turner Diaries*.

WWCR, Nashville, Tennessee, 7435 kilohertz.
This station carries the Liberty Lobby's *Radio Free America*.

Internet and the World Wide Web

The Internet and the World Wide Web house many conference and bulletin board connections with right-wing groups, along with home pages. Some discuss a broad range of conspiracy theories and political topics, others focus more narrowly on militias. The alt.conspiracy and alt.patriot lines frequently contain material forwarded by militias and their support groups, such as the Militia of Montana, the Michigan Militia, the United States Militia Association, and the American Justice Federation. There is a benefit and a danger in using the Internet. The benefit comes from exposure to the plethora of ideas bounced across cyberspace—the intensity of exchange can boggle the mind. The danger comes in concluding that the Internet represents the sum total of all ideas. Often, the Internet attracts only the most interested and most extreme participants. It should be used with caution.

Available through Usenet:

alt.conspiracy

Conspiracy theories abound here, including those advanced by militias. Recent messages have dealt with Ruby Ridge, Waco, the suicide of White House aide Vincent Foster, and the ever-present supposed threat from a One World government.

alt.politics.usa.constitution

This site contains messages from both the liberal and conservative wings of the political spectrum, including exchanges regarding militia activities.

alt.society.revolution

Discussion of radical ideas from both the left and the right can be found here.

alt.society.resistance

Messages posted here deal with resistance to government actions and social strictures of various types.

misc.activism.militia

Mostly pro-militia persons post messages here, but critics also voice their concerns. The Oklahoma City bombing and Senate hearings into the militias evoked a lively response. One participant told of plans by the Department of the Army to fight insurgency and terrorism through low-intensity conflict in the event of an emergency.

misc.survivalism

Messages are presented on topics of concern to survivalists in general, and thus not only militias. They deal with weapons, desert life, and winter bathing, among others.

talk.politics.guns

Discussions run the gamut on gun control. Many views are expressed here that follow the militia ideology about strict interpretation of the Second Amendment.

Mailing list:

patriots@kaiwan.com

Subscribing to this list ensures an extensive exposure to militia talk and conspiracy theories. This avenue of communication has been used by the American Justice Federation, among other prominent groups.

FTP:

ftp://tezcat.com/patriot

This is the Patriot Archives; many articles are available about militias and their activities.

ftp://ftp.shell.portal.com/pub/chan/militia/

Documents and articles relating to militias are available.

World Wide Web Sites:

http://www.rtside.com/rtside/

This is not a militia site, but one that expresses conservative ideas, some of which deal with the Second Amendment and religious issues. It provides access to the National Rifle Association and the Christian Coalition. It is known as the Right Side of the Web.

http://mmc.cns.net

This is the home page of the Central Michigan militia; it's an excellent resource for ideas circulating within the militia movement and permits subscription via e-mail to the organization's *Weekly Update*.

http://www.constitution/org/mil/tx/mil_ustx.htm

At this site, the Texas Constitutional Militia offers its views.

http://ourworld.compuserve.com/homepages/SCCM/

This is the South Carolina Civilian Militia home page with links to other sites.

http://www.infi.net/extra/militias/m-index.htm

Articles about the militia movement in North Carolina, prepared by the *Greensboro News and Record*, can be found here.

http://smartworld.com/perceptions/perceptions.html

This site is more New Age than right wing, but the conspiracy ideas communicated here resonate with conservative extremists and show the convergence that can occur between the two seemingly polar opposites. It contains sample articles from *Perceptions* magazine and commits itself to examining the New World Order, Big Brother, and general government interference with freedom.

http://www.copi.com/deepbook.html

Alternative political views of various ideologies are provided at this site.

http://www.sff.net/people/pitman/militia.htm

A highly informative site, it contains analyses of the early and modern militia movements by historians Sheldon Sheps and Mark Pitcavage. It presents an exhaustive fact sheet that poses important questions about militias and answers them one-by-one.

http://home.megalin.net/~eplurib/home.html

This is the home page for *U Pluribus Unum*, a publication of the Ohio Organized Militia.

http://www.eskimo.com/~hmcom/4/a.html

This is the home page for *Patriotic Justice in America*, a magazine dedicated to right-wing issues, including the rise of militias. A recent article detailed the alleged connection between top journalists and the Council on Foreign Relations.

http://paul.spu.edu/~sinnfein/arizona.html

Articles about the militia movement in Arizona as reported in the *Arizona Republic* and other newspapers are included here.

http://www.the-spa.com/constitution/

As the home page of the Constitution Society, which is based in Texas, it includes excerpts from the philosophers Machiavelli and John Locke along with suggestions on how to establish a militia.

http://afcomm.com/afc/

This is the home page for the American Freedom Coalition, a group that believes the United States has been in a state of emergency rule since 1933; it includes a Frequently Asked Questions section concerning federal war and emergency powers.

http://www.execpc.com/~jfish/na/index.html

This site contains articles from *American Magazine*, a right-wing publication supportive of militias; recent topics include conspiracy theories and the possibility that the federal government knew about the Oklahoma City bombing in advance.

http://www.execpc.com/~awallace/militia.html

Links to many militia issues and groups that both oppose and support the militia movement are provided at this site.

http://www.natall.com

This is a white-supremacist page that has some material on the militia movement.

http://nwcitizen.compublicgood

This is the home page for the organization Public Good, which monitors extremist activities, including militias. This organization considers itself dedicated to democratic values and the protection of them from intolerance. A recent article presented here covered the militia movement in Montana.

http://www.well.com/user/srhodes/militia.html

An extensive list of links related to the militia movement is found here.

http://www.worldmedia.com/caq/militia.html

A copy of the often-cited article "The Rise of the Militias" written by Daniel Jonas and published in *CovertAction Quarterly* can be found here.

http://www.usit.net/hp/patriots/ccla.html

This is the home page for the Christian Civil Liberties Association, publisher of the *Militia News*.

http://www.kaiwan.com:80/~patriot

This is the home page for "patriots" that includes links to several sites, including the National Rifle Association, State Militia Page, and Sovereign Citizen Resource Center.

http://paul.spu.edu/~sinnfein/berlet.html

An article on militias by analyst Chip Berlet can be found at this site.

http://paul.spu.edu/~sinnfein/fair.html

This contains an article from the publication *Extra!*, written by Leslie Jorgenson and covering the relationship between right-wing talk shows and the militia movement.

http://la.tcinet.com/~mrjohn

This is the home page for the Constitutional Militia of Southern California and includes its newsletter.

http://www.nidlink.com/~bobhard/mom.html

This is the home page for the militia of Montana and includes information about the Viper Militia in Arizona.

http://www.publiceye.org/pra

Maintained by Public Research Associates, a liberal group, this home page contains numberous articles about militias and right-wing activities, as well as links to far-right sites on the Internet.

Glossary

This glossary contains acronyms, references to words used in the overview section, and words that have special meaning to militias.

American Revolution Most Americans glorify the Revolution that founded their nation, and the militias are no exception; but they interpret the event in a different way, for to them the republic emerged only with the invaluable help of armed private citizens who cast down their farm tools to do battle for liberty. Modern militias see themselves as extensions of this patriotic heritage, acting, they say, with as much gallantry as their forefathers and according to the same principles.

19 April A sacred date for many militias; it signifies at least two historic developments in American history: the shots at Lexington and Concord in 1775 that began the Revolution and the government action at Waco, Texas, that showed the republic had been replaced by tyranny.

ATF or BATF The initials stand for the Bureau of Alcohol, Tobacco, and Firearms. From the standpoint of most militias, this is perhaps the most hated organization in the federal government. The militias believe the ATF is seeking to disarm Americans in violation of the Second Amendment, perhaps as part of a general plan to advance a socialistic One World government, and that it has on numerous occasions trampled fundamental liberties.

AK   Slang for AK-47, a popular assault rifle.

alternative media   The alternative media consists of shortwave radio; computer bulletin boards; the Internet with its home pages; videotape productions; and small, independent presses that publish pamphlets and books. Militia views about Waco and the federal government's supposedly conspiratorial actions are presented. This is the means of communication most preferred by militias to communicate their message, because it is not part of the mainstream media and is thus "uncorrupted."

angry white man   This term refers primarily to unskilled or lower middle-class workers, displaced by changes in the job market, perhaps unemployed, and definitely discontent about stagnant or declining income. Quite frequently these economic concerns are linked to social ones—a feeling that white males are being "dumped upon" in a society that has established special programs to help women and minorities. The angry white man is considered by militias and those outside the movement to be a prime candidate for recruitment into a militia.

assault weapons   A class of 17 semi-automatic weapons banned under a crime bill sponsored by President Bill Clinton. Congressional passage of this legislation in 1994 produced outrage among the more strident defenders of the Second Amendment and boosted the militia movement.

black helicopters   Numerous conspiracy theories popular within the militia movement refer to mysterious black helicopters roaming the American skies. Supposedly these are being used by the federal government to spy on people as part of a conspiracy to crush liberty. Videotapes released by the American Justice Federation, a militia support group, and the Militia of Montana, among others, purport to show the black helicopters in flight. The federal government, does, in fact, maintain black helicopters at a base in Kentucky as part of what it calls an anti-terrorism unit.

Branch Davidians   An offshoot of the Seventh Day Adventists, Branch Davidians are considered martyrs by many militias. To them the Davidians, including their leader David Koresh, were persecuted by ATF agents and tried bravely to protect their liberties regarding gun ownership and religious beliefs. The conflagration at Waco, Texas, in 1993 only served to show the true intents of the federal government to establish tyranny.

Christian Identity   A racist religious movement, derived from a British ideology and founded largely by Californian William Potter Gale in the 1960s, that considers white Northern Europeans and, by extension, white Americans of European heritage, to be God's chosen people as part of the Ten Lost Tribes of Israel. Jews are considered to be the children of Satan and thus subhuman, while nonwhites are considered to be inferior "mud people." There are numerous, small Christian Identity churches in the United States, with most located in the Pacific Northwest. Identity Christians are found in several white supremacist organizations, including the Ku Klux Klan and Aryan Nations. Most militias do not adhere to this religion, yet its ideas have permeated many of them, and Identity Christians themselves have organized paramilitary activities.

Christian Patriot militias This term generally refers to those militias tied directly to the Christian Identity movement. Some militias that are not Identity Christian, but are nevertheless strongly Christian, use this term to describe themselves.

Christian Reconstructionists Those who follow Christian Reconstructionism desire a theocratic state. Reverend Jay Grimstead of the Coalition on Revival—an umbrella group for Christian Reconstructionist organizations—has promoted county militias to enforce God's law and stop the invasion of socialists from Mexico.

concentration camp Militia literature often displays "proof" of concentration camps that have been established in the United States. Now empty, they are intended to be used by the military and foreign invaders as places to imprison militia members and other dissidents, and put them to death.

Constitutionalists These people consider the Constitution to be unchangeable and thus criticize any attempts at modern interpretation. They frequently believe that the true Constitution consists only of the original document and the first ten amendments (the Bill of Rights), and that, as a result, the only true citizens of the United States are white people (African-Americans having been accorded citizenship only through the Fourteenth Amendment).

county movement Groups and individuals who believe the county government is the ultimate authority. This movement expressed itself most radically with the formation of the Posse Comitatus.

demonize Militias use this word when they refer to efforts by the mainstream media to portray militias as evil. Militias insist they are protecting liberty—the United States government is in fact the evil entity, working its conspiracy to crush liberty with the active help or at least unwitting cooperation of the media.

domestic enemies To the militias these are people who undermine traditional American values—people such as liberals, environmentalists, and outcome-based educators. Domestic enemies, militias claim, support such measures as gun control and restrictions on the use of private property, tend to see issues globally, and thus cooperate with the One World agenda.

FERN This stands for Federal Reserve Note. Oftentimes militias refer to paper money as FERNS to emphasize they are a contrivance of the Federal Reserve System which they see as manipulated by a largely Jewish elite. Some militias refuse to accept FERNS—they deal strictly in gold and silver.

founding fathers Militias revere the founding fathers—George Washington, Thomas Jefferson, and Alexander Hamilton, for example—as having developed the Constitution and created a republic through the sacrifice of the American Revolution. These great white men, they believe, would never have stood for the recent liberal interpretations that have corrupted the Constitution.

gun control A "hot button" within the militia movement, gun control is considered to be a crucial step in taking all guns away from private citizens and establishing tyranny. In general, militias hold to a world view they consider tied to seventeenth and eighteenth century republican ideology, when it was argued that an armed citizenry is an absolute necessity in protecting liberty, that a government must fear its people. Militias deplore recent efforts by liberals and others to restrict certain types of guns and extend registration procedures.

leaderless resistance This is a tactic whereby militias organize in units, or cells, of no more than six to eight people. Each cell is to be under general orders but develops its own specific strategies. As its proponent Louis Beam described it, they would "operate independently of each other and never report to a central headquarters or a single leader for direction or instruction." The benefit of this tactic is that should any one cell be infiltrated by outsiders, the others would go undetected and the organization as a whole would remain strong.

martial law Martial law is invoked in times of war or widespread disorder and it entails the suspension of civil liberties. Many militias believe the federal government will soon invoke martial law throughout the nation as a means to arrest militia leaders and crush their organizations.

militia A militia is an armed self-defense group consisting of private citizens; thus it is not part of the professional army. The National Guard is not considered a militia because it has been largely federalized. Whether groups such as the Militia of Montana and the Michigan Militia are actually militias is debatable. Most states prohibit paramilitary activities or militias, and the Constitution places militias under state and, to a certain extent, federal direction. Hence if a group organizes and engages in paramilitary activity without state approval, then it is not a militia; it is, instead, an informal group of armed people, perhaps operating in violation of state law.

New World Order This refers to a rearrangement of the world political scene so that national boundaries are eliminated or become meaningless. Militias use this term synonymously with One World government.

Under this arrangement, the United States will lose its sovereignty and the American people their liberty, for the One World government will be tyrannical and, in economic terms, socialistic. The New World Order, militias charge, is being advanced by a conspiratorial elite.

Patriot The terms "patriot" and "patriot militias" are used in several different ways by militias. Patriot sometimes refers to the nation's founding fathers. At other times, it refers to those people today who stand for protecting the Constitution through a strict interpretation of it and vigilant defense of the Bill of Rights, particularly the Second Amendment. Such true patriots resist any encroachment by a One World government. To some, patriot is more narrowly defined as those in the militias. Hence, militias are "patriot militias."

Protocols of Zion This is a condensation of the title *The Protocols of the Meetings of the Learned Elders of Zion*. Written in the early 1900s, this book purports to be the minutes of secret meetings held by Jewish leaders who plotted to take over the world. The book is a fake in that no such meetings ever occurred. Many in the militias, however, believe in this anti-Semitic tract.

racist right A term referring to those in the extreme right who believe there are innate biological differences between groups of people based on race and ethnicity. Some militias hold to this view, particularly those connected to the Christian Identity movement.

Ruby Ridge This remote location in northern Idaho was the site of the showdown in 1992 between Randy Weaver and federal agents. The ensuing gun battle resulted in the death of Weaver's son, wife, and an agent. Militias see this as federal power gone awry.

Second Amendment The Second Amendment, part of the Bill of Rights in the U.S. Constitution, reads: "A well-regulated militia being necessary to the security of a free state, the right of the people to keep and bear arms shall not be infringed." This provision is held sacred by militias. Any erosion of it, they believe, will end American liberty, including the First Amendment right to free speech.

United Nations Militias believe that an international elite operates through the United Nations to advance a One World government that will end American independence and liberty.

Waco On 28 February 1993, agents of the Bureau of Alcohol, Tobacco, and Firearms raided the Branch Davidian compound at Waco, Texas. A gun battle ensued, and then a siege that eventually resulted in the deaths of 75 Davidians, including more than 20 children. Militias see this action as an example of government oppression, and while they do not necessarily support the Branch Davidian religion, they insist on the right of the Davidians to worship as they please. Along with Ruby Ridge, Waco is considered to be a major event that stimulated the growth of militias.

ZOG   This stands for Zionist Occupation Government, a phrase used to describe the federal government, especially under President Bill Clinton. The implication is that Jews run the political system and it is not responsive to the American citizenry.

Index

N eil A. Hamilton is associate professor and chair of the history department at Spring Hill College in Mobile, Alabama. He teaches American history and leads seminars on classroom effectiveness. His previous works include *Visions of Worth*, a biography of a prominent baseball manufacturer, and *Founders of Modern Nations: A Biographical Dictionary*, published by ABC-CLIO.

PUBLIC SCHOOLING IN AMERICA   by Richard D. Van Scotter

Designed to serve as both a one-stop information source and a guide to in-depth exploration, this volume examines the perennially volatile issue of public education in the United States, from its origins through the present and into an uncertain, yet hopeful, future.   6 1/8" x 9 1/4", 240 pages, ©1991

RAINFORESTS OF THE WORLD   by Kathlyn Gay

This book explains what rainforests are, where they are, how they are threatened, what is at risk in losing them, and what is being done to protect these vital resources.

Review **VOYA** Jun 94; **ARBA** 1995   6 1/8" x 9 1/4", 219 pages, ©1993

RAPE IN AMERICA   by Rob Hall

This handbook presents an overview of the historical and social context of rape in America. Major law enforcement, judicial system, and correctional system trends in dealing with both the rapist and the victim are discussed.

Review **CH** Dec 95; **BL** Nov 95; **VOYA** Feb 96; **BN** Oct 95; **BR** Apr 96; **S (RQ)** Spring 96; **ARBA** 1996   6 1/4" x 9 1/2", 225 pages, ©1995

RECYCLING IN AMERICA   by Debi Kimball

Here's an eye-opening look at the challenges facing a world recently awakened to the reality of limited resources.   6 1/4" x 9 1/4", 254 pages, ©1992

RELIGIOUS RIGHT   by Glenn H. Utter and John W. Storey

This book provides up-to-date information on the religious right in all its aspects—its origins and development, the personalities and groups, their religious and political beliefs, their agendas and strategies, their influences on society, and society's reaction to them.

Review **BL** Mar 96; **CH** May 96; **BN** May 96; **SLJ** Aug 96; **VOYA** Aug 1996   6 1/4" x 9 1/4", 220 pages, ©1995

SEXUAL HARASSMENT   by Lynne Eisaguirre

This timely handbook offers a balanced overview of the history, social context, legal precedent, and legislative background related to the issue of sexual harassment.

Review **VOYA** Jun 94; **ARBA** 1996   6 1/8" x 9 1/4", 217 pages, ©1993

SPACE EXPLORATION: A Reference Handbook   by Mrinal Bali

Designed to serve both as a one-stop information source and a guide to in-depth research, **Space Exploration: A Reference Handbook** presents the who, what, where, when, why, and how of humankind's excursions into space in a lucid, readable style.   6 1/8" x 9 1/4", 240 pages, ©1990

1333-1670815

SPORTS ETHICS
by Lawrence Berlow

From professional athletes in the Olympic games and the use of steroids to discrimination against women in sports and unethical college recruiting practices– there's no question, sports ethics is a topic of growing interest and concern.

Review BN Apr 95; **SLJ** Jan 96; **ARBA** 1996

6 1/4" x 9 1/2", 230 pages, ©1994

TERRORISM
by Stephen E. Atkins

Designed to serve as both a one-stop information source and a guide to in-depth exploration, this engaging volume examines the philosophies, psychologies, and issues involved in international terrorism.   6 1/8" x 9 1/4", 199 pages, ©1992

VIOLENT CHILDREN
by Karen L. Kinnear

Who are the children involved in violent acts, and who are their victims? This new volume presents a balanced survey of children and violence in the United States– specifically those children who commit an act such as murder, rape, and assault. The physical, cultural, social, economic, and legal aspects of this pressing social issue are explored in detail.

Review VOYA Feb 96; **LJ** Oct 95; **BL** Oct 95; **BR** Apr 96; **ARBA** 1996

6 1/8" x 9 1/4", 251 pages, ©1995

WATER QUALITY AND AVAILABILITY
by E. Willard Miller and Ruby M. Miller

Designed to serve as both a one-stop information source and a guide to in-depth exploration, this eye-opening volume examines the availability and quality of our most fundamental resource: water.   6 1/8" x 9 1/4", 430 pages, ©1992

WORLD HUNGER
by Patricia L. Kutzner

Designed to serve as both a one-stop information source and guide to in-depth exploration, this volume examines the who, what, where, how, and why of chronic and debilitating hunger.   6 1/8" x 9 1/4", 359 pages, ©1991

NEW-FALL 1996

ANIMAL RIGHTS
by Clifford J. Sherry

"A treasury of information on animal rights not easily found elsewhere. Recommended." **--The Book Report** Oct 95

Review ARBA 1996   6" x 9", 214 pages, ©1995

1333-1670815

HEALTH CARE CRISIS IN AMERICA
by Linda Brubaker Ropes

Designed to serve as both a one-stop information source and a guide to in-depth exploration, this volume places the current health care crisis within a historical, social, and ethical context. It offers a comprehensive and balanced overview of the practices, policies, and developments that have brought the United States to a point where highly advanced medical technology exists side-by-side with an inability to provide many citizens with the most basic health services. 6" x 9 1/4", 172 pages, ©1991

INTELLECTUAL FREEDOM
by John B. Harer

Designed to serve as both a one-stop information source and a guide to in-depth exploration, this volume provides a clear and thorough introduction to the issues that continue to be hotly debated in the United States. 6" x 9 1/4", 313 pages, ©1992

LEGALIZED GAMBLING
by William N. Thompson

From the industry's history and spread to its variety of ventures—including casinos, state lotteries, charity bingo, and horse racing—this reference offers insight into legalized gambling industry organizations.

Review **RRB** Feb 94; **ARBA** 1995; **CH** Mar 95; **BR** Oct 95

6" x 9 1/4", 250 pages, ©1994

ORGANIZED CRIME
by Patrick J. Ryan

The words organized crime tend to call to mind images from The Godfather, yet organized crime today takes on far more varied forms and guises. This volume explores the pervasiveness of organized crime, examines its history and chronology from La Cosa Nostra to Colombian drug cartels and Jamaican posses, and covers nontraditional organizations such as the Hell's Angels and the Pagans.

Review **SLJ** Mar 96; **CJ International** Feb 96; **BL** Nov 95; **BN** May 96; **ARBA** 1996 6 1/4" x 9 1/4", 228 pages, ©1995

OZONE DILEMMA
by David E. Newton ✳

Many questions surround ozone depletion in the earth's atmosphere, both in respect to the ozone holes detected above the Antarctic in the past 20 years and the overall decrease of ozone in the earth's stratosphere. This book offers a general scientific and technical discussion of ozone depletion and raises important social, political, and economic concerns. Scientific data are balanced with an outline of the uncertainties surrounding this phenomenon, both scientific and nonscientific.

Review **VOYA** Apr 96; **CH** Feb 96; **SLJ** Jan 96; **BN** Oct 95; **BR** Apr 96; **ARBA** 1996 6 1/8" x 9 1/4", 196 pages, ©1995

1333-1670815